ORAL WORKPLACE COMMUNICATION
Job Talk

Second Edition

THOMAS CHEESEBRO

Waukesha County Technical College

LINDA O'CONNOR

Waukesha County Technical College

FRANCISCO RIOS

College of Education, University of Wyoming

PEARSON

Prentice
Hall

Upper Saddle River, New Jersey 07458

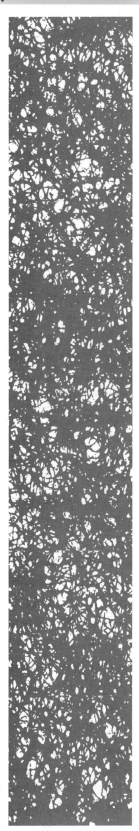

Library of Congress Cataloging-in-Publication Data

Cheesebro, Thomas, 1946–

　　Oral workplace communication : job talk / Thomas Cheesebro, Linda O'Connor, Francisco Rios. — 2nd ed.

　　　　p. cm.

　　Includes bibliographical references and index.

　　ISBN 0-13-170460-5

　1. Business communication. I. O'Connor, Linda, 1950– II. Rios, Francisco, 1956– III. Title.

　　HF5718 . C453 2006

　　651. 7'3—dc22

                                                    2004029599

Director of Production and Manufacturing: Bruce Johnson
Senior Acquisitions Editor: Gary Bauer
Editorial Assistant: Jacqueline Knapke
Editorial Assistant: Cyrenne Bolt de Freitas
Marketing Manager: Leigh Ann Sims
Managing Editor—Production: Mary Carnis
Manufacturing Buyer: Ilene Sanford
Production Liaison: Denise Brown
Production Editor: Ginny Schumacher/Carlisle Publishers Services
Composition: Carlisle Communications, Ltd.
Interior Cartoon Illustrations: Don Martinetti
Senior Design Coordinator/Cover Design: Christopher Weigand
Printer/Binder: Hamilton Printing
Cover Printer: Phoenix Color

This book was set in 10/12 New Baskerville by Carlisle Communications, Ltd. and was printed and bound by Hamilton Printing Company. The cover was printed by Phoenix Color.

Pearson Education Ltd.
Pearson Education Singapore, Pte. Ltd.
Pearson Education Canada, Ltd.
Pearson Education–Japan

Pearson Education Australia PTY, Limited
Pearson Education North Asia Ltd.
Pearson Educación de Mexico, S.A. de C.V.
Pearson Education Malaysia, Pte. Ltd.

10 9 8 7 6 5 4 3 2 1
ISBN 0-13-170460-5

CONTENTS

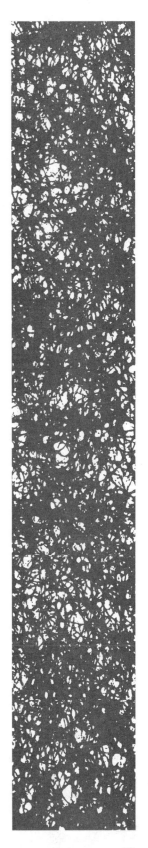

3

LISTENING BLUEPRINT   41

4

INTERPERSONAL BLUEPRINT   69

5

PRESENTATIONS BLUEPRINT   103

6

TEAMWORK BLUEPRINT   127

PREFACE

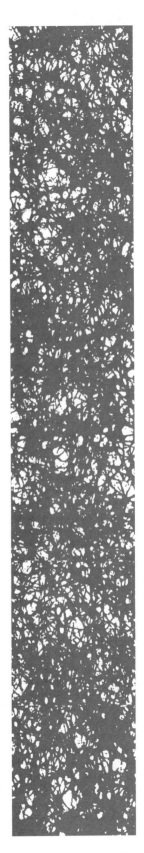

ABOUT THIS BOOK

Effective interpersonal communication skills are key to having success and happiness in life and in the world of work. The information contained in *Oral Workplace Communication: Job Talk* will help you develop these skills to become a valued employee, a good friend, and a respected family member.

This text presents concepts in a conversational manner and develops skills through hands-on applications. Rather than focus on theory and classical rhetoric, current communication concepts are discussed in a practical "let's-go-to-work" manner that will help prepare you for success in your career.

TEXT FORMAT: BLUEPRINTS, TOOLS, AND INTERACTIONS

Our goal is to make communication skills understandable, applicable, and practical for employees to function effectively on the job. The format is the most unique feature of this text. Each chapter includes three sections: Blueprints, Tools, and Interactions. The Blueprints sections present a brief theoretical basis for the chapters. The Tools sections offer a combination of guidelines and skills needed to improve our communication with others, particularly on the job. The Interactions sections provide an opportunity for hands-on application of the skills learned. In addition, each chapter includes a Tool Check as a review of the concepts discussed.

TEXT ORGANIZATION

Oral Workplace Communication: Job Talk provides a comprehensive foundation of the tools needed to communicate successfully on the job. This text builds upon the success of our earlier text entitled, *Communication Skills for the World of Work*. For those familiar with this book, you will find new chapters on diversity, teamwork, speech presentations, and customer service, along with an expansion of content throughout other chapters.

Chapter 1 begins with an overview of the communication process, its functions and barriers.

Chapter 2 reminds you that communication is culture bound and that understanding diversity can enrich our lives and enhance our effectiveness on the job.

Chapter 3 shows the importance of listening skills and the value of responding with effective feedback.

Chapter 4 shares the interpersonal skills that provide the information needed to help us resolve conflicts, express ourselves assertively, and cope with criticism.

Chapter 5 explains the speech preparation process: from phrasing central ideas and developing main points, to organizing and verbally supporting those points. Specific suggestions for rehearsing a dynamite presentation also are provided.

Chapter 6 explores the facets of teamwork. Special attention is given to organizing teams, developing strong participation skills, and employing problem solving strategies.

Chapter 7 helps you discover your qualifications for employment by inventorying your interests, achievements, skills, and values; studying your occupations; and discovering sources of job leads.

Chapter 8 offers an "extra" for an oral communication text by showing you how to prepare the written communications needed for seeking employment. Specifically, you are instructed in the preparation of resumes, letters of application, and thanks-for-the-interview follow-up letters.

Chapter 9 introduces you to an effective way of interviewing for jobs as you learn how to respond to behavior-based interviewing questions by providing qualifications with CAR stories, five saleable skills, and closing statements.

Chapter 10 shows how important effective customer service is and suggests ways of offering "top notch" service, including resolving customer complaints.

If you develop the skills discussed in *Oral Workplace Communication: Job Talk,* you can expect to experience a more satisfying work life, improved interpersonal relationships, and increased self-confidence.

INSTRUCTOR SUPPLEMENTS

The instructor's manual provides alternative course outlines: one for a 16-week semester with emphasis on oral communication skills, and a second outline with the inclusion of employability skills. A comprehensive test bank also is included. PowerPoint slides for each chapter visually reinforce the concepts and skills presented in the text.

ACKNOWLEDGEMENTS

We would like to personally thank reviewers of our manuscript for their insightful comments: Deborah Roebuck from Kennesaw State University, James Stull from San Jose State University, and Barbara Moran, Training Contractor. Our thanks also go to the following individuals from Prentice-Hall and Carlisle Publishers Services: Gary Bauer, Elizabeth Sugg, and Ginny Schumacher, for their help in preparation of this text. Additional thanks to Fred Dahl of Inkwell for securing permissions. We are also grateful to the Communication Skills Department at Waukesha County Technical College for their support throughout this endeavor.

ABOUT THE AUTHORS

Thomas Cheesebro has been a faculty member at Waukesha County Technical College for over 35 years, teaching courses in oral/interpersonal communication, public speaking, and workplace communication. He has previously co-authored an earlier edition of this text entitled *Communication Skills for the World of Work*.

Linda O'Connor has also taught in the Communication Skills Department at Waukesha County Technical College for the past 30 years. In addition to teaching courses in interpersonal communication, public speaking, composition, and business writing, Linda is the coordinator of WCTC's Speech Lab. She has previously co-authored an earlier edition of this text entitled *Communication Skills for the World of Work* along with Tom and Francisco.

Francisco Rios worked as a faculty member, along with Tom and Linda, at the Waukesha County Technical College for 13 years teaching courses in oral/interpersonal communication, public speaking, composition, human relations, and cultural awareness. He is currently a Professor in the College of Education at the University of Wyoming. Francisco is the author of numerous articles and four books, including *Communication Skills for the World of Work*.

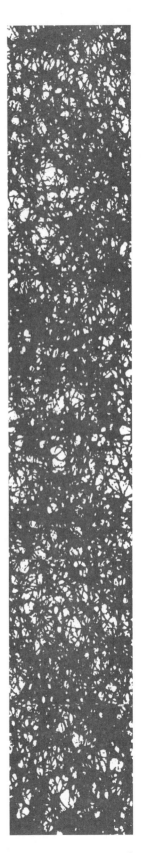

CHAPTER 1
COMMUNICATION BLUEPRINT

Communication Defined

Functions of Communication

Communication Process Model

Types of Noise

Communication Climate

COMMUNICATION TOOLS

Overcoming Barriers

Giving and Getting Feedback

Recognizing and Limiting Information Overload

Improving Relations

Remaining Sensitive to the Organization's Structure

TOOL CHECK

INTERACTIONS

Communication Process Model

Feedback Exercise

Personal Experience Talk

Communication Self-Assessment

COMMUNICATION BLUEPRINT

Introduction

What is communication? Why do we communicate? How important is communication in the workplace? What tools can we use to help improve our communication? We will explore these important questions throughout this text. They are tough questions with even tougher answers. How you answer these questions will affect your ability to get along with others as you attempt to make a valuable contribution to society through your career.

By studying effective communication, we can find new and perhaps better ways of dealing with those people who are important in our lives: those people we work with, learn with, and live with. This chapter will define communication, list reasons why we interact with others, develop a model of the communication process, discuss ways to improve the climate for communication, provide strategies for reducing noise, and identify suggestions for overcoming barriers to effective communication.

Communication Defined

What is communication? This is the first question that we must answer before we undertake the study of it. Obviously, communication means different things to different people. To the supervisor on a job, it is a way of making sure that the job gets done. To those who love us, it is a way of maintaining that relationship. To friends and co-workers, it is the tool that helps us to get along.

Communication is sometimes defined as the process of sending and receiving messages. When a customer explains a problem to you about the exhaust system of a car, a message has been sent, and you have, supposedly, received it. What if the language used, however, is not clear? For example, if the customer says, "Every time I'm driving, my car makes funny noises, and smoke comes from that thing in the back and from that little jobber over yonder." A message has been sent, and you have received it. Communication, as defined above, has taken place. But you still do not know what is wrong with the car or how the customer wants it fixed.

This situation suggests that more needs to happen for communication to be effective. For one thing, the customer needs to be more specific in describing the problem. You need to listen carefully and ask clarifying questions. The goal is to achieve *shared understanding* of the information.

In addition, effective communication involves more than just understanding the information. It involves the shared understanding of the feelings, thoughts, wants, needs, and intentions of the communicators, which may not be openly expressed in words. Note that shared understanding and agreeing with someone are different. For example, I may not agree with my boss on the correct way to file customer accounts, but I can still try to understand the message.

Functions of Communication

People communicate for a number of important reasons: to meet practical needs, to fulfill social needs, to make better decisions, and to promote personal growth.

Practical functions. We communicate to have practical needs met, such as buying food, renting an apartment, securing a job, and maintaining our health and safety. Travelers to foreign countries know how difficult it is to have these needs met when they do not speak the host country's language.

Social functions. We often communicate with others for the sheer pleasure of interaction. Communication also enables us to meet others, demonstrate ties, maintain friendships, and build intimate relationships. Are our social needs important? Failure to meet our social needs often results in serious consequences: loneliness, loss of job productivity, drug and alcohol abuse, marital problems, divorce, and even suicide. We all need to have the affection of others, to feel like we belong, and to exercise control over our lives.

Decision making functions. Communication can and should help us to make decisions about our own lives. Generally the more information we receive, the better the decisions we make. Let us say, for example, that the radio alarm clock goes off and you hear, "Good morning. It's 6 A.M. Sam Sunshine here. Rise and shine. It's 60 degrees out and clear." With this little bit of information, you can decide how much longer you can stay in bed, whether to wear your overcoat or windbreaker, and whether you will "bike" it or take the old "clunker" to work. Not all decisions are this simple. We use information to decide what job to take, where to live, and who to marry.

Personal growth functions. Communication can also be seen as the primary means of intellectual, emotional, social, and psychological growth. Through self-expression and feedback from others, we define and confirm who we are, feel appreciated and successful, obtain new information, increase our level of awareness, and expose ourselves to challenging new experiences. As a result, we grow as people.

Communication Process Model

One way to see how communication works is to examine a process model. A process model for communication is much like a schematic for an electrical appliance. They both show the internal workings of a complex process in a simplified way. A communication process model breaks down communication into its separate parts and puts it onto a two-dimensional surface for inspection. An interpersonal model of communication might look like Figure 1.1.

FIGURE 1.1
Communication Process
Model

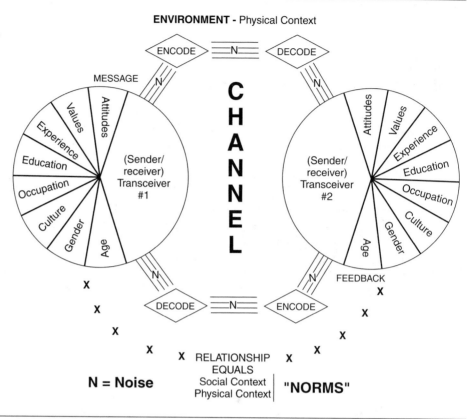

Sender/Receiver. The first component of communication is the sender/ receiver. Though we separate these two roles, it is important to keep in mind that we send and receive messages simultaneously. For example, while you are speaking to someone, you also receive nonverbal feedback, enabling you to act as a "transceiver," both sending and receiving messages.

Encoding. More specifically, senders originate a communication message. An idea comes into mind, and an attempt is made to put this thought into symbols (non-verbal gestures or words) that the receiver will understand. This process of changing thought into symbols is called encoding.

Decoding. The receiver, who is the destination of the communication message, must assign meaning to the symbols so they can be understood. This process of assigning meaning is called decoding. Like encoding, decoding happens so fast, we rarely are aware of its occurrence. As we read and listen, we simply assume we understand what the symbols mean. Each person, sender and receiver, is a product of experiences, feelings, gender (male/female), occupation, religion, values, mood, and so on. As a result, encoding and decoding are unique for each person. For instance, you could tell a co-worker that your new secretarial job has great benefits and mean you are satisfied because you get a three-week paid vacation. Your co-worker may think that you mean you have family insurance coverage.

Message. The message is the idea, thought, feeling, or opinion to be communicated. Sometimes the message is clear and direct, such as, "Get me a package of disks for the computer." Other times the message is unclear, as when a job interviewer says, "We'll keep your application on file." Does this comment mean you will be called for the next vacancy, or is this a polite way of saying you are not qualified, and you will never hear from the employer again? In addition, at all times, we are sending several messages simultaneously. Along with the actual content of a message, nonverbally we may be sharing a feeling or defining how we see our relationship with the other person.

Channel. The channel is the line through which the message travels from sender to receiver. In face-to-face communication, messages are carried by sound and light waves. Though we use sound and light primarily, people can and do use any sensory channel. How a person smells communicates, as does how firmly a person shakes hands. In addition, communication technology is requiring us to communicate in new and different ways. Whether we are using e-mail or voicemail, teleconferencing or audio-conferencing, we need to know how and when to use the proper technology.

Feedback. Feedback is the receiver's response to the message and indicates how the message is seen, heard, understood, and often how the receiver feels about the message and/or sender. In the case of oral communication, effective feedback comes after careful listening. Most students and employees spend more time listening than reading, writing, or speaking. Communication experts in general estimate that we spend close to 50 percent of our day listening. Part of a listener's responsibility is to provide feedback, making communication a two-person affair. In interpersonal relationships where understanding is the goal, we will want to stimulate as much feedback as possible. In short, feedback is the primary means of increasing personal awareness. We should give and get as much feedback as possible.

Context. Two factors affect what we say and how we say something—the social and the physical context. The social context deals with the relationship between sender and receiver. Obviously, what you say and how you say it will change, depending upon whether you are talking to your best friend, a total stranger, your boss, Reverend Rivera from your church, or Officer O'Malley of the Police Department. Also, the physical context will dictate what you say and how you say it. Your communication will change if you are at the local dance club, at work, at home, or in church. The context of communication determines the rules or norms for that interaction. These unwritten, expected ways of behaving vary from situation to situation. Their violation can result in negative consequences. For example, using foul language in a job interview may keep you from getting the job you want. No one is forced to adhere to expected standards, but society does make you bear the consequences for violating its norms.

Noise. Noise is any interference that prevents shared understanding. Because noise is such a significant impediment to effective communication, we will discuss internal, external and semantic noise in greater detail later in this chapter.

Types of Noise

Three types of noise contribute to communication breakdowns. These types of noise are internal, external, and semantic.

Internal Noise. Internal noise includes our attitudes, opinions, and beliefs toward what is being said, as well as who is saying it, and may inhibit our understanding of others. Our intrapersonal communication (the dialogues which occur inside our heads) is often a source of disruptive internal noise. Internal noise is also affected by our self-concept, how we feel, and what we expect. Daydreaming is the most obvious form of internal noise interfering with communication. Preoccupation with personal problems can be another form of internal noise. If your fiancée told you before you left for work that the wedding was off, you might have a difficult time listening to a training session on new safety procedures because of the "noise" inside your head.

External Noise. External noise deals with the noise in the environment: other voices, airplanes overhead, buzzing of machines, and so on; it most often affects our interpersonal communication—our communication between people which is "personal." This type of noise is more obvious than internal noise and is easier to cope with. Interestingly, most families who live near airports or train stations become extremely good at ignoring external noise even when it shakes and rattles their windows.

Semantic Noise. Semantic noise, the third type of noise, occurs when sender and receiver have different meanings for the words and/or gestures they use. Semantic noise often occurs when technicians and lay people talk to each other. When a printer tells the customer he will burn an image of the customer's picture, the printer means he will create a copy, while the customer may assume his picture will be torched and destroyed.

Describing the kinds of noise that interrupt communication is one thing; figuring out what to do about these noises is more difficult. In some instances, the only thing that needs to be done is to turn up the powers of concentration. In the case of internal noise, for example, being aware of the topics and words that send you reeling is an important preventative step. For external noise, turning off noises, tuning them out, or asking others to speak up increase the chance of understanding considerably. Finally, for semantic noise, being aware that people may have different meanings for the same words is a beginning. Using questions and paraphrasing to clarify meanings and confirm understanding can minimize semantic differences.

Communication Climate

Good communication does not just happen. Effective communication happens when the people involved work to create a climate of openness, honesty, and respect for one another. Effective communication also happens when the people involved act to minimize the breakdowns that are likely to occur.

Principles. Some breakdowns can be prevented by an awareness of the following communication principles:

1. **We are always communicating, whether we intend to or not.** Try to stop communicating. What would you do? Leave? Sleep? Go into a corner and put headphones on? If nothing else, you would communicate a desire not to communicate. It has been found that 75 percent of our waking day is spent communicating through reading, writing, speaking, and listening. This fact, however, does not include the amount of time we talk to ourselves (either silently or out loud).
2. **The message sent is not necessarily the same message received.** In fact, some experts claim 50 percent of our daily communication is misunderstood. While we are sharing information important to us, others spend half of the time dozing off, thinking of something else, or simply misinterpreting what we have said.

3. **A part of the message is who sends it.** It is impossible to divorce a message from who sends it. Assume, for example, you hear the message, "I love you." Would the meaning of the message change if it were said by a stranger, spouse, friend, or enemy? Of course it would.

4. **The meanings of words are inside of us.** Words don't "mean"—people attach meaning to words. When Farmer Fred and Biker Bob talk about their new "hogs," there's a good chance they mean different "animals."

5. **Communication is learned.** We learn the language, gestures, and customs of the culture in which we are raised. Consequently, communication is "culture bound." Since most communication is learned, we can learn ineffective ways of communicating, but we can also unlearn and relearn new and sometimes better ways of communicating.

COMMUNICATION TOOLS

Throughout this book, we will provide a series of guidelines and skills, "communication tools," for improving our interactions with others. In this section, we will describe five such tools that will assist effective communicators. We will describe the skills associated with overcoming barriers to effective communication, giving and receiving feedback, recognizing and responding to information overload, maintaining quality relations, and remaining sensitive to the organizational structure of the workplace setting.

Overcoming Barriers

We have thus far discussed how communication works and the kinds of noises that can produce breakdowns. Now we will identify four other barriers to communication that often contribute to misunderstandings, poor personal relations, and decreased quality in the workplace.

Gossip. As anyone who has played the party game "telephone" can tell you, messages become distorted as they move from person to person. Gossip has been the source of countless instances of poor communication. When you hear gossip, you can check the facts face-to-face with the people directly involved. Until then, you would be wise not to pass the message on and consider the message for what it is: unsubstantiated rumor.

Gaps. Gaps represent a second barrier to effective communication and occur because people are different. The greater the difference, the greater the likelihood of miscommunication. Gender gaps, generation gaps, supervisor-employee gaps, cultural gaps, and racial gaps can be fueled by the assumption that all people of a particular group "automatically" think or feel a certain way. Such assumptions can result in stereotyping. This stereotyping can produce divisions between people that may be difficult to reconcile. Organizations, for example, that are experiencing labor-management strife may see factions form that make the gaps grow larger, especially as people are expected to fulfill a particular role within a company (unionist versus management, for example). Those who represent these groups often feel that they have to present only one particular viewpoint of the group.

Gaps can be overcome by questioning the validity of your own stereotypes as well as questioning the stereotypes of others. In addition, gaps are minimized when we focus our communications on individuals rather than on representative members of a group.

Loss of emotional control. A third communication barrier is an inability to control emotions. Emotions that get out of control can quickly turn into barriers. When listening to a powerful motivational speaker or a skillful persuader, for example, audience members may become overly enthusiastic. Such reactions can short-circuit reasoning and prevent the listeners from receiving the information objectively. However, hostile or defensive responses can occur when speakers present disagreeable or offensive topics. As a result, listeners may mentally block out incoming messages, plan a response to the attack, or distort what is being said. In addition, "trigger" words or "hot buttons" can evoke strong emotional responses in the listener, although reactions to these words vary from person to person. Emotional words for some may include political labels, profanities, ethnic slurs, or stereotypes. Being aware of terms, phrases, or topics that create an emotional response in both you and the people with whom you interact is a necessary first step in overcoming this barrier. Recognizing that people have different views of the world and that these differences are indeed valuable will help considerably. Adopting a curiosity about other viewpoints and why they exist will also help.

Defensiveness. The tendency to misinterpret another's comments as a personal attack when that was not the intention is typical of defensiveness. For example, to make conversation, you might ask if a co-worker has heard about the missing equipment in the storage room; the co-worker might assume that you are making an accusation of theft and react defensively. As another example, an employer might mention that some employees are not working to their full capacity. Some of the employees may assume that the employer is talking about them. Defensiveness can be minimized by developing an accurate self-concept, by checking possible interpretations with the speaker, and by sharing thoughts and feelings honestly.

Giving and Getting Feedback

Feedback is almost always worthwhile for increased understanding; how we provide feedback or how we receive it can often be the source of difficulty.

When giving feedback, consider some of the following suggestions.

1. **Make the feedback appropriate.** Feedback is appropriate when it is requested from the sender or when it is necessary for the receiver to clarify the message. In addition, feedback tends to be most effective when it is provided as soon after the sender's message as possible. Of course, the timing involved in offering feedback is also dependent upon the nature of the message, the setting in which the communication occurs, and the attitudes

of the people present. For example, reprimanding a subordinate for not wearing safety glasses in the shop would best be done in the boss's office rather than out on the floor in front of others.

2. **Make the feedback specific.** Rather than telling a subordinate, for example, "Your quarterly report wasn't up to your usual standards," it would be clearer and more precise to say, "Your quarterly report needed to include total sales for the month of March."

3. **Make the feedback positive.** Make certain the tone of the feedback is positive, especially when it involves constructive criticism. In other words, rather than criticizing a co-worker for a mistake, offer suggestions that might prevent that same mistake in the future. Also, consider offering positive feedback before and after any negative feedback. For instance, "I liked the delivery of your presentation; you had great eye contact. Next time, you might consider using a visual aid or two to depict your statistics. The other supporting material you used worked well to prove your point."

When it is your turn to receive feedback, keep in mind some of these tips.

1. **Ask for feedback and then receive it openly.** Requesting feedback from your receiver may require you to be specific about the kind of information you are seeking. For example, "I need to find out what questions you have about the new pricing structure we just discussed."

2. **Acknowledge the feedback.** You might begin by thanking the receiver for the feedback given. Then you may consider paraphrasing the feedback to make sure you fully understand what the receiver meant. A paraphrase could be stated like this: "So I sense you are uncertain about how the new pricing structure will affect our current customers."

3. **Consider the feedback received.** Be open to suggestions, opinions, and concerns the receiver may share with you. This consideration doesn't necessarily mean you agree with the receiver but rather that you are willing to listen as openly as possible. The information you receive can improve your own decision-making and at the same time make the listener feel valued for providing the feedback.

In workplace settings, discuss with co-workers how feedback is given and received. Then develop a plan that will provide opportunities for co-workers to share feedback with each other. Some ways to promote feedback include suggestion boxes, open-door policies, internal/external customer feedback forms, team meetings, and so on.

Recognizing and Limiting Information Overload

At one time or another, all of us have been overwhelmed with workplace responsibilities. We may be trying to juggle customer demands with management's deadlines, co-workers' needs for help, and family commitments. In addition, advances in technology require us to continually update skills to meet the changing work environment. In short, these experiences can result in information overload.

Fortunately, a number of tools are available to counteract information overload. Let's examine some of these tools.

1. **Recognize overloads in others.** First, become sensitive to others who seem to be experiencing overload. Often they will give us cues that say, "I'm preoccupied; leave me alone." Avoidance of eye contact, hurried mannerisms, and a full in-basket clearly communicate overload. Acknowledge your

awareness of their overload and ask for a more convenient time to meet with them. Workers who are this busy are not likely to be attentive to your message. Far better for the sake of understanding to approach these individuals when they are able to be more receptive to you.

2. **Recognize overloads in self.** When you are experiencing overloads, ask for help if you need it and delegate work if possible. Also, let others know you are busy and not able to give them your complete attention. Suggest another time to meet. If a situation arises that must be dealt with immediately, you may have reorganize your own agenda to meet the present need.

3. **Limit overload situations.** We can often minimize overload by scheduling our communication in realistic time frames. We need to establish priorities and give interactions with others the time they require. For example, we may need to set aside a specific amount of time to deal with a customer complaint, a personnel problem, or business correspondence and then move on to the next task. Time management strategies can provide a means to accomplish what needs to be done while reducing problems of overload.

Improving Relations

While specific verbal strategies can be used as communication tools, so can certain attitudes improve relations with others. Four such attitudes include positive regard, empathy, openness, and trust.

1. **Positive regard.** Accept other people for who they are as human beings, regardless of race, attitudes, or behavior. Believe in the equality of all people rather than in the superiority of one person (or group of people) over others (based on money, power, gender, etc.).

2. **Empathy.** Develop an interest (indeed, even a curiosity) in other people and of wanting to know about their feelings, thoughts, and experiences by putting yourself in their shoes and understanding their viewpoint through active listening. Remain open-minded to new perspectives rather than closed-minded.

3. **Openness.** Communicate with others by sharing your own true feelings, thoughts, and experiences.

4. **Trust.** A positive communication climate also occurs when high levels of trust are evident. Trust is of two types: *task trust* is the trust associated with carrying out whatever is expected of you. This type of trust is evident, for example, when you mention to someone that you will turn in a request for a schedule change and then you turn in the request. The second, *interpersonal trust*, is evident in keeping secrets (when requested of you), in supporting colleagues, and in defending someone who is unfairly being criticized.

Remaining Sensitive to the Organization's Structure

As employees, we work within an organization's structure. This structure is characterized by two types of communication networks: formal and informal. Formal networks are those established by management and are often represented in organizational charts. These formal networks identify a chain of command, provide a feedback system, and regulate the kind of communication that occurs in day-to-day operations. Informal networks, however, develop as the result of friendships, common interests, and proximity workers have to one another. Following are some general guidelines for remaining sensitive to your organization's networks.

Formal networks. Know your responsibilities within the formal network. These responsibilities involve sending and receiving information through the proper channels. For instance, if you had a concern or complaint about a co-worker, you would probably want to approach your immediate supervisor first rather than contacting the plant manager. However, when you are listening to a superior explain a new procedure for completing accident reports, it is important that you accurately gather the information in order to pass it on to the next level in the chain. Likewise, it is necessary to listen to subordinates who may point out problems with a procedure or process and report those up the chain. Such information could save the company time and money in the future.

The greatest advantage of formal networks is the structure they provide for getting the work done. However, communication flow may be slow, cumbersome, and impersonal.

Informal networks. Develop informal networks with co-workers. Unlike formal networks, informal networks form when employees who share a common interest interact with one another on a regular basis outside the chain of command. One such network occurs when members of different departments bowl on the same team for XYZ Electronics. Another informal network might emerge among people within the same department who share common space like an office cubicle, employee lounge, or coffee machine.

These informal networks offer a variety of advantages for workers. They build morale and establish rapport by providing face-to-face contact, immediate feedback, and additional information that was not available in the formal networks.

However, these networks may generate inaccurate or incomplete information, fuel gossip, or cause resentment among workers who are not a part of the network.

In summary, sensitivity to organizational structure requires that you understand formal and informal networks. You can make the best use of these networks if you keep in mind the advantages and disadvantages of both and if you are sensitive to the people who make up these networks.

As the information in this chapter shows, communication is a process that satisfies basic human needs. In order for this process to work effectively, we need to understand the elements, principles, and barriers that influence this process. Finally, we need to develop strategies that will promote understanding. The remainder of this text is designed to develop those strategies more fully.

CHAPTER 1 TOOL CHECK

Directions: Use key words from the preceding chapter to complete the following sentences.

1. The communication inside our heads is called _____.
2. _____is the idea that we are both sender and receiver while we communicate.

3. When I have understood "completely" what was said, as the sender intended it to be understood, we have completed effective _____.

4. Daydreaming is a type of _____.

5. Communication helps us to make decisions, but we also communicate with others because it fulfills a _____.

Respond to the following in your own words.

6. Describe the difference between "task" trust and "interpersonal" trust.

7. Define and provide an example of each of the following:
   - Gaps –
   - Loss of Emotional Control –
   - Defensiveness –

8. List three strategies for giving feedback.

9. List three strategies for receiving feedback.

10. Explain how your communication might change given a formal versus an informal organizational structure.

CHAPTER 1 INTERACTIONS

INTERACTION #1—Communication Process Model

Use the space below to create your own map or model of the communication process that has been described on the previous pages.

INTERACTION #2—Feedback Exercise

This exercise will help you to discover the importance of feedback as it relates to "understanding" what is being communicated. Three different diagrams will be described to you. In each instance you are to draw, as accurately as possible, the diagram as it is explained. In all three situations, note how much time it took to draw the diagram (Time), how sure you were that you matched the original (Confidence Level), and how closely your drawing resembled the sender's (Accuracy).

For Situation 1, there should be no verbal or nonverbal feedback from the audience.

For Situation 2, there should be nonverbal but NO verbal feedback from the audience.

For Situation 3, use AS MUCH feedback as possible.

Diagram 1	**Diagram 2**	**Diagram 3**
Accuracy_____	Accuracy_____	Accuracy_____
Confidence	Confidence	Confidence
Level_____	Level_____	Level_____
Time	Time	Time
_____	_____	_____

FEEDBACK EXERCISE WORKSHEET

Answer the following questions after completing the feedback exercise:

1. Which diagram took longest to explain? the shortest? Why?

2. Which diagram was most frustrating to listen to?

3. Which diagram had the highest degree of accuracy?

4. How did your confidence level differ throughout the three diagrams?

5. What conclusions can you draw from this experiment about the role of feedback in communication?

INTERACTION #3—Personal Experience Talk

The purpose of this exercise is to give you the opportunity to speak in front of the class. The goal is to increase your confidence in speaking before groups. You are asked to share a personal experience from your life and to explain the lesson you learned from that experience.

The guidelines for this speech experience are as follows:

1. Choose a personal experience that was meaningful and true. The talk may be serious or humorous. The experience you share should also be one you feel will be of interest to the class.

2. Be sure to share all the necessary details of the experience by including answers to the questions of who, what, where, when, and why. Create a storytelling atmosphere by using specific and vivid language.

3. Finish your talk with a short and clear statement of what you learned from the experience.

4. The amount of time suggested for this presentation is between two and three minutes.

5. Practice the speech several times before the actual classroom presentation. Practice in front of a friend and ask for some suggestions for improvement.

6. Include *who, where, when, what,* and *why* in your talk. You are encouraged, however, to speak extemporaneously—carefully prepared but delivered without notes.

INTERACTION #4—Communication Self-Assessment

This survey is intended to give you an opportunity to see your strengths and weaknesses as they relate to your communication abilities. This survey is not going to be used by any person other than yourself, so you should be honest in answering the questions. When completed, this survey will give you some idea of which areas you may want to pay particular attention to as you proceed through the course.

Scoring should be based on the following scale: 3 points = a definite strength, 2 points = an area I would like to improve, 1 point = a definite weakness

1. _____ Listen completely and attentively without distraction.

2. _____ Respond to others in a way that shows you were listening to them.

3. _____ Detect main ideas and their supporting points.

4. _____ Use clarifying questions to promote understanding.

5. _____ Summarize directions, statements, or feelings shared with you by others.

6. _____ Spell and define technical terms as they relate to your job specialty.

7. _____ Talk freely and confidently to employers about your favorable qualities in a job interview.

8. _____ Clearly state important information about work experiences, educational experiences, and personal qualities on a resume.

9. _____ Fill out applications for employment accurately, neatly, and completely.

10. _____ Write and send business letters regarding employment.

11. _____ Give instructions to others which are clear, concise, and direct.

12. _____ Express feelings to others at work and at home.

13. _____ Separate fact from opinion.

14. _____ Skillfully discuss differences of opinion with others.

15. _____ Employ successful problem-solving techniques when faced with a conflict.

16. _____ Choose specific words to communicate your ideas in writing.

17. _____ Write a clear, accurate set of directions.

18. _____ Draft letters and memos that are free of wordiness and extra information.

19. _____ Write logically organized ideas.

20. _____ Verify factual information in your writing.

COMMUNICATION SURVEY SCORING KEY

Use the following scoring key to assess your perceived ability to communicate. Total your points for items 1–5, 6–10, 11–15, and 16–20. When finished scoring, check your rating and answer the questions which follow.

LISTENING SKILLS	**EMPLOYABILITY SKILLS**	**WRITING SKILLS**	**SPEAKING SKILLS**
(1–5) _____	(6–10) _____	(11–15) _____	(16–20) _____

Rating Scale for Communication Survey

No perceived problem with these communication skills. 11–15 points

Need work to improve these skills. 6–10 points

Need maximum efforts to develop communication strengths. 5 points

Answer the following questions:

1. What do the results of this survey tell you about your ability to communicate?

2. How close do these results compare to your own personal assessment of your communication ability?

3. In what areas do you need special improvement? How might you go about improving your ability in these areas?

CHAPTER 2
DIVERSITY BLUEPRINT

Acknowledge Intercultural Interdependence

Picture Intercultural Communication

Understand Principles of Intercultural Communication

Intercultural Communication Styles

DIVERSITY TOOLS

Overcome Personal Biases

Relate Culture to Communication

Empathize with Non-English Speakers

Develop Cross-Cultural Competence

TOOL CHECK

Intercultural Personality Profile

Making Intercultural Contact

INTERACTIONS

Describing American Culture

Nonverbal Intercultural Differences

Verbal Intercultural Differences

DIVERSITY BLUEPRINT

Acknowledge Intercultural Interdependence

Today we are more likely to interact with people in our communities, in our schools, and in our workplace settings who are ethnically and linguistically different from us. Advances in transportation, the move toward a global economy, and the movement of people in search of increased living standards all mean that diversity is part of the landscape in our communities and in our places of work.

It is important that we understand that we are not just interacting with people who are different from us, but we rely on them for our health, for our education, and for our food. These people are our customers, our neighbors, our employers, and our fellow workers.

Much has also been made of our *global* interdependence. When OPEC raised the price of oil in the 1970s, people in the United States had to sit in waiting lines at gas stations while paying four to five times more for gas. When a nuclear reactor accident occurred in Chernobyl, Russia, nuclear emissions did not stop at the Russian border. Political borders did not stop the killer bees first introduced in Brazil as they made their way into the southern part of the United States. Viruses from the Hong Kong flu to AIDS did not stop at our borders either. And of course, drugs, some of which ravage our communities, and others of which show the promise to heal, come from other countries, too.

Our workplaces are also influenced by our global interdependence. Many of the jobs that we work at are dependent, either directly or indirectly, on foreign trade. Often, the products that we rely on to do our jobs and live the lifestyles we have been accustomed to are manufactured abroad. Indeed, many of the companies we work for are owned by people who are not born in the United States.

In considering these changes, we cannot focus on the changes that come with increased "internationalization" alone. We also need to consider the increases in U.S. born ethnic minority and language minority people. The 2000 U.S. Census data characterized 12.5 percent of the U.S. population as Latino, 12.3 percent as African Americans, and 10 percent as other (American Indian, Native Alaskan, Asian, Native Hawaiian, Other Pacific Islander, etc.) (U.S. Department of Commerce, 2001). In addition, the number of people who classify themselves as "bi-racial" is 2.4 percent. Collectively, we are describing more than 100 million United States citizens. In short, more than one of every three Americans can be classified as an ethnic minority. We also would be remiss if we ignored the number of people born in the United States but who speak languages other than English at home. Consider that the number of school-aged children for whom English is not a first language rose from 2.2 million in 1989 to 4.4 million in 2000 (a 100 percent increase since 1989) (Kinder, 2002).

Importantly, these are not just numbers. They represent the people we know, care about, and depend upon. These people enrich our lives because of their differences, and they help us to imagine new ways of thinking and behaving. They have helped us to understand what "culture" is and the profound influence it has on a person's life.

People from diverse ethnic and linguistic backgrounds also have made us more aware of variations in ways of communicating. We might observe, for example, that when some individuals communicate, they are more expressive, while others more reserved; some are more relationship-oriented, while others are more task-oriented; and some are more individual-focused, while others are more group-focused.

Consider how these differences might play themselves out in a work setting. If your supervisor wanted to consider a new process for creating a work schedule due to problems expressed around the current process (a process the supervisor established), she might gather all the employees together to brainstorm their "concerns" about the current work schedule system. However, some workers may be hesitant to share their concerns since such sharing might make the supervisor "lose face" (a concept generally associated with Asian countries that means one's dignity, rank, image, and respect is threatened). Afterward, she might get a small group of the employees to form a task force, with the specific responsibility of coming up with a new system that addresses the concerns with the current system. The near exclusive focus on accomplishing a task and the use of a group in making decisions may be uncomfortable for some employees based on their cultural values and world-view. Clearly, these differences exist, and they play a powerful role in the overall ability of a department, unit, or company to create inclusive and productive work environments.

Before progressing further, perhaps we need to explain our focus on "diversity." It seems that there are as many types of diversity as there are diverse people. At one end, it is certainly true that we are all "diverse" since we are unique in the combination of genetic makeup, personality, experiences, and groups to which we belong. At the other end, some people have a narrow definition of diversity focused largely on social groups that have been the target of individual and societal oppression. The focus of this chapter will be on diversity with respect to those groups that are protected by Title VII of Equal Employment Opportunity law (that is race, national origin, gender, religion, age, and disability). We also will focus on international encounters due to the increasing globalization of our economy and immigration with its direct implications for workers.

Consider, for example, that much has been written about differences in gender (especially important considering that women today have a better chance of moving into managerial positions than they had in the past). John Gray's (1993) bestseller book, *Men Are From Mars, Women Are From Venus* details some of the communication style differences of men and women. Clearly, we need to acknowledge differences in communication style based on many different characteristics and use these to maximize understanding and workplace productivity in increasingly diverse workplace settings.

Picture Intercultural Communication

Recall that, in Chapter 1, we looked at how we in the United States typically think communication works. Mainstream U.S. culture tends to value sending messages directly, assuring that nonverbal messages are complementary, and taking turns between being either a speaker or a listener. However, not all cultures view the communication process from this perspective.

Consider, for example, the Enryo-Sasshi Japanese model of communication as described in Klopf (1997). To understand this model (Figure 2.1), consider this extended example: You want to tell a customer that you can't fill an order as requested. To begin, the model represents all the possible information that a person could potentially express. In our example, that information could include all of the following: "I can't complete this task because it's not part of my job description"; "My job is on the line"; "I don't like you"; "My boss is standing over us listening to our conversation." The speaker carefully narrows the message (*enryo* means to be discrete, hesitant, restrained) and once the information has been selected, the symbols (words and nonverbal cues) available to the speaker, and the context where communication is taking place, all limit what is eventually expressed: "Completing this order will be most difficult."

FIGURE 2.1 Enryo–Sasshi Model (reprinted with permission of Dr. Satoshi Ishii).

THE JAPANESE ENRYO-SASSHI COMMUNICATION MODEL

By Satoshi Ishii

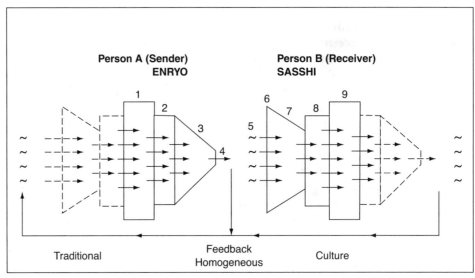

KEY:

1. Sender's potential experiences
2. Sender's chosen ideas (*enryo* filtering)
3. Sender's encoding (filtering)
4. Narrow, limited sending (filtering)
5. Channel
6. Wide, open receiving
7. Receiver's decoding
8. Receiver's expanded ideas (*sasshi*)
9. Receiver's experiences

Enryo: reserve; reservation; restraint; diffidence; retenue (French); coyness; discretion; hesitation; deference; regard.

Sasshi: conjecture; surmise; guess; judgment; understanding; consideration; considerateness; sympathy.

The receiver, whose job is more important than the sender's in this model, must be wide open to receiving not only the verbal message but also the nonverbal message while paying attention to where this dialogue is occurring. As the receiver decodes the message, he/she expands upon all these messages (*sasshi* means to be sympathetic, surmise, guess), adds them to his/her own experiences, and reaches an understanding of what is being communicated. Consequently, what goes on inside the receiver's head significantly influences the interpretation of the message.

This model works efficiently because the Japanese, a very homogeneous people in comparison to the U.S. population, find it easier to understand each other and can, therefore, guess about a person's real meanings more accurately. The closest that Americans get to this model is in intimate relationships. In these relationships, we recognize certain cues as reflective of the sender's true thoughts and feelings. If you know, for example, that your spouse goes out and works in the garage while banging things around when upset or angry, you'll likely know "something is up" the next time he or she retreats to the garage and starts making noise. Indeed, the better we are at understanding each other, the better we will be at making our own communication more efficient and effective.

Understanding these different perspectives about "how communication works" is a necessary first step in communicating cross-culturally.

Understand Principles of Intercultural Communication

Just as there are certain principles that govern communication in general, so are there important principles for communicating cross-culturally. Keeping these principles in mind, as adapted from Sarbaugh (1993), will help you move toward effective communication, regardless of the specific differences you encounter while interacting with people from different ethnic and linguistic backgrounds.

The first principle states that the greater the cultural/linguistic difference between people, the greater the likelihood that there will be a communication breakdown. For example, communicating with customers from Iran will more likely lead to communication difficulties than would be true when communicating with customers from England. Differences in world-views, values, and communication styles can all contribute to misunderstandings.

A second principle suggests that when communication breakdowns occur during cross-cultural encounters, the breakdowns are most often attributed to cultural differences. While these differences may be the cause of breakdowns, effective communicators also think about other possible causes as well. Such breakdowns could be the result of a misunderstanding based on personal differences or any of the breakdowns described in Chapter 1 (such as gaps, noise, or defensiveness).

A third principle illustrates that communicating across cultures often leads us to be more conscious about our own communication. We may, as a result, choose our words more carefully, ask clarifying questions, and refrain from discussing "politically incorrect" topics. Also, we may be conscious of how our nonverbal messages might be misinterpreted. When we consider, for example, that hand gestures that signal victory or "OK" among Americans may signal something quite different to those from other cultures, we are more apt to be cautious about the gestures we make. Note, too, that this increased awareness can make us uncomfortable and more self-conscious about communicating with people from other cultures.

A fourth principle states that cultures vary with respect to the number and kind of "do's and taboos" that are required of its members. Some cultural groups, for instance, have very formal rules that are rarely violated by its members or by anyone who desires to have strong relationships with members of that group. Other cultural groups have few formal rules of communication. However, all groups have some do's and taboos; the effective cross-cultural communicator learns what they are and is respectful of them. Roger Axtell, former CEO of the Parker Pen Company, has written extensively about the do's and taboos of interacting cross-culturally, including do's and taboos for interacting around the world (1993), using gestures, (1998), and hosting international visitors (1990). For example, Axtell (1990) recommends that you provide a small gift for Japanese visitors. However, you would not wrap the gift in white paper (a sign of death) nor should the gift ever be a knife (suggests the visitor commit suicide).

A fifth principle urges us to keep in mind that learning about the norms and variations in communication styles of a particular cultural group helps ensure understanding. You may find it especially helpful to understand the world-view and/or value systems different groups of people hold, since communication patterns reflect these orientations. We can learn about these groups by consulting books, by talking with people who have interacted with these groups, and from our own experiences with cross-cultural communication. While pursuing this information, recognize these sources may fail to provide us with all we need to know about another culture.

For example, variations within the same culture exist from community to community; changes in cultures occur over time; and the biases of the writers of books and people you consult may paint a less than complete (or accurate) picture.

The last principle asserts that if people see each other as friendly, cooperative, and trustworthy, barriers will be more easily overcome. When communicators sense these qualities in others, both parties are more likely to work together to achieve understanding despite differences in culture, language, and world-view.

Intercultural Communication Styles

Let us now examine specific variations in styles of communicating. First we will describe variations in our spoken communication. Then we will describe variations in nonverbal communications. The intention here is not to describe every possible difference but rather to make you aware that tremendous variations exist in how we communicate.

Variations in spoken communication. Variations in language begin with the value cultures place on language itself. U.S. Americans generally value the power of the spoken word. Consider the numerous "talk shows" on radio and television, the popularity of motivational speakers, and the acclaim we give to performing celebrities. The emphasis we place on the spoken message is so powerful that we often feel uncomfortable in silence and quickly talk to fill the voids. In contrast, other cultures are skeptical of language. They believe language can never reveal the truth, and idle babble is to be avoided. Consequently, they are more comfortable with silence. Raymond Tong in *Language of the Buddha* (1975), for example, says that ". . . the Buddha values restraint of words, knowing that silence is often more expressive than the finished poem." Consider a salesperson pitching a new computer-operated welder in Japan. After the salesperson highlights the features of the new welder, the Japanese customers are silent. Assuming that this silence signals that the customers are unimpressed, the salesperson offers to include free packing and shipping. When the Japanese buyers still are silent, the salesperson adds a complete overhaul of the machine at company expense in the third year. Thus, when the Japanese buyers finally agree, the net profit margin for the company is significantly decreased because the salesperson didn't understand the meaning of his customers' silence.

In addition to these different values about language, various cultures view the purpose of language differently as well. We as Americans, for instance, are concerned primarily with language that helps us to accomplish tasks, and, therefore, wish to get to the point quickly. However, different cultural value variations emphasize the use of language for the purpose of strengthening relationships (Axtell, 1998). Therefore, in Mexico, for example, we would talk about family, friends, and co-workers before even considering discussing the task at hand. Paying attention to language variations also helps us learn a little about the ways people regard relationships (formal or informal). In English, we would refer to "you" whether we were talking with a friend, a stranger, our employer, or the President of the United States. In German and Spanish, in contrast, distinctions would be made between those we can refer to informally as "you" ("tu" in Spanish, for those who are friends, peers, or subordinates) and those we regard formally ("su" in Spanish for those who are bosses, Presidents, or superiors). This variant suggests something about the ways you would address a manager differently in the United States ("Just call me Bob") versus in other countries ("I am Mr. Robles").

In addition to these value differences around language are differences in the structure of language. We often use subject-verb-object format for communicating in English as in "She hit the ball." However, in other languages, such as Spanish, the order of the words doesn't matter. For example, in Spanish, one could say, "She the ball hit," to communicate someone hitting a ball. There are differences in the sounds used in a language (phonology is the study of sounds of a language). While there are over 800 sounds in human languages collectively, any one language will use between 15 to 80 (Hawaiian has 18 sounds; depending on the dialect, English has about 45).

Most languages are tonal, meaning that changes in the pitch of a syllable changes the meaning of the word. In Chinese, consider also that there are certain letters or sounds that just are not used together. For example, in English, we would not know how to pronounce a word that starts with "ng" or "ts" (though we have words that end with them as in "moving" or "cats"). In Spanish, words do not begin with "sp" but words can begin with "es". So you will often hear a Spanish-speaker pronounce "speech" as "espeech."

Additionally, there are differences in word meanings. There are *denotative* differences (the object the word refers to) that are often difficult to get around. In English, for example, we say "chair" for the object you sit in and the head of a committee or department. In Korean, different words would be used for each version of "chair" that you mean.

Connotative differences refer to the emotional meanings that come along with words. In English we might want to describe our new supervisor, a woman, as "aggressive," whereas we refer to the previous supervisor, a man, as "assertive." Both words might be used to convey the same behaviors (sharing feelings and ideas, direct eye contact, persistence in getting the department's needs addressed, etc.) but each of the two words invokes a different emotional response. In English, we usually have a negative feeling about "propaganda," but in Spanish "propaganda" has no such negative meaning as implied in "propagating" (or spreading out or publicizing) to the faithful.

Differences also exist based on our use of figurative language. Imagine what your co-worker from Russia would think if you said to her, "Are you pulling my leg?" Conversely, consider if your Filipino customer, in response to being told that you can't be sure when the project will be completed, described you as "hipongtulog." Even if you went to a Filipino/Tagalog-English dictionary, it would read "fish sleeping." What would this mean to you? Does it mean you are lazy, boring, or inattentive? In fact, the word is used for someone who is "wishy-washy" (as a fish would go with the flow of the tides).

Another cluster of variation in language has to do with language use. In fact, knowing how language is used (called "pragmatics") is often as important as knowing the language itself (Heath, 1983). Consider, for example, your Hawaiian co-worker who tends to violate the clear "turn-taking" rule we often expect. Instead, this person consistently talks while you are talking. You might also get frustrated with your Native American friend who responds to your questions by telling a story that, at first glance, is completely irrelevant to the topic. Also, consider that there are differences in what we in the United States consider "appropriate" topics and inappropriate topics based on the gender of the communication participants, their age, and their status. The appropriateness of topics changes from culture to culture (Axtell, 1990). Would you know how to respond to a co-worker from Honduras who you have just met asking how old you are and how much money you make? All are examples of knowing the appropriate use of language that is culture-specific.

Finally, we all tend to make modifications to our communication depending upon where we are and with whom. It is helpful to consider how we change our speech depending upon whether we consider the relationship as formal or informal, how we think people will respond to our use of slang or regional variations in dialect, and variations we make to our speech when talking with children or non-English speakers (talking louder and slower).

Understanding all these language variations helps to explain why customers and co-workers, for whom English is not the first language, speak in the ways that they do and why they may misinterpret you as well.

Variations in nonverbal communication. While language differences are more obvious, we must also recognize the great variability that exists in the "hidden dimension" of our communications: our nonverbal messages (Hall, 1990). We will briefly describe just six of these nonverbal variations. As you read these, consider how they might play out in work settings as you interact with customers and fellow employees.

To begin, there are variations in how we come to regard time (*chronemics*). Time is important to most Americans as evidenced in all the ways we talk about "time" (losing time, killing time, saving time, time is money, etc.). Time is so important that we often stop a really valued activity (having a good conversation with a friend) because "time is up." The Swiss and Germans are also very time conscious. In contrast to this time orientation is a relationship orientation where the quality of the interaction dictates how much time will be spent.

A second nonverbal variation is related to our personal space (*proxemics*). This nonverbal variation refers to differences in the distance we stand when talking with one another. Compared to the United States, others have a shorter distance for personal space (people in the Middle-East, generally) and still others have a larger distance (the British, generally).

Related to this variation are variations in eye contact (*oculesics*). We generally like a soft eye contact where people look at us but, from time to time, look away. In other cultures, there is very little eye contact made (especially with people considered your superiors). Alternately, in some cultures there is an intense stare. Combining a short interpersonal distance and intense stare makes most Americans feel very nervous. But for the Middle-Easterners (generally), the eyes are the windows to the soul and a short personal space combined with a "looking through" the eyes helps them to "read" our "true" messages.

Nonverbal communication also has variations in gestures (kinesics), touch (haptics), and voice (vocalics) (Axtell, 1998; Morris, 1995). Hand gestures are by no means universal. Consider, for example, the hand gesture we often use to indicate that everything is "okay" (thumb and pointer finger making a circle; all other fingers standing up). In other cultures, the same gesture describes a specific body orifice and has the same significance as our social middle finger. While we regard touch as appropriate among friends, certainly for those with whom we are intimate, it was, until recently, just cause for being arrested in China. Alternately, in Argentina as well as much of Latin America, a hug (an "abrazo") and a kiss is a typical greeting even among strangers. Finally, Americans are often regarded as too loud in comparison to the vocal volume deemed appropriate in other cultures.

Barriers to effective intercultural communication. While we hope it is clearly evident that variations in communication abound, based on cultural differences, it is also important that we identify specific barriers to effective intercultural communication (Barna, 1998). We will identify four such barriers to effectiveness in intercultural communication.

The first barrier to effective intercultural communication is "walking on eggs." Certain topics create tension for ethnic minorities. This tension can make those communicating with ethnic minorities hesitant to approach these topics. Further, it is difficult to know exactly what these topics are or what comments spur this tension in communication: different people have different "eggs." One particularly tension-producing topic it is wise to avoid are ethnic jokes. Several things can help with this barrier. Foremost, if you think it is difficult walking on eggs, remember that the ethnic minority herself feels as if she *is* the egg! That is, these topics are profoundly personal and have implications for how people feel and think about themselves. It also helps to learn to handle defensiveness and to communicate your support for ethnic minority people. It might work to invite ethnic minority people in to discussions and ask them to share their perceptions of the topic at hand. Importantly, remember that listening is a vital link in any constructive communication interaction. Finally, it might be best to avoid these topics about ethnicity issues with ethnic minority people until a stronger relationship (marked by trust) is established.

Related to walking on eggs are "hot buttons." Hot buttons are words that invoke an emotional response in another person. Calling someone an "affirmative action hire," for example, does little to produce positive working relations. Sometimes words used are simply misunderstood (as previously described). Realize that for ethnic minority people who have a more formal view of the world, swearing can become a hot button. Other hot buttons are derogatory words used for people from specific ethnic minority groups. It will help for you to identify both the hot buttons for you and for those with whom you work most closely. Then learn to avoid these hot buttons. And when they are used, work hard to control your emotional responses. At some other point, when tension is minimized, talk about your reactions to these hot buttons as well as why they produce that reaction. In this instance, the hope is that having now provided some explanation of why and how these words bother you, the other will cease from using these hot buttons.

A third barrier is described as the "container myth." The container myth is the assumption that words mean the same thing across all cultures. Sometimes the word is simply misunderstood, as when one of us told students that "foul" language was not allowed in class. A concerned student from Turkey came to the office to ask why we couldn't talk about chickens and birds ("fowl") in class. At other times, it is simply differences in the meaning (denotation as previously described) or emotional response (connotation as previously described) of the words. Again, having a relationship built on trust will go a long way to creating a climate where people will share alternative understandings with you. It would be helpful to be curious about language use across cultures. We urge you to also stay away from jargon (the specialized language of an occupation) until these are fully understood. To assist, when using language that might be misunderstood or that absolutely must be understood, consider the phrase "we describe it as. . . ; how do you say this in your language?"

The fourth barrier is "language, vernacular, and accent bias." Almost all people, including mainstream Americans in the United States, have a particular affinity for their language. With language comes identity, access to ideas, and a level of comfort. To suggest that one language is better than another does little to create constructive relations with those who speak other languages. All languages are capable of communicating every possible thought. Related to language bias is bias related to vernacular (the specific language used in particular communities—such as that spoken by people in the Appalachians—or by certain ethnic groups—such as Black English) (the film *American Tongues* is excellent for its exploration of these). Finally, there are certain biases that come with a particular accent (Valley Girl, Southern Drawl, or Midwesterner). Again, keeping in mind the very personal relationship people have to their language, the vernacular of that language, and their accents is a productive starting point. It helps to identify your biases about language, vernaculars, or accents and actively work to overcome these. We suggest you develop a curiosity about other languages and the specific vernaculars of those languages. In addition, we urge you to recognize that there is power in learning new languages and that there are advantages to being able to use multiple languages.

We recognize that English is the international language of business. Nonetheless, relationships are strengthened with others for whom English is a foreign language when you can demonstrate some competence in their language. The message that you care enough about them to learn another language goes a long way to communicate respect and concern.

DIVERSITY TOOLS

The specific tools for effective communication across cultures are easy to list and describe but difficult to employ. In this section, we will discuss four such tools: overcoming personal biases, relating culture to communication, empathizing with non-English speakers, and developing intercultural competence.

Overcome Personal Biases

Racism, stereotypes, and discrimination negatively impact our communication with others. These are the source of hurt feelings and result in miscommunication, damaged relationships, and loss in productivity. The history of ethnic relations in America makes it difficult to overcome our current struggles with racism, since the philosophy and mentality that justified slavery, the forced removal of the first Americans from their ancestral lands, and exploited the existing communities in the southwestern United States still pervades much of this country's consciousness. Relations become strained when many Euro-Americans assert that these historical practices are over (and, thus, ethnic minority people should "just get over it") or when feelings of guilt keep them from creating meaningful relationships with ethnic minorities.

First, develop an understanding about what these words mean. We provide a set of definitions that we hope you will find helpful (see Figure 2.2). Second, recognize that racism and discrimination are still a powerful part of the American landscape. Make a commitment not only to be sensitive to the possibility of your own racism, but also develop strategies to actively resist the racism that may occur in your workspace. Third, be especially attuned to how we communicate our prejudices. In this regard, Brislin's (1988) description is helpful. His description moves from the most obvious and derogatory to the least. As we describe these in the next paragraph, ask yourself if you have heard (or perhaps have made) comments like these in the recent past.

Overt racism is communicated when people make some statement that would, by most people, be identified as racist. Such statements as "All. . . are lazy" or ". . . should go back where they came from" fall into this category. *Symbolic racism* is attacking some symbol of importance to a particular group of people. These symbols might be affirmative action, bilingual education, or reparations for land lost. By not attacking the people themselves, individuals fool themselves into believing that they are not racist. This doesn't mean that there's not genuine disagreement about these programs. Symbolic racists reject these symbols without being fully informed about them (for example, saying that affirmative action required companies to hire people who were not

Prejudice – A set of rigid and unfavorable attitudes toward a particular group or groups that is formed in disregard of facts. An unsupported judgment usually accompanied by disapproval.

Stereotype – A preconceived or oversimplified generalization involving negative beliefs about a particular group. Negative stereotypes are frequently based on prejudice. The danger of stereotyping is that it no longer considers people as individuals, but rather categorizes them as members of a group who all think and behave in the same way. We may pick up these stereotypes from what we hear other people say, from what we read, and from what people around us believe.

Discrimination – The differential treatment based on unfair categorization. It is denial of justice prompted by prejudice. When we act on our prejudices, we engage in discrimination. Discrimination often involves keeping people out of activities or places because of the group to which they belong.

Racism – The coupling of the false assumption that race determines psychological and cultural traits with the belief that one race is superior to another. Based on their belief in the inferiority of certain groups, racists justify discriminating against, scapegoating, and/or segregating these groups.

Scapegoating – The deliberate policy of blaming an individual or group when the fault actually lies elsewhere. It means blaming another group or individual for things they did not really do. Those that we scapegoat become objects of our aggression in work and in deed. Prejudicial attitudes and discriminatory acts lead to scapegoating. Members of the disliked group are denied social privileges (e.g., housing, employment, etc.). They are usually politically powerless to defend themselves. Scapegoating can lead to verbal and physical violence, including death.

Institutional Racism – Ideologies and structures that are used to systematically legitimize unequal division of power and resources between groups that are defined on the basis of race and resources between groups. The term "racism" is being used here in a broad sense to include discrimination against both ethnic and racial minorities. The discrimination is brought about both by the ways particular institutions (e.g., schools) are organized or structured and by the (usually) implicit assumptions that legitimize that organization. There is usually no intent to discriminate on the part of educators; however, their interactions with minority students are mediated by a system of unquestioned assumptions that reflect the values and priorities of the dominant middle-class culture. It is in these interactions that minority students are educationally disabled.

FIGURE 2.2 Definition of Terms

---

qualified is a distortion of the actual policy); the response is emotional and not based on fact. *Tokenism* is communicated by people who say "I can't be racist; one of my best friends is. . . ." Believing that knowing one person is enough to prove that she or he is not racist is illogical at best. *Arms-length racism* is suggesting that you don't mind ethnic minority people (to work with or to socialize with) but that you would oppose any closer relationship (for example, dating or marrying a person from a group).

These forms of racism are distinguished from general likes and dislikes about people. These general likes or dislikes are usually behavioral in orientation (disliking when people show up late for work) and are not applied to groups of people but to individuals. It makes sense to learn whether these are culture-specific ways of behaving or just an individual's way of acting. If it were a culture-specific behavior, communicating the cultural orientation of the organization to the individual would be an appropriate response. Finally, we are all skeptical of those things we are unfamiliar with. Only through genuine communication can we move beyond the unfamiliar and create cooperative relations with others who are different from us. As Martin Luther King suggested:

> People fail to get along because they fear each other; they fear each other because they don't know each other; they don't know each other because they have not properly communicated.

Relate Culture to Communication

We hope that as a result of this chapter you have now come to understand the powerful connection between culture and communication. Culture is not simply a matter of the foods, fashions, or folklores of a particular group of people. Consider, for example, that we cannot teach someone about "American culture" by simply having him or her wear jeans, eat hotdogs and apple pie, and listen to the legend of Johnny Appleseed.

Likewise, every aspect of communication is impacted by culture. Language and culture are intimately connected. In fact, it is hard to know a language without simultaneously learning the culture of that people. Nonverbal communication is impacted by culture-specific meanings that we would be remiss to ignore. Finally, the way we communicate conveys much about the values and world-view orientations of the people with whom we interact.

Keep in mind that culture is invisible, and most people are not aware of how culture impacts them. We do not know, for example, where the idea (and what purpose is fulfilled) of throwing rice at a wedding, wearing a tie in a business meeting, or kissing a "boo-boo" on the skinned knee of a child came from (Tejula, 1999). Asking someone why people of their culture "act in certain ways" might result in a quizzical response. It's true that we often have very little clue about the purpose behind culturally appropriate behavior (even our own) beyond explaining that it is "tradition."

The skillful intercultural communicator first will not trivialize culture and cultural differences. Rather she will seek to understand these cultural differences. She will then seek to affirm these differences and recognize that tremendous value results in the variation of human orientations. She will recognize the interdependent nature of groups (as described in the opening pages of this chapter). She will seek culture-specific knowledge that includes the history, current social issues, and perspective of that group about a wide range of topics. She will especially note the culture-specific differences in communication that characterize intercultural interactions. She will then seek to become an ally of people from diverse groups as a person who is committed to social equality and justice.

Empathize with Non-English Speakers

Speaking a language that is not the dominant language of the people with whom you work/live is difficult. Likewise, learning to speak a second language is a most difficult activity. It is difficult because learning a second language involves many, many factors including how you feel about the new language (and yourself as a second language learner), the degree to which you experience anxiety in language learning situations, and the learning style differences when it comes to language learning.

The skillful intercultural communicator develops empathy for second language learners. One way in which this is best facilitated is by learning a second language yourself. You will quickly come to appreciate the difficult task facing someone for whom English is the second language. Additionally, you communicate that you value languages and appreciate the attempts by others to learn your language. Above all, keep in mind that a person's intelligence has nothing to do with his or her ability to speak English. Maintaining a respectful orientation will be critical in this regard.

The two primary things you want to do when communicating with those for whom English is a second language is to minimize the level of stress and to work to make the message as understandable as possible. Minimizing stress is important to enable the language learner to be open to messages presented in a language not fully understood and encourages "risk taking" in efforts to speak the new language. Making the message more understandable by providing as many clues as possible (via visuals, gestures, pictures, objects, etc.) also enhances the likelihood that the message will be more fully understood.

Develop Cross-Cultural Competence

While the above areas are critical to cross-cultural effectiveness, it is also important to work to develop the full range of cross-cultural competency skills (Spitzberg, 1999). The kind of competence meant here is an ability to accomplish goals while also reducing misunderstandings and building strong interpersonal (cross-cultural) relationships. This is a lifelong process and must be engaged in purposefully (that is, it will not "just happen"). We believe that these competencies will enhance the overall quality of your life (as well as your relationships with all the people with whom you live and work).

We provide a brief list of these skills. Think about these and assess where you stand with respect to these. Identify a couple that you want to work toward and then move toward effectiveness in that area. Cross-cultural competency skills include the following:

- An ability to acknowledge one's own prejudices and biases and the lifelong work to overcome them.
- An ability to work toward equal status relationships with people who are different.
- An ability to challenge one's own personal assumptions about the skills and competencies of employees who are different.
- An ability to learn as much as possible about how one's own culture is different from others, and how that difference contributes to a particular way of viewing the self and others.
- An ability to take risks in an effort to communicate with people from other cultures.
- An ability to learn about how individuals and groups of people like to be treated and to accommodate them as much as possible.

CHAPTER 2 TOOL CHECK

Directions: Use key words from the preceding chapter to complete the sentences below.

1. The idea that we rely on others is described as our _____.
2. _____ is the study of "space" when communicating.
3. The emotions that come along with words we chose is called _____.
4. The Japanese notion of being wide "open" and guessing about a speaker's meanings is defined as _____.
5. _____ means the actual object to which a word refers.

Respond to the following in your own words.

6. Describe three differences in how our verbal communication changes across cultures.
7. Define the words below and give an example of a cultural difference for each:
   * Oculesics –
   * Kinesics –
   * Vocalics –
8. The idea that our intercultural communication might involve "walking on eggs" is. . . .
9. Explain the meaning of "arms-length" racism.
10. List three strategies for communicating with people for whom English is not their first language.

CHAPTER 2 INTERACTIONS

INTERACTION #1—Intercultural Personality Profile

Directions: To assess how easy it will be for you to interact with people from a different culture, complete the questionnaire below. Use a scale of 1 to 5 to indicate how strongly you agree with each statement.

low agreement   1   2   3   4   5   high agreement

1. I am constantly trying to understand myself better. I feel I know my strengths and weaknesses and generally feel good about myself.

2. I respect the opinions of others, though I may not always agree.

3. I interact well with people who are very different from me in age, race, economic status, gender, and sexual orientation.

4. I can usually apply what I learn to real-life situations.

5. I do not need to understand everything going on around me.

6. I am able to change my plans or expectations to fit new situations.

7. I often find humor in difficult situations and can laugh at myself.

8. When I have to wait, I am patient.

9. I constantly seek new things, new people, and new places.

10. I am resourceful and able to entertain myself.

11. I tackle problems confidently without needing the help of others.

12. When things go badly, I am able to keep my mind clear and my attitude positive as I attempt to resolve the problem(s).

13. I realize that my culture is not "better" than other cultures.

14. In an unfamiliar situation, I watch and listen before acting.

15. I am a good listener and can put myself in another's place.

16. When I am lost, I ask for directions.

17. When working with others, building a good relationship is just as important (if not more important) as completing our task.

18. I like people and can accept them as they are.

19. I am sensitive to the feelings of others and observe their reactions when I am talking. I sincerely do not want to offend others.

20. I like new ideas and try new ways of doing things.

Now re-read each and identify the cross-cultural competency underlying each.

These competencies are:

Those that I best exhibit are:

Those that I need to work on are:

INTERACTION #2—Describing American Culture

Much of what we do, feel, and believe is influenced by our culture. Yet we rarely consider our cultural practices and perspectives. It is part of our "collective unconscious." That is, we're not aware of our culture, but we share it with lots of people. Therefore, it is not easy for a person to respond to a question that asks her to "explain" her culture. We hope that you will have a better awareness of this phenomenon at the end of this interaction. Consider the following:

Sieko, a new friend of yours who has recently arrived from Japan, is sitting having lunch with you one day when she suggests she's having a hard time understanding Americans. You ask her to explain. She then relates several activities she has seen Americans engage in and has heard numerous statements that don't make sense to her. She asks you not only to explain the meaning of the behavior or statement but also to tell you what it says about "Americans" (that is, the cultural value). How would you respond to these? Select any four of the eight listed below

A. Throwing rice on a couple emerging from a church after just being wed.
    Why do we do this?
    What value orientation does it imply?
B. Seeing all "businessmen" in ties (men)
    Why do we do this?
    What value orientation does it imply?
C. Wearing high heels (women)
    Why do we do this?
    What value orientation does it imply?
D. Putting candles on a cake, lighting them, and then having the birthday person blow them out.
    Why do we do this?
    What value orientation does it imply?
E. The saying: "Pull yourself up by your bootstraps"
    Why do we say this?
    What value orientation does it imply?
F. The saying: "Don't split hairs"
    Why do we say this?
    What value orientation does it imply?
G. The saying: "If at first you don't succeed. . . ."
    Why do we say this?
    What value orientation does it imply?
H. The saying: "What's good for the goose is good for the gander"
    Why do we say this?
    What value orientation does it imply?

INTERACTION #3—Nonverbal Intercultural Differences

In this interaction, you will discover differences in nonverbal (specifically gestures) communication cross-culturally. In a study by Morris and his colleagues (1980), pictures of gestures were shown to over 1,200 people in 40 different locales (mostly in Europe). Respondents were asked to describe what each gesture meant.

On this page, mark what you think each gesture communicates. Compare their response with your own.

The Nose Thumb

_____ Mockery	_____ Buzz off
_____ Idiot	_____ You're crazy
_____ Get lost	_____ Up yours

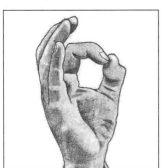

The Ring

_____ O.K.-Good	_____ Orifice
_____ Zero	_____ Threat
_____ Insult	_____ Thursday

The Thumb Up

_____ Directional	_____ Hitch-Hike
_____ O.K.	_____ One
_____ Sexual Insult	_____ Obscenity

Answers based on 1,200 informants, 40 locations, mostly in Europe

Nose Thumb:	**The Ring:**	**The Thumbs Up:**
Mockery 1,058	O.K.-Good 700	O.K. 738
Others 14	Orifice 128	One 40
Not Used 128	Zero 115	Sexual insult 36
	Threat 16	Hitch-hike 30
	Others 27	Directional 14
	Not Used 214	Others 24
		Not Used 318

Gestures, Their Origins and Distributions. Morris, Marsh, and O'Shaugnessy (1980). Reprinted with permission.

INTERACTION #4—Verbal Intercultural Differences

In this interaction, you will discover differences in verbal (specifically word meanings or semantics) communication cross-culturally. In a study by Szalay and Fisher (1987) and Takahara (1974), distinctions were identified with respect to word meanings across cultures.

For each of the two words below, list as many words as you can that come to your mind when you think of these words. When completed, refer to the bottom of the page and see the word meanings that were associated with marriage and family in other cultures.

Marriage

_____

_____

_____

_____

_____

Family

_____

_____

_____

_____

_____

Word meanings as described in other cultures follow below. How do these compare with the words you associate with both family and marriage?

Family

Korean and Americans offered the following different designations for "family."

Korean Top 3	USA Top 3
*Mother/Father	*Mother/Father
*Children, brother, sister	*Children, brother, sister
*Relatives	*Love, Friendship

Marriage

"Marriage" produced interesting results when comparing American, Japanese, and French respondents.

USA Top 3	Japan Top 3	France Top 3
*Love	*Trust	*Love
*Respect	*Family	*Passion
*Responsibilities	*Understanding	*Sex

What do these differences mean to you?

What did you learn about word meaning differences generally?

How will knowing these differences impact your communication with other cultures?

INTERACTION #5—Making Intercultural Contact

We believe that "experience is often the best teacher." For this interaction, we ask that you interview someone ethnically different from yourself. It could be someone in your community, someone in your school, or someone from your place of employment. We list some guidelines we hope that you seriously consider. We provide questions that you might want to ask. And finally, we ask that you take notes and explain to the teacher and/or your class what you have learned about cross-cultural communication.

Guidelines

1. Get the person's permission to conduct an interview. Tell her/him that you will not "identify" her/him in your class report. Explaining that this is a school assignment and explaining the purpose of the assignment might be helpful in getting the person's assistance.

2. Adopt a "genuine curiosity" about the other person. Don't argue with anything said. Listen and be open.

3. Begin by trying to build a relationship of trust before asking the questions that make up this assignment. Remember that some cultures are more relationship-oriented than they are task-oriented.

4. As you ask a question, consider "follow-ups"—questions that ask for clarifications, examples, or extensions of what the person just said. These follow-ups are usually the best source of specific information and are, therefore, more enlightening.

5. At the end, thank the person for participating and for helping you to learn.

Possible Questions/Probes

1. Tell me about your (or your family's) history in the United States.

2. How would you describe your culture's main value orientations?

3. How is your culture different from "mainstream" American culture?

4. What differences do you notice in gender relations within your culture?

5. What is one thing you wished people understood about your culture or people from your culture?

6. Explain a time when you and another person miscommunicated and you believed that it was as a result of cross-cultural communication differences. What was the basis of the miscommunication? How did you respond?

7. What words/phrases/topics that people engage in are especially uncomfortable for you to discuss?

8. How would you characterize cross-cultural relations in America? In your community? In your school? In your workplace?

9. Have you ever been discriminated against? If so, what happened? Why do you think it happened? How did you respond?

10. What piece of advice can you offer me to be a more effective communicator when interacting with people from your culture?

    Be prepared to answer the questions on the following page.

Reporting Differences

1. What differences did you note in how the person communicated verbally? Nonverbally?

2. What answers to questions asked most surprised you? Why?

3. How did you cope with the person's accent or language dialect (if she/he had one)?

4. How did you feel the communication interaction went? What competencies did you demonstrate? What competencies would have helped make the interaction more productive?

5. What have you learned most from this assignment?

REFERENCES

Axtell, R. (1998). *Gestures: The do's and taboos of body language around the world.* New York: John Wiley & Sons.

Axtell, R. (1993). *Do's and taboos around the world.* New York: John Wiley & Sons.

Axtell, R. (1990). *Do's and taboos of hosting international visitors.* New York: John Wiley & Sons.

Barna, L. (1998). Stumbling blocks in intercultural communication. In M. J. Bennett (Ed.), *Basic readings in intercultural communication: Selected readings* (pp. 173–190). Yarmouth, ME: Intercultural Press.

Brislin, R. W. (1988). Prejudice in intercultural communication. In L. A. Samovar & R. E. Porter (Eds.), *Intercultural communication: A reader* (5th ed., pp. 339–343). Belmont, CA: Wadsworth.

Gray, J. (1993). *Men are from mars, women are from Venus.* New York: HarperCollins.

Hall, E. T. (1990). *The hidden dimension.* New York: Anchor Books.

Heath, S. B. (1983). *Ways with words.* Cambridge: Cambridge University Press.

Kinder, A. L. (2002). *Survey of the states' limited English proficient students and available programs and services, 1999–2000 summary report.* Washington, D.C.: National Clearinghouse for English Language Acquisition.

Klopf, D. W. (1997). *Intercultural encounters: The fundamentals of intercultural communication* (4th ed.). Englewood, CO: Morton.

Morris, D. (1995). *Bodytalk: The meaning of human gestures.* New York: Crown Publishing.

Morris, D., Collett, P., Marsh, P., & O'Shaugnessy, M. (1980). *Gestures, their origins and distributions.* New York: Stein and Day.

Sarbaugh, L. E. (1993). *Intercultural communication* (2nd ed.). New Brunswick, NJ: Transaction Books.

Spitzberg, B. H. (1999). Communicating interculturally: Becoming competent. In L. A. Samovar & R. E. Porter (Eds.), *Intercultural communication: A reader* (pp. 373–387). Boston, MA: Wadsworth Publishing Co.

Szalay, L. B., & Fisher, G. H. (1987). Communication overseas. In L. F. Luce & E. S. Smith (Eds.), *Toward internationalism* (2nd ed., pp. 166–192). Cambridge, MA: Newbury House.

Takahara, T. (1974). Semantic concepts of 'Friendship,' 'Marriage,' 'Work,' and 'Foreigner' in the American, Japanese and French cultures. In J. Condon (Ed.), *Patterns of communication in and out of Japan.* Tokyo: International Christian University.

Tejula, T (1999). *Curious customs.* New York: Galahad Books.

Tong, R. (1975). Language of the Buddha. *English Language Teaching, 30*(1), p. 3.

U.S. Department of Commerce (2001). Overview of race and Hispanic origin: Census 2000 brief. (U.S. Census Publication No. C2KBR/01–1). Washington, D.C.: U.S. Government Printing Office.

CHAPTER 3
LISTENING BLUEPRINT

| Recognize Importance of Listening | Identify Types of Listening | Minimize Bad Listening Habits | Interpret Nonverbal Behaviors |

LISTENING TOOLS

| Attending Tools | Remembering Tools | Evaluating Tools | Responding Tools |

TOOL CHECK

Self-Assessment

Paraphrasing Practice

INTERACTIONS

Response Styles Questionnaire

Information Passing Exercise

Active Listening Identification

LISTENING BLUEPRINT

Recognize Importance of Listening

How well do you listen? Do you comprehend fully what you are being told by supervisors, co-workers, friends, and family? How would they rate your listening skills or lack of them? In what kinds of situations do you find it most difficult to listen? Finally, how do you attend to and respond to others who attempt to share their personal or occupational concerns with you?

Chapter 3 addresses all of these important questions. When one considers the time and money spent correcting errors because somebody didn't listen properly, it's no wonder that employers rate listening as a communication essential.

In *The Business of Listening,* Diane Bones relates the story of a costly mistake when a dispatcher didn't listen to an entire message and sent a fleet of trucks to Portland, Oregon, not Portland, Maine. This incident illustrates the problems that can occur when listening is incomplete or absent. The costs of poor listening affect both profits and promotions (Bones, 1994, p. 5).

Listening is by far the most frequently used communication skill. On its web page, the International Listening Association presents interesting quotes, facts, and statistics that describe the importance of listening in our lives. Included recently were the following:

"85% of what we know we have learned by listening."

"We remember only 20% of what we hear."

"Less than 2% of us have had any formal educational experience with listening."

"Being listened to spells the difference between feeling accepted and feeling isolated" (*www.listen.org*).

Furthermore, the hurt feelings generated when we fail to actively demonstrate our listening skills can damage our personal and occupational relationships with others. People are fired, customers are lost, and working relationships are strained because of ineffective listening. Likewise, friendships suffer, marriages fail, and families grow apart when individuals fail to listen with genuine concern.

No doubt, the importance of listening seems self-evident. In fact, on the average, we spend nearly half of our communication time listening. Yet studies suggest that we are mediocre listeners at best. Estimates of listening efficiency barely reach 25 percent, meaning that we generally will miss three-quarters of what we hear.

Yet when we do listen and are listened to, we experience a confirming connection that brings about a shared understanding, which is the goal of effective communication. Ask someone to describe his or her best friend; a co-worker that is easy to work with; or an effective, valued subordinate, and you will likely hear a description of a good listener. Ralph Nichols, who pioneered the study of listening, described the highest compliment that you could pay to a supervisor as, "I like my boss; he listens to me!"

Identify Types of Listening

The term "listening" has different meanings for different people. For some, listening involves paying attention and maintaining eye contact with the speaker. For others, "listening" means remembering what has been said word-for-word, while for others, listening is all about "reading between the lines" to perceive the unspoken message. While each of these perceptions focuses on one aspect of listening, none of them contains all of the elements that characterize effective listening. In addition, some individuals make the mistake of confusing listening with hearing. Consider the following illustration.

Technicians of all kinds use hearing skills to monitor procedures, judge the smoothness of operations, spot malfunctions, or locate problems. They hear "whirs," "pings," "screeches," "pops," "thunks," and "squeals" to name but a few. Hearing these sounds can trigger the listening process to begin. After the recognition of aural stimuli, the technician decides whether the sound deserves attention or not. With attention focused on the sound, the technician can identify the sound, determine its origin, analyze its cause, and take appropriate action.

As you can see from this illustration, hearing involves the physical recognition of sound, while listening goes beyond simple recognition and can be defined in terms of the following elements: attending to the speaker, both mentally and physically; assigning meaning to both the verbal and nonverbal messages; verifying accurate understanding of these messages; evaluating the importance of the messages; and then responding appropriately.

In their book, *Listening*, Wolvin and Coakley (1996) describe the types of listening that we do. Included are discriminative listening, comprehensive listening, therapeutic listening, critical listening, and appreciative listening. Discriminative listening involves recognizing different "auditory and visual messages and identifying their distinguishing features before we process the messages at any other level. The comprehensive listener strives to understand the message in order to retain, recall, and possibly—use that information at a later time"(p. 164).

The therapeutic listener may provide help to someone who needs to talk out a concern by being a sounding board for a troubled friend, by suspending all judgment, and by empathizing with the sender. Therapeutic listening is common when friends face choices in their lives, when problems need to be aired, when strong feelings need to be expressed and heard. "The successful therapeutic listener must have the willingness to listen, the capacity to care, the desire to understand, honesty, and the patience to assume the role of sounding board" (Wolvin & Coakley, 1996, p. 320). The therapeutic listener does not give advice or pass judgment; rather, therapeutic listeners ask clarifying questions and summarize the thoughts and feelings of the speaker.

However, after comprehending the message, the critical listener evaluates the content of the message. Critical listening entails separating facts from inferences, assessing logical fallacies, analyzing source credibility, evaluating evidence, and recognizing emotional appeals. Critical listening is used when negotiating, making decisions, and assessing persuasive messages. Effective critical listeners summarize message content, ask questions, and make evaluative responses.

Appreciative listeners enjoy the aesthetic experience listening can provide. For some listeners, background music is essential to soothe their concentration. For others, the blare of heavy metal sets the pace for work or pleasure. Still others enjoy the spoken word of "Books on Tape," a Garrison Keillor monologue, or a Dylan Thomas tape-recorded poem. Most have enjoyed the appreciative listening experience as children with bedtime stories from books or grandparents.

Regardless of the type of listening that you are engaged in, several factors may keep you from being an effective listener.

Minimize Bad Listening Habits

We don't listen very effectively for many reasons. Listening problems can be grouped into five general categories: lack of specific training, message overload, yielding to distractions, losing emotional control, and failing to use the thought-speed advantage.

One explanation for poor listening skills is that most of us have not been taught how to listen. Throughout our formal education, we are offered courses in reading, writing, and speaking, but rarely are we offered training in listening skills. Certainly we learned how to listen as we watched and modeled those around us whom we admired: parents, family, and friends. But they, like most of those untrained in listening, probably were only mediocre listeners themselves.

Another factor that contributes to poor listening is the mistaken belief that because we are bombarded with an overwhelming number of messages daily, we somehow learn to listen automatically. Radio commercials scream at us as we drive to work; machines grind, whir, and hum the noises of production; a barrage of chatter deafeningly echoes as we sit in the student center reviewing for an upcoming exam; and stereo systems "whoof and tweet" us into oblivion with nonstop rock. Such an overload, instead of helping us to listen better, teaches us to tune out many of the messages we receive.

Even when we choose to listen, we are influenced by external and internal distractions. Problems occur when we choose to focus our attention on these distractions instead of on the speaker's message. Examples of external distractions, as previously mentioned, constantly compete for our attention and may be both visual and verbal.

We may also tune out a speaker because of distractions that exist inside of our head. When we doubt what the speaker is saying, when we begin to formulate a re-

Actions and attitudes keep the listener
involved in the listening process.

sponse before the speaker has concluded, or when we are preoccupied with our own personal problems, internal distractions keep us from listening well.

Losing emotional control is a fourth problem many listeners face. Our listening effectiveness drops as our emotional responses increase. Listening while you are experiencing intense anger, happiness, or boredom, for example, can make listening very difficult.

Sometimes the emotional reaction is directly related to what the speaker is saying or how it is being said. For instance, listening to a pro-union speaker when you are strongly against collective representation is difficult because such opinions oppose your attitudes, values, and beliefs. Likewise, if the speaker begins labeling those who express anti-union beliefs as "scabs," chances are your listening effectiveness will drop to zero. Emotional control, though not easy to achieve, is essential for successful listening.

Finally, failing to use the thought-speed advantage is a major source of our listening problems. Because we can think so much faster than anyone can talk, we often fool ourselves by believing that we can take mental holidays, daydream, plan, or worry and still listen at the same time.

The fact is that the more we allow our minds to wander, the stronger the tendency to tune out the speaker. The result might be sitting in a meeting on shop safety and not hearing a word the speaker is saying. By no means are these the only reasons why we don't listen well, but they constitute the bulk of our listening problems. In any case, the first step to solving a problem is to become aware of the problem; you must find out what causes your bad listening habits and take steps to overcome them. Unfortunately, these poor listening patterns may come from well-established habits. Fortunately, these listening problems can be improved if we learn new and better habits to replace the old ones.

Interpret Nonverbal Behaviors

Although most listening focuses on the verbal message, to understand the total message we must receive both the verbal and nonverbal components. Nonverbal messages can replace, strengthen, or contradict the verbal message. In face-to-face communication situations, factors such as distance, body orientation, eye contact, facial expressions, posture, tone of voice, gesture, and touch all can provide information necessary to understand the total message. Nonverbal communication can be classified into several categories: kinesics, proxemics, chronemics, touch, and appearance.

Kinesics refers to the many behaviors of the body, for example, postures, gestures, body orientation, facial expressions, and eye behavior. The body speaks in many ways, and each message must be interpreted by considering the uniqueness of the individual, the physical and social setting, and the cultural context in which the communication occurs.

Sometimes our words say one thing and our body posture and attitude say something different; confusing the receivers of our messages.

Proxemics is the language of space, territory, and distance. In large part, proxemic behavior is culture-bound. Edward Hall (1969) and others have noted different uses of space for North Americans: intimate messages are shared from physical contact to about 18 inches; personal messages are shared from 18 inches to 4 feet; social messages are communicated at a distance between 4 to 12 feet; and public messages are shared beyond 12 feet. Also, messages match the distances. You are more likely to share confidential information in the intimate zone than in the public zone. In addition, North Americans have a perceived "personal space" that surrounds them and extends out to about 30 inches. When this personal space is invaded by someone standing too close for comfort, we may react defensively. Territoriality, the final element of proxemics, refers to our relationship to fixed space. Our seat in a classroom, our work area, or our favorite chair at home are all examples of fixed spaces that we regard as our own for specific periods of time. We mark our territories in a number of ways, often with belongings or other identifying markers. As employees, we need to be aware of others' personal space, territory, and distance when we communicate at work.

Time can also be a part of the total message. An awareness of chronemics includes a sense of time: when a message is shared, the urgency with which it is shared, and the length of time it takes to communicate the message. Although cultural differences may complicate our interpretation of time, individuals also have a unique sense of timing. Some are constantly rushed, while others exhibit a more laid back attitude toward time. Some focus on one thing at a time, while others pride themselves on doing multiple tasks at the same time. As listeners, we need to know our standards for appropriate use of time and share our time needs with others. If we don't, saying we need a report ASAP may not get us that report "on time."

Touch is another powerful form of communication that can share a range of feelings from a warm greeting, to a congratulatory pat on the back, to a push away. While touching behaviors take many forms, they, too, must be interpreted in light of culture, status, gender, and personality traits. The boss' hand on the listener's forearm may signal, "pay attention." A supportive hand to the shoulder may signal, "I'm here"; while similar signals may say, "move over." Accidental touching is usually accompanied with an apologetic, "Excuse me." And we all know people who are "touchers," and that their behavior may make some uncomfortable. Guidelines for appropriate touching vary from one culture to another, but in the workplace, when touch is a part of communication, it should be purposeful and clear to both sender and receiver.

Appearance as nonverbal communication includes the body, clothing, and possessions. People assign meanings to our body types, skin color, manner of dress, hairstyle, and accessories we display. Think about the stereotypes you may have when you see someone with a nose ring, a Mohawk haircut, or an obscene tattoo. Unfortunately, some people do not see past the obvious item of appearance to see the traits and skills of the person. Remember that appearance is only a part of the total message and may work to reinforce it or contradict it.

LISTENING TOOLS

Attending Tools

While many suggestions are offered to help us become better listeners, real improvement requires a caring attitude and attentive, responsive behavior. The central attitude important to listening effectively is "I WANT to understand you." Until you make this decision as a conscious choice, you will be easily distracted from the important listening task at hand. This attitude is rooted in wanting to know about others: their experiences, perceptions and feelings, while withholding any judgments of the speaker.

Until we go beyond our own personal preoccupations and focus our concentration on the speaker, effective listening will be haphazard at best. After we've made the decision to really listen, proper attending behavior is an initial skill that the listener needs to use. Attending behaviors are a combination of the attitude already mentioned and actions that communicate involvement with the speaker and demonstrate interest and concern. Equally important, this caring attitude and attentive behavior keep the listener involved in the listening process, focus the listener's attention on the speaker, and reduce both external and internal distractions.

Actions associated with good attending behavior include eye contact that is appropriate in duration, frequency, and intensity; body posture that reflects your interest and involvement; and interpersonal distance that is suitable for the message being shared.

Each of these three components has a best or optimum level of effectiveness. Much like a carburetor setting in which "too rich" or "too lean" is ineffective, the good listener uses an appropriate amount of eye contact, an attentive body posture, and a comfortable interpersonal distance. Good attending behavior shows concern, strengthens the relationship, and sets the stage for effective listening.

Finally, we offer the following suggestions:

1. Stop talking. You can't listen and talk at the same time.
2. Hear the speaker out. Wait until the speaker has completed the message before offering a response of your own.
3. Tune out distractions. Eliminate distractions whenever possible, and practice good attending behavior to minimize distractions that can't be eliminated.
4. Don't lose your "cool." Develop an open-minded tolerance for ideas and opinions different from your own; learn which loaded words produce strong emotional reactions for you; and stop mentally debating with the speaker before you fully understand what is being said.
5. Take advantage of thought-speed. Review what the speaker has said; relate the message to your own past experiences and present knowledge; and anticipate the speaker's next line of thought.

Certainly this list is not complete. But it is a start. It's up to you to identify the listening problems that affect you most and find ways to overcome these problems.

Remembering Tools

After paying attention to the speaker, the second challenge to the listener is remembering what the speaker said. Many listeners have difficulty remembering the speaker's name, let alone the content of the message. In *Listening*, Wolvin and Coakley (1996) suggest that we remember information more easily when it is "(1) meaningful, useful, and of interest to us, (2) particularly striking/out of the ordinary, (3) organized, and (4) visual" (p. 226). When a listener needs specific information, his or her capacity and motivation to remember is increased.

With the desire to remember in place, the concerned listener can employ any number of memory techniques to improve recall. Lyman Steil in *CAUSE for Listening* suggests repeating, linking, picturing, and grouping as basic steps to strengthen memory. Another more structured technique includes the loci system. Simple mnemonic devices also help listeners remember. Let's explore some of these techniques further.

At times the listener must recall the exact words of the speaker. In such cases, repeating the message or making notes will help the listener remember. Some work areas have signs near the phones that remind employees to "Write it down!" New employees may feel self-conscious about taking notes on the job, but using a pocket notebook may save a costly mistake. Other times, recall can be enhanced by paraphrasing, restating the meaning in our own words.

Linking works best when remembering lists of items. The listener creates ridiculous, vivid images of the first item linked to the second, the second to the third, and so on. If your grocery list included: potatoes, tomato soup, toothpaste, milk, and detergent, you could make a list or try to create a vivid picture of white potatoes floating in blood red tomato soup, covered with striped toothpaste, in a gallon milk container with a label saying New Blue Cheer. Just try to forget this image!

Pictures work well for receiving directions. The listeners create a mental image of the location being described. Let's say, for instance, you are receiving directions from a customer to make a delivery. If the customer tells you to drive east until you reach a "T" in the road, you could picture the letter "T." You might also be told that at this intersection you will find a pizza parlor on the right-hand side of the road. If you are already familiar with this territory, the customer's directions are easy to picture. If you are not familiar with the location, the comparisons to letters and easily recognizable landmarks still help you recall the directions you've been given.

Grouping occurs when employees give their social security number, phone number, or some other lengthy bit of information to you. This information is easier to remember when it is broken into smaller chunks, like the area code, exchange, four-digit number, and extension of an office phone. Most of us learned our A, B, C's this way. Some memorized long spelling words by grouping letters into shorter segments.

A more structured system for recall employs a spatial connection with the items to be remembered. With the loci system, the listener takes a familiar space, like a car, a living room, or even a toolbox, and mentally places the objects to be remembered in different locations in these spaces. To recall the items, the listener visualizes the space and, "Voila!" the items are recalled. The Greeks used this system centuries ago to recall lines for their plays. Employees can use it to record where they have stored files.

More basic techniques include mnemonic devices. Most have used "HOMES" to remember the Great Lakes or "My very educated mother just served us nine pizzas" to recall the order of the planets. Few listeners make use of these mnemonic devices, although they are really very simple and easy to use. Motivated listeners who want to understand will find ways to make memory aids that work for them.

Evaluating Tools

As the attentive listener gains an understanding of the total message, the critical listening process begins. The critical listener sorts facts from inferences, detects logical fallacies, spots relative terms, and maintains emotional control. Let's examine each of the tools in turn.

Separate facts from inferences. Communication barriers and misunderstandings between people occur for a variety of reasons. One of these reasons involves the failure to separate fact from inference or opinion.

As a result of our different backgrounds, physical traits, and present feelings, we all have formed an infinite number of opinions on topics ranging from politics to the weather. Indeed, the varied opinions we hold are, in part, what make us unique and interesting human beings.

But there is an inherent danger in the opinions we possess, especially if they are strong and/or long-standing. The danger is that subtly, and often unconsciously, we cross the fine line that frequently separates fact from opinion and begin to view our own opinions as factual and, therefore, incapable of being in error.

Let's say, for instance, that you firmly believe women should be given equal opportunity to pursue work in nontraditional occupations such as welding, automotive repair, or electronics. Your friend and co-worker, however, thinks a woman's place is in the home fulfilling the role of homemaker and mother, or at the very least, doing jobs "nature intended" for women which include being a teacher, nurse, or secretary.

Now if both of you have forgotten that your opinions are just that—opinions—and subject to change and error, it is highly probable that neither of you will be able to calmly discuss this topic without trying to convince the other of the "facts!"

However, if you both recognize your opinions for what they are—nonfactual—you will be more willing to listen open-mindedly to conflicting views and to respect the right of others to think as they do even if you do not personally agree.

Some of the characteristics that separate facts from inferences or opinions are listed below. Statements of fact must be:

1. Based on observable sense data—observations report what you can see, hear, taste, touch, or smell—sensory data.
2. Only about the past or the present, never the future—statements about future events are purely inferential since they have not yet occurred and are, therefore, not observable.
3. Objective and devoid of any interpretations, conclusions, or assumptions about what has been observed. Observing a man with a Harley-Davidson logo tatooed on his arm is a fact, and assuming he must belong to a motorcycle club is an inference that goes beyond the observable data.

Statements of inference, in contrast:

1. Go beyond what has been observed, as in the case of the "biker" with the tatoo;
2. Are about the past, present, or future.
3. Include interpretations, conclusions, or assumptions about what has been observed and are, consequently, subjective.

As a final note, it's often a good idea to state your opinions to others in non-factual terms by including the use of an "I" message. For example, rather than saying, "Women should have the right to pursue work in nontraditional occupations," say instead, "I have come to believe women should have the right to pursue work in nontraditional occupations." Phrases such as "I think," "To me," and "From my point of view," also work equally well.

Fact inference confusion exercises. The exercises below will help you to become more aware of the differences between factual and inferential statements and to realize how easy it is to confuse the two. From the following stories, determine whether the statements are true (T), false (F), or inference (?). Base your decision on the information in the story. True statements will be verified in the story; false statements will be contradicted in the story; and inferences will leave you guessing.

The owner of Webster's Auto Repair, who was getting ready to close shop for the evening, turned and noticed one of the mechanics stuffing impact and torque wrenches, sockets, and a micrometer into a knapsack. The owner called to the mechanic, but the mechanic picked up the knapsack, ran out of the garage, hopped into a waiting vehicle, and drove off. The garage owner immediately called the police.

T   F   ?   1. The garage owner was named Webster.

T   F   ?   2. The mechanic was seen stuffing tools in a knapsack.

T F ? 3. The man with the knapsack ran out of the garage and into a waiting vehicle.

T F ? 4. The car with the mechanic in it drove off.

T F ? 5. The mechanic stole the tools.

Terry, who was the first one to punch in on Friday, arrived at Department 325 and noticed the job which had been worked on Thursday afternoon had been moved to another machinery area. Another casting with "RUSH" painted on its side had been moved into Terry's machine. Friday's assignment called for Terry to work on the same machine as on Thursday. The supervisor for Department 325 was at a staff meeting all Friday morning.

T F ? 1. Terry's work assignment had changed for Friday.

T F ? 2. The supervisor forgot to tell Terry about a new rush job.

T F ? 3. Terry was not the first person in Department 325 on Friday morning.

T F ? 4. The job Terry had been working on had not been moved.

T F ? 5. Terry has been reassigned to another machinery area.

Sandy and Pat, both data processors, are especially good at their jobs. Their combined experience totals some 30 years. They are reliable, hardworking, and very strong individuals. In fact, Sandy lifts weights for a hobby, and Pat plays basketball.

T F ? 1. This story concerns two men named Sandy and Pat.

T F ? 2. Sandy and Pat are both hard workers.

T F ? 3. Sandy is handicapped.

T F ? 4. Pat and Sandy are married to each other.

T F ? 5. Sandy never lifted weights.

Detect logical fallacies. A critical listener follows the reasoning of the speaker to be certain that errors of logic do not create misunderstandings. Specifically, the critical listener looks for common logical fallacies: faulty causation, hasty generalization, either/or thinking, circular reasoning, and faulty comparison. Faulty causation occurs when coincidental events are seen as having a cause-effect relationship. Because a machine broke down after the operator completed a specific job does not mean that the job caused the breakdown or that the operator caused the damage. Simplistic cause-effect reasoning has limited application in complicated problem solving.

Hasty generalizations happen when only a few examples are selected to represent the whole of the conclusion. Sampling only a small or unique portion of a universe limits the conclusion that one can derive from the selected sample. To conclude too quickly or without qualifications can result in a hasty generalization. If only two people in this room of 25 people have cell phones, we might conclude that cell phones are not very popular. Because many of our friends in the United States have computers, we may think this is true worldwide. In reality, only one of every one hundred people has a computer when we look around the world.

Either/or thinking presents two alternatives when, in fact, many more possibilities exist. Rather than seeing only two choices, the critical listener must look for other possibilities that may not be stated. Whenever an "either/or" decision is presented, the critical listener must ask what other choices exist. If a report states that, "We must invest in new equipment, or we must subcontract the work to a vendor," careful thought should be given to other alternatives. Perhaps used equipment is available, or a new design could modify our parts needs.

Circular reasoning merely restates what you are trying to prove without providing evidence. For example, "This car is a really good deal because it's the greatest deal I could get." No comparisons are offered, no support is presented, no testimonials are offered. The proof is in itself. It's good because "it's good." The critical listener notes what follows the "because" to be certain new information supports the claim being presented in more than circular logic.

Although comparisons with figurative language can give color and life to our descriptions, faulty comparisons suggest that similarities outweigh differences and that unique situations can be treated the same. "This order for the XYZ Company is a lot like the one we did for Acme last week." The critical listener looks for differences when only similarities have been presented. Mentally asking, "Are these the same?" or wondering, "But what about ____?" will help the critical listener avoid faulty comparisons.

Detecting each of these problems requires careful attention to the details and thoughtful assessment of the message. For a fun exploration of these and more logical fallacies, check out Stephen's Logical Fallacies Index at *www.datanation.com/fallacies/index.htm*.

A critical listener also must be aware of relative terms that cloud the exact meaning of a message and may create misunderstanding. Relative terms, such as, "several" "many," and "most" lack specific meaning to communicate clearly. Likewise, terms like "inexpensive," "affordable," "limited warranty," or "average" may suggest different meanings to critical listeners. Be careful to question the exact meaning of such terms in critical listening situations.

Finally, critical listeners must be sensitive to loaded words that label, call names, generalize, or otherwise distort information. These terms stereotype people or situations making a clear understanding difficult. The strong emotional content of these words makes them offensive to some listeners. Terms like "geek," "nerd," "liberal," or "radical" provide more information about the speaker than the person spoken about, and as loaded words, they are of little value to the critical listener.

Responding Tools

In addition to the attitudes and actions already described that promote clear understanding, the listener must choose how to respond to the message received.

The choice of response becomes especially important when someone shares a personal or professional problem. In such situations, you have an opportunity to respond in several ways. Your response reflects your reaction to the situation as well as your intentions and may encourage open communication and problem solving or inhibit further sharing and understanding.

Take a closer look at the choices that are available to you as you react. Does your response help you to listen? Does your response help the person with the problem?

Suppose Shawn, your classmate and friend, comes to you and relates the following: "I don't know about this program. I thought I wanted to work in Appliance Servicing, and now I find out how much electricity and electronics are involved, and I don't know. I hate electronics. Schematics look like puzzles to me. I don't know if I'm going to make it in this program or not."

As you respond to Shawn's problem, you may feel evaluative or judgmental, curious, concerned, analytical, supportive, or empathic. The feelings and reactions that you have can be shared clearly with Shawn if you are aware of the different responses that are available to you.

Research has identified several types of responses. The following is a partial list of common responses that you can chose from as you provide feedback to the concerns of others.

1. **Evaluating** judges, evaluates, advises, or solves. There are two types of evaluating responses, those that judge and those that advise. Those that judge say what is right or wrong, good or bad. Examples might be: "That was stupid! That's right! You're great! That's important!" Responses that advise offer a solution to the person's problem by telling him what to do. Examples might include these: If I were you, I would. . . . You really should. . . . You ought to. . . . Why don't you. . . . ? An evaluating response to Shawn might be, "You're in over your head. I'd bail out as fast as I could if I were you and go into another program."

2. **Interpreting** interprets, explains, or teaches. This response explains why something happens, or states cause(s) for actions and feelings by adding information not stated in the original problem. Examples might include these: You may feel that way because. . . . She probably did that because. . . . Maybe the reason this problem came about is due to. . . . An interpreting response to Shawn might be, "Maybe you're afraid of burning yourself with the electrical wires because of that time you were burned while fixing that television."

3. **Supporting** reassures, pacifies, or comforts. Supporting responses attempt to make people feel better, cheer them up, or offer help, encouragement, or comfort. Probably one of the most effective supportive responses is one that states how you are able to help in terms of being available and offering your services, time, or possessions. Examples may be: I'm sure things will be better. . . . Look at the progress you have made since. . . . We all feel that way once in awhile. . . . If there is any way I can help. . . . I'd be willing to come over and help you with. . . . A supporting response to Shawn might be, "I feel that way about school also. If you would like, we can work on the homework together for awhile and see how it goes."

4. **Questioning** probes, clarifies, questions, or seeks more information. Questioning requests more information or clarity of information. Two types of questions are "open" which require more than yes or no answers and encourage greater freedom of response, and "closed" which can be answered with a yes or no. Examples include these: What makes you think that? How long have you felt that way? Where were you. . . ? What do you mean by that? A questioning response to Shawn might be, "How come you're having such a hard time with those classes in particular? What can be done to make you feel more comfortable taking them?

5. **Paraphrasing** summarizes, restates, or reflects. This response shows what you've understood by restating in your own words what you think the speaker meant or by summarizing the content and/or feelings in the message. Examples might be these: You mean you're feeling. . . . So what you are saying is. . . . In other words. . . . If I understand, you've. . . . A paraphrasing response to Shawn might be, "You're unsure of your own ability in some of the courses and are wondering whether you should just bail out of the program?"

An important point to remember is that these responses are not right or wrong. They all have their place in effective interaction with those who have problems. What's needed is practice in developing the skillful and appropriate use of these responses.

Using the response styles. Approximately 80 percent of all the feedback we give to senders can be categorized as evaluating, interpreting, supporting, questioning, or paraphrasing responses.

The evaluating response appears to be the one used most frequently when senders share problems with listeners. The frequent use of the evaluating response may be the result of listeners feeling responsible to solve the senders' problems. In contrast, paraphrasing tends to be used least often, most likely because it is a response we must be specifically taught to use.

One response is not necessarily better to use than another. Rather, the overuse, underuse, or inappropriate use of any response is what can make feedback ineffective. According to psychologist Carl Rogers, if we use any response 40 percent of the time or more, people tend to see us as always responding that way. Consequently, if we use a large number of evaluating responses in communication, we may be perceived by others as being judgmental and closed-minded individuals, which can lessen our effectiveness as listeners.

Certain guidelines can enable us to use the response styles more effectively. In addition, senders give us some cues to let us know when a particular response is working (i.e., helping the sender to deal with a problem). When senders come to us with problems, try to keep in mind the following suggestions:

Evaluating. The evaluating response normally does not help a sender in coping with a problem unless the sender specifically asks for advice. Even if advice is requested by a sender, the listener should feel confident that the sender is ready to accept the advice and is unlikely to blame the listener if the advice does not work out. An indication that advice is working occurs when the sender willingly accepts the advice, almost as if it represents a solution the sender hadn't thought of previously. If the sender openly disagrees with the advice or responds with, "Yes, but. . . " and proceeds to explain why the advice won't work, chances are the evaluating response is not being effective.

Interpreting. This response works best when the listener's intention is to offer insights into the problem's causes. Interpreting also tends to work more effectively when stated non-absolutely, such as, "Maybe you feel this way because. . . " or "Perhaps you're feeling undecided as a result of. . . ." This non-absolute language acknowledges that the listener may not be completely accurate in the analysis, and therefore, potential defensive or argumentative reactions in the sender are likely to be reduced. If the sender agrees with your interpretation, this response is working. If the sender disagrees and proceeds to tell you why you're wrong, the interpreting is unsuccessful.

Supporting. Support and reassurance work best when the sender has already determined how to solve the problem and simply needs the strength and encouragement that your support can provide. If this response is working, the sender will accept your words of comfort and assume a more relaxed nonverbal posture; if not, the sender may say something like, "But you don't really understand."

Questioning. When additional information is genuinely needed, questioning works best. If questions are used, ask them one at a time; ask them only as often as necessary; and keep them open-ended. You may also want to ask questions that make the sender think more deeply about the problem such as, "What might be some underlying causes of this problem?" "How do you feel about this?" "What do you think you can do about this?" If questioning is having the desired effect, the sender will gladly provide the information requested; if not, the sender may begin sharing less.

Paraphrasing. This response seems to work best when a sender communicates a problem to a listener because paraphrasing reveals a sincere desire to understand the sender's thoughts and feelings. The sender can then talk through the problem and arrive at a solution in an atmosphere of acceptance. If paraphrasing is being effective, the sender will continue to share thoughts and feelings in greater depth or correct you if your understanding is inaccurate. If the sender retreats and begins to share less, the paraphrasing is probably not successful.

Response Style Summary

Response	Intent	Example
Evaluating, judging	Values as good/bad or right/wrong.	That's stupid. You're right! What a smart aleck!
Evaluating, advising	Shares solution or offers advice.	If I were you. . . . You really should. . . .
Interpreting	Explains why something happened, gives reasons not stated in the problem for feelings or behaviors.	You may feel that way because. . . . S/he probably did that because. . . .
Supporting	Reassures, pacifies, reduces intensity of feeling.	I'm sure things will be better. . . . Look at the progress you've made. We all feel that way once in a while.
Questioning	Solicits more information, clarifies meaning, expands details.	What makes you think that? How long have you felt. . . ?
Paraphrasing	Shows what you understand, restates in your own words what you heard. Summarizes content and/or feelings of the speaker's message.	You mean you're feeling. . . . So what you are saying is. . . . If I understand you. . . . You feel _ because. . . .

CHAPTER 3 TOOL CHECK

Directions: Find the key words from the preceding chapter to complete the sentences below.

1. The type of sounds made by jackhammers, rock bands, and computer printers that compete for our attention and make it difficult to listen is called _____.

2. A response that states "why a person's problem exists" is called _____.

3. The goal of effective listening is _____.

4. A response which rephrases in your own words the speaker's content and/or feelings is called _____.

5. Good eye contact, forward leaning body posture, and a comfortable distance between you and the speaker are aspects of _____.

6. The response that asks for additional information or clarity of information is called _____.

7. When listening to ourselves while someone is talking to us, we are being distracted by _____.

8. Reviewing, relating, and anticipating are all ways to use _____.

9. A response which tells a sender what "ought" to be done or which offers a judgment is called _____.

10. Making a conscious effort to listen involves the attitude: _____.

CHAPTER 3 INTERACTIONS

INTERACTION #1—Self-Assessment

1. On a scale from 0–100, how would you rate yourself as a listener?

   I___I___I___I___I___I___I___I___I___I___I   Place (X) to indicate rating.
   0   10   20   30   40   50   60   70   80   90   100

2. How do you think others would rate you as a listener? Use the letters and the scale below to indicate where you think the following people would rate you as a listener:
   A. Your best friend
   B. Your boss
   C. Co-workers
   D. Subordinates
   E. Intimate other

   I___I___I___I___I___I___I___I___I___I___I   Place letters to indicate rating.
   0   10   20   30   40   50   60   70   80   90   100

3. What kind of listening habits do you have? Indicate how frequently you do the following:

LISTENING HABITS	FREQUENCY					
	A lot				Very little	
Call the subject uninteresting	5	4	3	2	1	0
Criticize the speaker's delivery	5	4	3	2	1	0
Disagree with the speaker's message	5	4	3	2	1	0
Listen only for facts	5	4	3	2	1	0
Try to outline everything	5	4	3	2	1	0
Fake attention to speaker	5	4	3	2	1	0
Tolerate distraction	5	4	3	2	1	0
Avoid difficult material	5	4	3	2	1	0
Overreact to emotional words	5	4	3	2	1	0
Waste the thought/speed advantage	5	4	3	2	1	0

4. What two terms best describe you as a listener?
   4A. _____, 4B. _____

5. Describe your listening behavior in four different types of listening situations. Record your strengths and weaknesses as a listener in each type of situation.
   5A. Listening to directions or work assignments _____
   _____
   _____
   _____
   _____
   _____

   5B. Listening for factual information (lecture material) _____
   _____
   _____
   _____
   _____
   _____

5C. Listening for opinions _____
_____
_____
_____
_____
_____

5D. Listening for feelings _____
_____
_____
_____
_____
_____

6. List three changes that would improve your listening skills.

6A. _____

6B. _____

6C. _____

INTERACTION #2—Response Styles Questionnaire

Read each of the 10 situations listed below, and write a response that is typical of what you normally say as a listener. Then go back and read the sample responses for each situation. Circle the letter of the sample that most closely resembles the intention of the response you've written, even though the wording may be different. If there are no matches, circle the one that sounds like something you might say in response to the problem.

After you complete the Response Styles Questionnaire, answer the questions posed in the Response Styles Analysis. Finally, practice making each type of response by completing the Response Styles Practice Worksheet.

1. The union just told us we have to take another 10 percent cut in pay because the company is in bad economic straits. I don't know what I'm going to do. With a family of three kids to support, it will be hard making ends meet.
   1. Your Response:

   _____

   _____

   _____

   A. You have no right to complain. Just be thankful you've got a job.
   B. I know what you mean. My company cut back on our vacation time because of financial problems.
   C. It sounds like you're feeling depressed about that salary loss?
   D. You may be concerned because you've never been forced to budget your money before, and you're not sure how to go about it.
   E. How much was the other cut you had to take?

2. I'm seriously thinking about the boss' offer to have the company send me to school part-time to upgrade my skills. But I don't know—I was never much of a student in high school, and I don't know if I've got what it takes to go on to a technical school.
   2. Your Response:

   _____

   _____

   _____

   A. What do you mean when you say you weren't much of a student in high school?
   B. You're having doubts about your ability to succeed in school?
   C. You'll be sorry if you don't take the boss up on this offer, especially since the company agreed to pay for it.
   D. Most people have apprehensions about returning to school. But you can make it!
   E. Perhaps you're worried about being embarrassed in front of the boss if you don't get all A's and B's.

3. I'm really having a hard time getting along with the new supervisor. He's the company owner's son, and he seems to feel he can push everybody around because his mom owns the business.
   3. Your Response:

   _____

   _____

   _____

   A. How has he been pushing you around?
   B. If I were you, I'd go and complain to the owner about it.
   C. I get the idea you're unhappy with the way this supervisor is handling the people in your department?

  D. It could be that he feels the need to prove his supervisory ability to his mother.
  E. If you can just hang in there a little longer, the situation is bound to improve.

4. I just can't talk to my parents anymore since I told them Terry and I are getting married. They are always asking questions about where I go and what I do. They keep track of me like I am a two-year-old. I don't know what's happened to them.
   4. Your Response:

   _____

   _____

   _____

   A. Why don't you tell them to butt out? They shouldn't be hassling you.
   B. What do they want to know?
   C. You sound really upset about this.
   D. They're probably just finding it hard to let go of you now that you're getting married.
   E. Lots of parents are like that all the time. I'm sure it will pass.

5. Lupe, I hate it when those customers call and say their appliances konked out on them after we just fixed them. Half of the people barely know how to plug them in, much less run them. Then I get stuck listening to all their problems on the phone.
   5. Your Response:

   _____

   _____

   _____

   A. They really do get you upset, don't they?
   B. What was wrong with that last caller?
   C. Just tell them to read their owner's manual.
   D. Sometimes they worry more about something when it's new or fixed. That's why they call so much.
   E. I had the same grief when I had your job; you'll get used to it.

6. The crew on the line keep inviting me to join them at a bar after work. I feel obligated to go, being the new employee and all. Sometimes I can't afford to buy a round, but everybody usually buys one. I hate to be rude, so what do I do?
   6. Your Response:

   _____

   _____

   _____

   A. Don't go just because you feel obligated. That's dumb.
   B. Perhaps you think you need to do this to feel accepted by them.
   C. So you're worried about fitting in with the crew on the assembly line, but you're not sure you can afford being one of the group.
   D. Where do you usually go anyway?
   E. I was in the same situation at the last place I worked. I guess it's the normal thing to do when you're new on your first job.

7. I really like working here. The opportunities are great; the conditions are excellent; the pay is good. I've learned a lot. But Kerry, that perfectionist boss we have. . . I just can't seem to do enough right. There's always something wrong with the work I've done.

7. Your Response:

_____

_____

_____

A. Hey, you'll get through okay. I'm sure Kerry will see that you're working up to your potential.
B. You think the boss demands too much from you?
C. Kerry's boss used to treat him the same way. Kerry probably thinks that's what a good boss does.
D. What did Kerry say to you last night?
E. If I were you, I'd find something else to do or somebody else to work for.

8. My boss is really rude. Three months ago I asked if I could have a vacation in early July and was told yes. I've made all kinds of plans to go out west, and now the boss said that if I go, I'll be fired.
    8. Your Response:

_____

_____

_____

A. After promising you vacation, your boss has threatened action if you take it?
B. Why do think the boss changed so suddenly?
C. I'd go to a union officer and file a grievance.
D. A lot of the workers around here feel the same about their boss.
E. The company must have just gotten a new order in, and now they need your help.

9. It's really hard being the only female in an all-male shop. All the employees who don't think I'm serious about diesel mechanics tease me to death.
    9. Your Response:

_____

_____

_____

A. You're being too sensitive about the issue. Just ignore their remarks.
B. That must really be a hassle. If there's anything I can say or do to help change things, just let me know.
C. What do they say that is most irritating when they tease you?
D. You seem fed up with the other employees' comments?
E. Maybe they're intimidated by a woman in this occupation.

10. It's totally useless! Everywhere I go for jobs, I'm told that nothing is available or that I don't have enough experience. How can I get any experience unless somebody is willing to give me a chance?
     10. Your Response:

_____

_____

_____

A. What kind of jobs are you applying for? What are your qualifications?
B. You want to work, but you lack the needed experience?
C. You're going about it all wrong. You should go to school and get an advanced education in that area.

D. The economy is in such a mess that employers have a greater pool of potential workers. They can now afford to be really choosy.
E. You're only one of many people in the same boat.

RESPONSE STYLES ANALYSIS

Answer the following questions about your response styles.

1. What was the dominant style of your written responses?

2. Did the dominant written style match with the selected style? If not, explain the differences.

3. Describe the dominant response style used by each of the following:
    A. Your significant other
    B. Your boss
    C. Your major instructor
    D. A significant family member

4. How will your knowledge of response styles affect the messages you send?

5. How will your knowledge of response styles affect the feedback you give to messages you receive?

RESPONSE STYLES PRACTICE WORKSHEET

For each of the three situations below, write an example of all five responses.

1. "This co-worker in my carpool is constantly criticizing and complaining about the other people at work. I'm getting sick and tired of these comments. I never hear anything positive about anybody."

    Evaluating:

    Interpreting:

    Supporting:

    Questioning:

    Paraphrasing:

2. "Wow, I just got fired. My boss walked up to me, gave me my last paycheck, and told me that they didn't need me any longer. I didn't even get an explanation why."

    Evaluating:

    Interpreting:

    Supporting:

Questioning:

Paraphrasing:

3. "What do you do when somebody wants to borrow your tools or test equipment? This new assembler doesn't have everything that's needed for the job. I don't mind lending some of my stuff, but I can't keep up with my own work without the tools I need. I hate to be selfish, but I don't know what to do."

Evaluating:

Interpreting:

Supporting:

Questioning:

Paraphrasing:

INTERACTION #3—Information Passing Exercise

Imagine that you have been asked to inform a new employee about the responsibilities of the job. In a short paragraph of three to five sentences, write an original set of instructions that contains at least five specific details for completing a specific task, such as making a delivery, completing an order, or maintaining equipment.

Following the paragraph, prepare five quiz questions that could be asked to determine if the new employee fully understood your message. Pair up with another student and take turns reading your sets of directions and asking your questions to one another.

After you've completed this exercise, discuss the following:

1. What difficulties did you have as a listener understanding the instructions as given?

2. What steps could you take to make your listening more effective?

3. What might be the consequences of failing to understand these directions exactly?

WRITE INSTRUCTIONS HERE:

WRITE QUESTIONS HERE:

INTERACTION #4—Active Listening Identification

Listed below are a variety of messages. Following each statement are several responses. Select the one that most accurately paraphrases the statement. The best paraphrase is one that restates the feeling and meaning heard. Remember that your goal is to listen only—not to agree or disagree, give advice, or end the feeling.

1. Boy, I hate working for this company. They have the cheapest wage and salary program I have ever heard of, and they make us work like dogs.
   ( ) A lot of places are like that. Just forget it.
   ( ) Why do you say that?
   ( ) This company doesn't pay you what you deserve and you're irritated by that?
   ( ) You just complain too much. If it's not one thing it's another.

2. If that supervisor tells me to change the setup on that machine one more time, I'm going to scream.
   ( ) Screaming is not going to solve the problem. You'll probably just end up getting fired.
   ( ) You're furious at being told to change the machine setup so often?
   ( ) What do you mean when you say machine setup?
   ( ) I know what you mean. I worked for a supervisor that did the same thing.

3. That circuits teacher is really a jerk. The other day we were told that we would not have any tests for a while; then the teacher comes in and gives us a unit exam!
   ( ) Yeah, I had that teacher before. The same thing happened in our class.
   ( ) What was the test on? Do you think you did well?
   ( ) Maybe the teacher had a fight with a student and is taking it out on your class.
   ( ) You're irritated with a teacher who gave a test after saying there wouldn't be one?

4. Geez, was that customer angry. He said that he'd brought that computer in about 15 times, and we still haven't fixed it right. I never know how to handle customers who complain like that.
   ( ) Just be as nice as possible. Remember that the customer always comes first.
   ( ) An angry customer has you wondering how to deal with irate people?
   ( ) What's wrong with that unit?
   ( ) I'd be mad as hell, too, if I brought my computer in three times.

5. Did you ever notice that when all the dirty work comes in, I have to do it? That's really unfair.
   ( ) You feel cheated because you have to do all the unpleasant work?
   ( ) You should have seen the work I had to do for my company.
   ( ) What kind of work are you talking about?
   ( ) The Philadelphia 76ers are going to be in town tonight. You want to go see the game?

INTERACTION #5—Paraphrasing Practice

From the previous exercises, you have had the chance to identify and write the five response styles. Because we believe strongly in the benefits which come from the paraphrasing response (greater openness, listener attention, and understanding) and because it is not as automatic as the other responses, additional practice will help you perfect this valuable response.

For each of the following situations, identify at least two probable feelings the sender may be experiencing. These feelings may be stated directly or implied. Next, write a paraphrase. Remember, the best paraphrase is one that includes both the speaker's message and feelings.

Example: "The weekends go so fast, and before you know it, we're back to the grind of another week."

Probable Feeling: Anxious, trapped, restless, inhibited, frustrated.

Paraphrase: You feel frustrated when your time off goes so quickly?

1. "Guess what? I was called for that job interview I've been waiting for. The only problem is that the personnel manager asked me to bring along a resume, and I've never made one up before."

   Possible Feelings:

   Paraphrase:

2. "My folks have been trying to get me to work in their travel agency after I graduate, but I want to find a job and try to make it on my own."

   Possible Feelings:

   Paraphrase:

3. "I've got three hot reports to get out before Friday, and Lee just called in sick. How am I ever going to get all this work done on time?"

   Possible Feelings:

   Paraphrase:

4. "I'm not sure what's wrong with this generator. We've been doing the regular maintenance on it, but we did have it apart once for cleaning. Now the blasted engine won't even start."

   Possible Feelings:

   Paraphrase:

5. "I really can't stand it any longer. My fiancée keeps nagging and nagging me to get married. We haven't finished school or saved up enough money. Geez, we don't even have decent jobs yet."

   Possible Feelings:

   Paraphrase:

6. "Jumpin' jelly beans. . . I can't believe that I did it. That communication skills test I thought I would fail turned out to be easier than I thought. Now I'll be able to get straight A's. Fantastic!"

   Possible Feelings:

   Paraphrase:

7. "Wow. That's the first compliment I ever got from my boss. After my six-month review, my supervisor told me that I'm on the right track for promotion to chief operator."

   Possible Feelings:

   Paraphrase:

REFERENCES

Bones, D. (1994). *The Business of listening: A practical guide to effective listening.* Menlo Park, CA: Crisp Publications.

Hall, E. T. (1969). *The hidden dimension.* Garden City, NY: Doubleday.

International Listening Association. Listening factoids. Retrieved June 28, 2001, from the World Wide Web: *www.listen.org/pages/factoids.html.*

Steil, L. K. (1985). *CAUSE for listening.* Princeton, NJ: Sperry Corporation.

Stephen's Guide. The logical fallacies index. Retrieved September 6, 2001, from the World Wide Web: *www.datanation.com/fallacies/index.htm.*

Wolvin, A. D., & Coakley, C. G. (1996). *Listening* (5th ed.). Dubuque, IA: Brown & Benchmark.

CHAPTER 4
INTERPERSONAL BLUEPRINT

- Build Positive Workplace Relations
- Define Conflict Types
- Recognize Conflict Styles
- Consider Conflict Strategies

INTERPERSONAL RELATIONSHIP TOOLS

- Using Skillful Language
- Using Assertion Messages

TOOL CHECK

INTERACTIONS

- Sending Combined Assertion Messages
- Responding to Criticism

INTERPERSONAL BLUEPRINT

Chapter 4 identifies some ways people share information to build a positive workplace climate, resolve conflicts, and solve common problems people have when expressing themselves, by focusing on how to state perceptions, feelings, consequences, assumptions, and requests to others in a clear manner. Expressing yourself by using the right language is certainly essential, but you also need to be aware of how to send messages so that the receiver is willing to listen to them. Chapter 4 also examines conflict types, styles, and strategies to help employees understand the many facets of conflict in the workplace. Finally, Chapter 4 offers three methods to deal with criticism in a helpful manner.

Build Positive Workplace Relations

People do not express themselves clearly for many reasons. Some of these problems relate to the message structure, while other problems relate to sending the most appropriate message for the situation and the relationship.

We believe four specific qualities will improve workplace relations. Clarity, respect, assertiveness, and flexibility are necessary to create a positive communication climate in the workplace. In the first instance, unclear messages often result when we intentionally hide feelings and experiences from others for fear of rejection. At other times, our lack of clarity stems from our inability to put our thoughts and feelings into words. The words we use may not reflect our inner world. Sometimes our words say one thing, and our tone of voice, body posture, and facial expressions say something entirely different, confusing the receivers of our messages. We need to find the right words that clearly and thoughtfully present to others our observations, wants, needs, and feelings. Our nonverbal behaviors need to reinforce the words we share if we are to send a clear message. For instance, greetings need to convey positive words and body language.

A second quality involves sending respectful messages that do not create defensive responses. Above all, in our dealings with others, we must communicate a feeling of mutual respect for one another. Often we express our thoughts and feelings in ways that make others feel threatened and cause them to react with anger or silence. Defensiveness results when others perceive that we are attacking them, evaluating them, acting superior to them, or communicating with them for some hidden motive. Respect is shared by listening with empathy and understanding to others and speaking in ways that show a feeling of equality and caring for the receiver.

A third quality is our ability to communicate "assertively." We often react in two distinct ways when we feel that someone is violating our rights. Many people respond passively by letting others "walk all over" them, saying nothing, sacrificing their needs for the needs of others or for the relationship. Also, we may respond with aggression, which tends to put the other on the defensive, thereby increasing the resentment to a dangerous level in the relationship. By acting assertively, we show respect for our rights and needs and also treat others as we would like to be treated.

The final quality we need to build positive workplace relations is flexibility to cope with criticism in a constructive way. When confronted with criticism, we often find the need to justify our behavior in a defensive way rather than to listen for information which may help us improve, correct a serious fault, or deal with manipulative criticism in a tactful way. All of these problems can be dealt with more effectively if the sender has the appropriate attitudes and skills necessary for communication.

These qualities have corresponding communication tools that may be employed to bring about more positive workplace relations. Attitudes that reflect a desire to improve relationships underlie each specific tool. Both the skills and the attitudes will be developed fully in individual worksheets throughout this chapter.

For now, let's preview the skills necessary to solve these problems.

The quality of clarity can best be achieved by using specific and tentative language to report our opinions. These skills combined with attitudes that reflect openness, honesty, and empathy will improve communication. Similarly, the best deterrent to defensiveness demands the skills of respectful informing statements and tentative expression. Both of these are based on the attitudes of equality, open-mindedness, and honesty.

Effective assertion messages include behavior descriptions, impression checks, feeling messages, consequence statements, request statements, and combinations of these. Assertive skills are based on the assumptions that conflict is best managed through a problem-solving approach that makes use of direct, honest, and appropriate messages.

Criticism can be handled constructively by analyzing the type of criticism in the situation, using fogging (acknowledging), negative assertion (strongly agreeing), or negative inquiry (clarifying). Each of these tools reflects two basic assumptions about conflict and the judgments of others: conflicts are problems to be solved, and individuals are the best judges of their own behavior.

The qualities for building workplace relations, which include clarity, respect, assertion, and flexibility, will be valuable in our personal and professional lives. They can be developed through the acquisition of specific tools and the cultivation of positive, supportive attitudes.

The challenge to you, the communicator, is to incorporate these tools and attitudes into your natural communication system so that you seem honest, open, and genuine in your communication.

Define Conflict Types

Despite our best efforts to build positive workplace relations, conflict is inevitable and is bound to occur in all work environments. Joel Edelman and Mary Beth Crain in the *The Tao of Negotiation* (1994) have identified the most common causes of conflicts at work. They found that poor performance of an employee is seldom the cause of conflict, but rather the five leading causes of conflict are as follows:

1. Misunderstanding–Miscommunication
2. Disrespect or disregard for other people
3. Conflicting egos
4. Impatience
5. Fear and insecurity over loss of control (p. 238).

Any of these factors can cause conflict in the workplace. Regardless of the cause, experts tell us that many types of conflicts challenge us every day. Verderber and Verderber in *Inter-Act* (1998) describe several different types of conflicts that we typically encounter: pseudo-conflicts, fact conflicts, value conflicts, and ego conflicts (pp. 337–340). In addition to these types, conflicts can also be centered on our needs.

Some conflicts are called "pseudo-conflicts." As their name suggests, they are not real conflicts, but are only perceived as conflicts. Pseudo-conflicts can result from two causes: faulty assumptions and false dilemmas. Take the situation that occurs when you and your partner agree to clean the office on Friday afternoon. At noon on Friday, you see your partner leave the building. Your first reaction may be that your partner is ducking out on the cleaning job. When you assume that your partner left you to clean by yourself, you may be setting yourself up for a pseudo-conflict. Although you may be right in your assumption, your partner may have gone shopping for cleaning supplies. Mistaking inferences for facts may explain many pseudo-conflicts.

Pseudo-conflicts that result from false dilemmas occur when the parties involved see only two choices as solutions to a problem. For example, assume your boss has asked you to attend a 20-hour training workshop, and you have a full schedule of inventory duties to complete. You may see only two choices: either complete the training and fall behind on the inventory or complete the inventory and disappoint the boss. In reality, other choices may be available: attend the training and ask for help with the inventory or postpone the training until the inventory is complete.

A fact conflict is at hand when individuals disagree about information that could be easily verified. What are the tolerances for machining a particular part, who has the best ERA record in the National League, or how many miles per gallon the hybrid cars are getting are all questions that can be answered by consulting some reference. Unfortunately, some people choose not to seek answers; rather, they turn "fact conflicts" into ego conflicts.

Ego conflicts occur when a dispute centers on status or power. The initial arguments may be over some factual question that could be answered easily. However, the ego conflict results when we argue over who has the "right" facts. The question of who hit the most home runs in the major leagues last year becomes who knows more about baseball, you or me? Rather than solving problems or answering questions, those engaged in ego conflicts spend their energy proving their self worth, their power, or their status to others.

Value conflicts focus on personal beliefs that you hold. You may value the right to organize workers and engage in collective bargaining. Or you may believe that employees should have the right to choose their own health care providers. Perhaps you have difficulty with the way your co-worker treats customers. These issues are in the realm of values conflicts.

Conflicts of needs usually occur when the needs of one individual are at odds with the needs of another individual. When I need a tool to finish a job and so do you, when I need time to complete my report and you want my help right now, or when I need to schedule a meeting at 2:00 and you can't be there until 3:00, we have a conflict of needs.

Sometimes these conflicts are easily resolved be redefining or restating the needs in a way that allows a mutually satisfying solution. For example, while I may need to start the meeting at 2:00, I could schedule your presentation later on the agenda. Or, I can give you the help you want right now, if you help me finish my report afterwards. Finally, if we can't share the tool to finish our jobs, maybe one of us could borrow someone else's. Often the needs of each person can be met if those needs are specifically stated and clearly understood by both parties.

These conflict types can overlap and complicate situations by masking the real issues and making status, values, or assumptions more important than problem solving. Many of us have witnessed the mixture of needs conflicts, values conflicts, and ego conflicts. We have felt uncomfortable as we watched others argue and attack one another. We have perhaps questioned the benefit of conflict or wondered what good could come from such behavior. Unfortunately, many conflicts are poorly managed, and people often let conflicts bring out the worst in them and their relationship.

Recognize Conflict Styles

Alan C. Filley in *Interpersonal Conflict Resolution* describes five individual styles people use in conflict situations (1975, pp. 49–55). These five styles represent choices that people make as they communicate in conflict situations. Included among these are avoiders, friendly helpers, tough battlers, compromisers, and problem solvers. Each meets a different need for participants in conflicts.

Avoiders steer clear of conflict for a variety of reasons. They may lack the time, energy, confidence, or skills to engage in conflict. In addition, they may be fearful that the conflict will escalate, or they may be doubtful that either party's needs can be met in the conflict. Avoiders try to stay away from conflict by leaving the situation, changing the subject, or simply agreeing to disagree without discussing the issues that precipitated the conflict. Although constant use of avoidance is not recommended, you may choose this style as a means of buying time in order to think through the problem, as a way of temporarily defusing strong emotions, or as means of limiting your involvement in a conflict that does not seem worth the time or effort required to resolve it. However, avoidance may keep those involved from seeking a long-term solution to a conflict.

Friendly helpers, or accommodators, allow others to determine the outcome of the conflict. These individuals prefer to maintain relationships by meeting the needs of others. They will "give in" to keep the peace. Friendly helpers value smooth relationships and don't want to make waves or cause trouble for anyone. Accommodation may be most appropriate when the issue in conflict is not that important or when it is easy to make concessions to others. Repeated attempts to accommodate others, however, may result in resentment and failure to get one's own needs met.

Tough battlers expect to get their needs met regardless of the costs. For the tough battler, winning may provide a sense of accomplishment. In conflicts, the tough battler's needs come first and sometimes with little or no regard for the needs of others. These individuals see conflict as a win or lose situation in which they must be the winner. Tough battlers employ persuasion with emotional appeals, forceful deliveries, and persistence to get their needs met. They frequently are more interested in implementing their solution to a problem rather than listening to the opinions, needs, and feelings of others. Tough battlers are often impatient with others who do not see things their way. While battling can lower morale, jeopardize relationships, and stifle creativity, in some situations, this approach may be appropriate. For example, when decisions have to be made quickly or when a crisis must be addressed, battling may be the most reasonable option.

Compromisers think that those involved in the conflict must each be prepared to give up something in order to reach a solution. These individuals expect to settle for less than what would meet their needs. They subscribe to the principle, "We must both give a little." Compromisers usually employ maneuvering, negotiating, and trading in an attempt to find a solution. Finding some middle ground may provide a partial solution to a conflict. However, unmet needs may still remain, and for those involved, the commitment to the solution will be only lukewarm at best. Sometimes we choose compromise because we can both "live with" the solution, even though neither of us gets our needs met. Other times, a compromise is the best we can do in negotiating a solution, and we embrace the solution as "something we can live with."

Different from compromisers, problem solvers believe that both parties can and will get their needs met. The underlying belief of problem solvers is that if we understand each other's needs, we will be able to find a way to meet both parties' needs. The question is not whose needs will be met, but rather how will we meet the needs of both parties. Problem solvers share specific information about what they need and listen to understand what the other party needs. Trust and openness make searching for possible solutions a creative experience. Both parties feel committed to the process and the solution because both sets of needs are met. This style has the advantages of promoting collaboration, creativity, and commitment. However, problem solving can seem unattainable when the needs of those involved are not clearly understood, stated, or listened to.

Filley suggests that each conflict style may be appropriate in different circumstances, and that we must learn to assess how well each style is meeting our needs. He further suggests that if a particular style is not working for us, we need to be flexible and try another style. Most of us have seen people switch from being tough battlers to being avoiders, compromisers, or friendly helpers depending on how they read the situations. Conflict styles may be used habitually, or they may be a conscious choice. Examine these styles to determine which you use most frequently in your attempts to manage conflict.

Consider Conflict Strategies

Regardless of the conflict style you select, establishing some ground rules for conflict may enhance your success. Most competitive sports have rules and officials to enforce the rules during the event. At work or at home, however, the rules may not be spelled out as clearly. Two men, George Bach and Herbert Goldberg, who have spent decades studying how people behave in conflict situations, describe the following "Nine Steps in a Fair Fight" in their book *Creative Aggression*:

1. Agree upon a date, time, and format to discuss the conflict.
2. Rehearse what you will say and how you will respond to what the other may say about the issues before the actual meeting.
3. Confront the other by stating the problem, describing your feelings, and identifying the consequences.
4. Provide feedback using the following format: Each person must paraphrase the previous speaker before commenting on what was said. This controlled feedback encourages listening and promotes understanding of the other's position. Feedback is best when it summarizes the content and feelings of the other.
5. Make a specific request of the other person that you feel would resolve the conflict.
6. Allow the other person to respond to your request. Then listen and paraphrase his or her response.
7. Continue the process of listening, paraphrasing, and asserting throughout the discussion of the issue and request.
8. Acknowledge closure of the discussion. Closure occurs when agreement is achieved, a stalemate is reached, or a recess is needed. As the initiator, you should state how you the see closure occurring, for example, "In other words, you will change the times that you work on maintenance so we can complete our production," or, "It looks like we will continue to disagree

about this," or, "It seems we need to take a break and maybe talk about this problem later this afternoon."

9. Arrange a follow-up that provides an opportunity to review the implementation of the solution or renews discussion in light of the time passed. At the time of closure and follow-up, you should express thanks and appreciation to the other person for listening and trying to resolve the conflict (1974, pp. 307–311).

These may not be the rules at your house or your place of employment, but certainly they have merit for those times when you are ready to sit down and talk things out.

Other basic rules for "fair fighting" may include the following:

1. Select the right time to fight. Avoid conflicts at mealtimes, bedtime, or when you or the other is too upset to discuss the matter. It is better to set a time that allows both parties to prepare for the discussion.

2. Try to maintain control of anger and strong feelings. Consider time-outs to calm down when they are needed. Be aware of others' "beltlines" and inform them of yours. In other words, be fair and sensitive to the feelings of others by avoiding topics that may cause pain or embarrassment.

3. Limit your fighting to one issue and stay focused on that one issue. Make sure that the one issue is the real issue and not just a presenting argument to test the waters.

4. Take turns clearly expressing your concerns and listening to the other's response. The most difficult communication challenge that you will face is to switch from being an asserter to being an active listener.

Remember that conflicts have at least two important factors, the issue and the relationship. To solve a problem at the expense of the other person can destroy a relationship, yet to maintain a relationship where issues are not addressed can be equally frustrating. Meeting both parties' needs is the best way to resolve conflicts.

INTERPERSONAL RELATIONSHIP TOOLS

When individuals or a group set out to solve a problem, their chances for success increase if they follow a problem-solving approach. Of the many variations of Dewey's problem-solving method, consider the one presented by Robert Bolton in *People Skills*. In "Chapter Fourteen: Collaborative Problem Solving: Seeking an Elegant Solution," Bolton explains the following six-step process:

1. Define the problem in term of needs, not solutions.

2. Brainstorm possible solutions.

3. Select the solution (or combination of solutions) that will best meet both parties' needs.

4. Plan who will do what, where, and by when.

5. Implement the plan.

6. Evaluate the problem-solving process and how well the solution worked. (1979, pp. 243–248).

Robert Bolton cites Peter Lawson's ideas about the importance of each of these steps and the strong message that they send. Consider the unspoken message, or meta-communication, sent with each step:

1. When you define the problem in terms of needs, not solutions, the message is, "Your needs are important to me," or "We really can understand one another."
2. When you brainstorm possible solutions, the message is, "I value your creative thinking and believe that together we can be even more creative in dealing with our common problem."
3. When you select a solution that will best meet both parties' needs, the message is, "I want you to have your needs satisfied. I want my needs satisfied."
4. When you plan who will do what, where, and by when, the message is, "You and I are willing to make joint decisions and coordinated plans to get our needs met."
5. When you implement the plan, the message is, "We have the power to change our behaviors in ways that can improve our relationship."
6. When you evaluate the problem-solving process and how well the solution worked, the message is, "We can get better at problem solving. We are not locked into this or any solution. We are flexible." (pp. 248–249).

USING SKILLFUL LANGUAGE

Specific Language

Perhaps one of the single most frequent causes of misunderstandings between people involves their use of general rather than specific language when communicating. If we become more observant of events around us at home and on the job, chances are we will become aware of these misunderstandings as a daily occurrence. Consider the shipping clerk who mistakenly sends a company its order by air rather than truck because the invoice read "RUSH"; the assembly line supervisor who replaces a costly automatic control unit instead of fixing it because the boss said to "get rid of the trouble"; the person who gets upset with a spouse for not helping out with household chores after just stating, "You never do anything around this place!" And the list goes on and on.

We tend to be general in our communication with others because we assume they'll know what we mean. The company manager who writes "RUSH" on the order form assumes the shipping clerk will send out the parts needed immediately, but not by air, which is twice the cost of truck transport. The boss assumes the assembly line supervisor will fix rather than replace the automatic control unit after being told, "Get rid of the trouble." The spouse is supposed to understand that the garbage needs to be taken out when told, "You never do anything around this place!"

It's important to keep in mind that we all have different perceptions of the world around us. No two people will ever process information from their environment in the exact same way. Whenever we receive a message from another person, we interpret that message from our own unique point of view, and the meaning we attach to the message may not be the same meaning intended by the sender.

So, to avoid the communication breakdowns caused by language that is general rather than specific, keep in mind the following suggestions:

1. Do not assume that receivers should know what you mean.

2. Avoid the use of absolute or general words like "always" and "never" (such as, "You're always late"). Be specific by saying, "You were 20 minutes late for work this morning."

3. Whenever you are expressing needs, wants, thoughts, or feelings, state your message in the most concrete or specific words possible. For example, it's better to say, "I need you to answer the phone and take messages while I attend the 1:00 p.m. meeting," versus saying, "I want you to help out this afternoon."

4. Encourage the receiver to paraphrase the message. "I'm not sure I made myself clear. What do you believe I meant by my last comment?"

SPECIFIC LANGUAGE WORKSHEET

Some of the following 15 statements are stated specifically. Put an "S" next to those statements that are specific—that is, those statements which create a clear picture of what is being said. Put a "G" next to those statements that are general and have broad areas of meaning and may result in varied interpretations.

_____ 1. Your workstation is a mess!

_____ 2. The grass in my backyard needs to be cut today.

_____ 3. That's the third time you've gone jogging this week.

_____ 4. You certainly let your boss take advantage of you.

_____ 5. There's a 30 percent chance of rain in the forecast today.

_____ 6. Send us some of those fancy switches for the control panel.

_____ 7. Place the cost forms for XB4773 on the computer terminal in my office for entry.

_____ 8. Never buy that brand of tool. It is really junk.

_____ 9. From the force of the collision, that car will require extensive repair. It's impossible to fix.

_____ 10. Let's get some help around here. Try pitching in and doing something worthwhile to assist.

_____ 11. The September 13th concert in the park was enjoyable because we had 80-degree sunny weather and third row center seats.

_____ 12. He is a poor worker based on that project he turned in.

_____ 13. Juan has not missed one day's work since being hired at this job.

_____ 14. Get the blue, two year-old Grand Cherokee in the second row of the used parking lot, section 1.

_____ 15. You're really doing a good job on that project.

NOTE: Now change the statements that you labeled as "general" to make them more specific and clear.

Tentative Language

A skill that is closely allied with our effort to be specific rather than general in our communication involves being tentative rather than absolute in the messages we send to others.

We all have our own perception of the objects, events, and people in our environment. We not only perceive these external stimuli through our senses, but we also interpret what these stimuli mean to us and go one step further to formulate opinions about them.

For instance, let's say you look out your living room window and observe a brand new, expensive, Italian sports car parked across the street. You may conclude that the owner must be wealthy. This interpretation may be followed by your personal opinion that money isn't required for happiness or that people should buy American cars as opposed to foreign imports. There's nothing wrong with forming opinions like these; we all do, every day of our lives. However, we can run into trouble in our relationships with others when we describe our opinions as if they are *always* true or absolute.

Receivers tend to become defensive and unwilling to listen to our opinions with an open mind when these opinions are stated in such strong terms that they leave no room for conflicting views.

Imagine that you work for a company with a strong union and that you personally believe unions are necessary and valuable to protect employee rights. Your friend who works in a non-unionized shop feels just the opposite, and tells you, "Companies, if left alone, would take care of their workers. Unions always cost their members money in dues and don't really provide worker protection." Now, since your views are in direct opposition to your friend's, your response to this statement is likely to be defensive and may trigger an argument.

However, if your friend had said, "I believe that some companies really care about their workers, like where I work at Acme Tool, and that some unions don't necessarily guarantee worker protection," chances are your reaction to the statement will be different. Why?

Notice the slight change in the wording of the second opinion statement. This time your friend prefaced the opinion with "I believe." This phrase is an example of tentative language as are such other phrases like "I think," "I've come to the conclusion," "It seems to me," "I personally feel," "My belief is," and so on. These qualifiers make the language more tentative and open to change for both the sender and the receiver.

Tentative language makes it clear to a receiver that your opinions are just that, *opinions*, not facts, and are, therefore, subject to error. Notice, too, that in the second example, your friend omitted the absolute word "always" and related the opinion to a specific company where an employer provides worker protection. Elimination of words like "always" and "never" reduces the tendency we all sometimes have to overgeneralize. Avoidance of these words can be especially helpful when we are commenting on another person's behavior.

Examine the difference between the absolute statement, "You never listen to me when I talk to you," and the tentative version, "You don't seem interested in listening or talking right now." It should be apparent that the first statement stands a greater chance of arousing defensiveness than the latter.

This skill doesn't demand that all of your opinions, however unimportant, be stated tentatively. Chances are it won't make much difference in a conversation if you say, "This is a beautiful day," instead of, "I think this is a beautiful day." But certainly if you are expressing opinions that are controversial, that may conflict with your receiver's view, or that focus on some aspect of your receiver's behavior, it will probably be more effective to keep your language tentative. By using this skill, you will also be less likely to view your own opinions as "facts" and will, consequently, be more open to conflicting points of view.

TENTATIVE LANGUAGE WORKSHEET

Absolute language reports a definite, unchanging, unqualified point of view, whether or not it is correct. Tentative language, in contrast, reports what seems to be and acknowledges limitations in our perceptions of things, events, and people—all of which can and do change. Tentative language also opens up the sender to other viewpoints.

Put a "T" next to those statements that are stated tentatively and an "A" next to those that are absolute.

_____ 1. Breaks should be more than 10 minutes long.

_____ 2. I believe women should have an equal opportunity to compete with men for job openings in the skilled trades.

_____ 3. Foreign cars are engineered better than American models.

_____ 4. You need to exercise if you want to stay healthy.

_____ 5. It appears to me that unemployment contributes to increased crime rates.

_____ 6. Mr. Mendoza is the best teacher in the world.

_____ 7. Getting a student loan is one of several ways of paying for school.

_____ 8. That gauge isn't accurate. Don't ever trust it.

_____ 9. Supervisors spend too much time in meetings and not enough time out on the floor.

_____ 10. I think Sam made some good points about that grievance you wrote up.

Informing Language

No one likes to be ordered around: not children, not adults. We put up with orders when we know we must, but resentment often results. Sometimes orders are necessary; we cannot do away with them completely. However, very often we can give information instead of orders. Informing statements will often get the same results without creating defensiveness.

Ordering statements command the receiver of the message to behave in a specific way. They remove any choice or decision making from the receiver. Orders are called "You" messages, and, as such, they direct, control, or command a given course of action.

Whether orders are presented in a polite tone of voice or shouted in an unskillful manner, they usually represent one-way communication that doesn't encourage feedback from the receiver. By giving orders, one sends the message, "I don't want to talk about it. Just do as you are told!"

However, informing statements provide information that the receiver needs to make a decision. Informing statements reveal thoughts, feelings, wants, and needs. They tell the receiver, "It's important that you know this. I want to share this with you." With adequate information, most receivers will respond in a constructive way. The disclosure of informing statements opens the door for two-way communication and encourages similar sharing from the receiver.

As an example of the difference informing statements can make, let's suppose a manager tells a group of service representatives in the shop, "You've got to write down a customer's complaints more fully on the work order form." Although this "You" message may get the reps to change their behavior, it may also increase defensiveness and resentment at being told what to do.

Informing messages may be more effective here. To the service representatives, the manager might state, "The technicians spend much of their time figuring out what's wrong with a piece of equipment when specific information is not written on the order form. They'd like to be better informed of the trouble so that they know what to look and listen for."

This response will allow the service representatives the chance to offer their own solutions (e.g., write out the specific complaint on the order form, explain the complaint directly to the technicians, or revise the format of the order form) while not increasing defensiveness or resentment.

Furthermore, the service representatives will, once they've decided on a course of action, be more likely to follow through since they're the ones who proposed the solution.

Again, although orders do have a place in communication, they are not the foundation of a healthy relationship.

INFORMING LANGUAGE WORKSHEET

Some of the following 10 statements give information, and some give orders. Put an "I" in front of the informing statements, and put an "O" in front of the ordering remarks.

_____ 1. When you don't close the walk-in cooler door, the compressor overheats.

_____ 2. A Wednesday night meeting is not convenient for me because I have a dental appointment right after work.

_____ 3. Let's talk about something other than politics.

_____ 4. Twice you've asked to use my tools, and I said "no." The answer is the same.

_____ 5. Give me a break! You can't expect me to keep track of everything that happens when the machine breaks down.

_____ 6. Believe me; you've just got to buy this computer software!

_____ 7. I need more help to complete these calls this week.

_____ 8. You have to share the overtime with Ronnie and Kim.

_____ 9. I feel hurt when you yell at me.

_____ 10. Don't you know that you have to pick up your boss at 6:00 this morning?

USING ASSERTION MESSAGES

Behavior Description Statements

You have probably begun to notice that the sharing skills discussed so far are all closely related to one another. This same connection will be seen as we talk about behavior descriptions.

How we interpret other people's behavior influences our thoughts and feelings. If someone's behavior violates our personal rights, prevents us from meeting our needs, or causes us unnecessary inconvenience, we may think we are being treated unfairly and respond with feelings of frustration, irritation, or annoyance.

Expressing feelings is certainly healthy, both physically and psychologically, but such expressions can be even more useful if we let a receiver know what behavior we are reacting to. We cannot force a person to change behavior that is having a negative impact on us, but we can increase the chances of a person changing the behavior voluntarily when we describe that behavior in specific, factual, nonjudgmental terms.

Notice the difference between saying to someone, "You've really been inconsiderate lately," as compared to, "You've borrowed my reference manuals twice this week without asking me if I needed to use them."

In the first instance, your receiver may not only become defensive at being called inconsiderate but also may have no idea what behavior led you to make that judgment. In the second instance, the receiver now knows precisely what behavior you are reacting to, minus the personal judgment you make about the behavior.

The receiver is more likely to ask permission to borrow your manuals next time (which is really what you wanted all along) because you've clearly identified the behavior, and you've avoided any evaluation of character, motives or intentions, thereby reducing defensiveness.

We can never know for certain what motivates people to behave as they do, so it's wise to simply describe the behavior we observe with our senses and then identify how we are feeling in response to that behavior.

Behavior descriptions should meet the following criteria:

1. They should report only behaviors we can observe with our senses.
2. They should exclude any evaluation of the behavior or statement of what we believe may be the feelings, motives, or intentions that prompted the behavior.
3. They should be specific and tentative rather than general and absolute (i.e., avoid words like "always" and "never").

As a final note, you may find it helpful to describe others' behaviors that affect you positively and not just negatively as we've been discussing thus far. For example, let's say your friend makes the following statement to you: "When you canceled your plans to go up north last weekend so you could help me move, I was really grateful because I couldn't have done it alone." This comment shares a very specific behavior, along with personal feelings and results of the behavior. You would probably feel more appreciated for your actions if your friend makes this kind of statement rather than simply saying, "Thanks for helping me move."

Describing others' behaviors that affect us positively not only reinforces such behaviors but also promotes relationships in which feelings of warmth, caring, and appreciation are fostered.

Problems with Behavior Descriptions

In *People Skills*, Robert Bolton explains the following most common problems that students encounter when sending behavior description messages to others:

1. Using general, "fuzzy termed" statements.
2. Presenting inferences about the other's motives, feelings, attitudes, and so on.
3. Including character assassination, profanity, or other loaded words that introduce judgments into the description.
4. Using absolute terms, such as "never," "always," or "constantly."
5. Extending the description to include more than one specific act, thus making it too lengthy or "windy" (1979, pp. 145–147).

RECOGNIZE BEHAVIOR DESCRIPTIONS WORKSHEET

Some of the following statements describe only observable behavior while others go beyond and deal with motives, feelings, attitudes, and so on. Put an "X" next to those statements that describe specific behaviors only.

_____ 1. When you never pay your fair share, I get upset.

_____ 2. When you waste my time with stupid questions, I get angry.

_____ 3. When you gave me a dirty look for telling an ethnic joke at the party, I was furious.

_____ 4. When you asked for my help locating that center, I was surprised.

_____ 5. When you said you got that new job offer and may leave here, I was worried.

_____ 6. When I just saw you punch in on Stewart's time card, I was curious.

_____ 7. When you were really annoyed because I wouldn't change vacations with you, I was surprised.

_____ 8. When you called the service department and said Job #2217 was ready, I was impressed.

_____ 9. This morning when you interrupted me while I was on the phone with a customer, I was alarmed.

_____ 10. When you look at the newspaper while I am talking to you, I feel slighted.

_____ 11. When you were rude to that customer because you're prejudiced, I was appalled.

_____ 12. When you took the parts from your machine and put them in the boxes without checking them for the correct size, I was surprised.

_____ 13. When you twisted the way the accident occurred to fit your version, I could tell you were worried.

_____ 14. When you changed my work schedule on Friday for next week's work, I felt pleased.

_____ 15. When you ignore safety policy so you can get the job done faster, I wonder how long you will last.

NOTE: Change all non-behavior description statements into statements that describe observable behavior only.

WRITING BEHAVIOR DESCRIPTIONS WORKSHEET

Use specific, clear language to write six behavior descriptions. These should present behaviors that please you in three situations and behaviors that upset you in the other three incidents.

1. _____

   _____

   _____.

2. _____

 _____

 _____.

3. _____

 _____

 _____.

1. _____

 _____

 _____.

2. _____

 _____

 _____.

3. _____

 _____

 _____.

Constructive Feeling Messages

As human beings, we all experience a wide range of emotions. Psychologists theorize that those individuals who skillfully express emotions to others tend to experience a higher degree of physical and psychological health, which is often the result of more satisfying interpersonal relationships, than those individuals who do not.

We could all lessen misunderstandings, reduce stress, and avoid unnecessary conflict if we learned to voice our feelings constructively at home and in the workplace. The skill of expressing feelings doesn't imply sharing our deepest inner emotions with everyone and anyone. The inappropriate expression of feelings can be just as destructive as the failure to express any feelings at all. However, more people seem to fall into the category of underexpressing rather than overexpressing their feelings; therefore, our goal is to achieve a balance between these two extremes.

Four general guidelines can help us to determine when expressing our feelings is appropriate. Feelings should be expressed:

1. In ongoing relationships (e.g., parent-child, husband-wife, friend-friend, etc.).
2. When there is a greater likelihood of helping the relationship rather than harming it.
3. In the face of conflict that threatens the relationship.
4. When the expression of those feelings moves gradually to a deeper level of sharing (i.e., you don't share highly personal feelings with someone you've just met).

Knowing when to express feelings is not enough. Equally important is knowing how to express them. Constructive feeling messages contain these elements:

1. An "I" message that makes it clear to a receiver that you are claiming ownership of and accepting responsibility for the feelings you are expressing.

2. Identification of the precise feeling you are experiencing (e.g., hurt, annoyance, happiness, uncertainty, confidence, etc).

The following are examples of how these elements can be combined into effective expressions of feelings:

1. "When you use my car and then don't refill the gas tank, I feel irritated."
2. "I'm so pleased with the seven extra hours you've put in on the blueprints."
3. "When you tried to talk to me during the meeting, I got really upset because I missed the change in work hours that the supervisor was explaining."

In the beginning, you may feel awkward and mechanical using this skill, but with practice, feeling messages will become a part of your overall style of communication and become a natural way of responding to the people with whom you interact.

Problems with Feeling Messages

Over the many years of watching students learn to write and share skillful feeling messages, we have noticed several problems that occur frequently. Below are some of these problems with expressing feeling messages:

1. Misplaced ownership occurs when speakers substitute "that," "it," "you," or "they" for "I." The responsibility for the feeling is assigned to some external event or person. Consider these examples: "You upset me when you say things like that"; "It makes me unhappy when you ignore me." Without the personal "I" message, these unskillful attempts can sound like accusations or blaming statements.
2. "Feel" is often used when the speaker means "think." When "think" can replace "feel" with no change in meaning, then the speaker is sharing ideas rather than feelings, as in, "I feel the Packers will win on Sunday." The speaker would not likely say, "I think depressed about the test results."
3. Rather than share how they do feel, speakers tell how they **don't feel**. For instance, they may say, "I don't feel confident about that new procedure." This problem can be eliminated with statements that share how the speaker **does** feel: "I feel confused about that new procedure."
4. Future feeling statements forecast feelings the speakers will have in a few minutes or when some condition is met. Saying how they would or will feel after something happens doesn't share how the speaker feels right now. Contrast these two statements: "I would be happy if you finish that report by the beginning of the week," versus "I am worried about making the deadline for that report."
5. When speakers say "I feel like" or "I feel that," chances are they will not name a feeling. Most likely they will report an action they feel urged to take, present some figure of speech, or offer some advice. Consider the way these statements fail to express an emotion: "I feel like throwing in the towel," or "I feel that you should change the setup on that project."
6. Trite expressions, such as, "I'm sorry" or "I'm afraid," lose their meanings as feeling messages when speakers overuse them.
7. When speakers combine skillful feeling messages with unskillful messages, the resulting mixed message will be confusing at best. Rather than challenge the listener to sort out these conflicting messages, speakers should strive for clear, skillful feeling messages. Consider the result of a message like this: "I am worried about your attendance. Why don't you think about how your missing work affects others?"

As you begin to write and share your feeling messages, try to become comfortable saying, "I feel. . .", " I get. . .", or "I am. . .". Then try to zero in on the single word that names the feeling you are experiencing. Try to avoid the problems mentioned above with skillful feeling messages.

RECOGNIZE CONSTRUCTIVE FEELING MESSAGES WORKSHEET

Following are 15 statements, some of which describe feelings directly and specifically. Put an "X" next to those statements that constructively describe what the speaker is feeling.

_____ 1. I feel it's time for us to take a break.

_____ 2. I'm really grateful you loaned me your car while mine was being repaired.

_____ 3. I get annoyed when you turn up the stereo while I'm studying.

_____ 4. My feelings are hurt when you tell me I'm inconsiderate of others.

_____ 5. You are such an easygoing person.

_____ 6. This darn fighting all the time is a pain. It has me really worried.

_____ 7. Apart from all the work I have to do, I feel a sense of accomplishment with this job.

_____ 8. I'm surprised that you could say that to the supervisor. I thought you did it just right, though.

_____ 9. I don't feel good about being here; Sam's always complaining about something.

_____ 10. I feel that going on second shift if you don't have to is really stupid.

_____ 11. I feel you could practice more.

_____ 12. When you're late from work, I feel concerned.

_____ 13. I feel nervous about that speech assignment coming up.

_____ 14. I am clumsy—always have been, always will be.

_____ 15. I feel like I'm on top of the world.

Now rewrite those statements that unskillfully express feelings so that they clearly state the speaker's feelings.

WRITING CONSTRUCTIVE FEELING MESSAGES WORKSHEET

Refer to the worksheet titled, "Write Behavior Descriptions" you completed earlier. For each of the behavior description statements you wrote, add an appropriate feeling message. Use the form, "When you _____ I feel _____."

1. When you _____

_____ I feel _____.

2. When you _____

_____ I feel _____.

3. When you _____

_____ I feel _____.

4. When you _____
   _____ I feel _____.

5. When you _____
   _____ I feel _____.

6. When you _____
   _____ I feel _____.

Consequence Statements

All of our actions have consequences; these consequences affect our lives in many ways, both positively and negatively. This simple fact of life comes home to us in countless ways. Our job performance, when reviewed, can be the source of reward or punishment. Our conduct on the job can either impress or turn off co-workers. Our behavior in public places can win the respect of family and friends, or it can get us arrested. What we do can have a very definite impact on others and our relationship with them.

The consequences of our actions can be tangible and concrete, or they may be intangible. Thomas Gordon, Robert Bolton, and other communication experts have written about the importance of tangible and concrete effect statements when expressing feelings to others. They note the strengths of telling others how behavior has real, lasting effects on our **time, money, work, possessions, and effectiveness on the job**. To this list we have added **health and safety** because people do act in ways that endanger or enhance our health and safety. We need to comment about the times when others act in these manners. These tangible, concrete effects can be measured in terms of gains, savings, or losses. As such, they represent the most potent form of consequence by showing how someone's behavior affects us directly.

Different from the tangible, but in many ways no less important, are the intangible effects which occur when others take action that has a definite impact on our lives as well. The feelings we enjoy or suffer through, the sense of accomplishment or being cared for, and the notion of power or belonging can directly or indirectly spring from our reaction to the behavior of others. Hearing that someone loves you, that your son wants a Mohawk haircut, or that a good friend is moving away may produce effects which cannot be measured by a clock, in your pocketbook, or in your productivity, yet the consequences affect you in very significant ways.

Both tangible and intangible effects may be positive or negative. They can save, enhance, add to, or enrich; however, they also can cost, diminish, waste, or destroy. Effective communication requires the sharing of consequences both positive and negative, tangible and intangible. Consequence statements provide information that clarifies our feeling reactions and makes our messages more appropriate to the receiver.

Consequence statements answer the question "why?" They provide a "because" for thoughts and feelings. Here are some examples of these statements:

"... because I have to pay money that I don't have."
"... because I have to spend extra time repairing the equipment."
"... because I couldn't hear the customer."

These, of course, are tangible, negative effects; they could also be positive:

"... because I save money and time when you rebuild that carburetor for me."
"... because I saved extra work and trips when you helped me move across town last week."

Likewise, the intangibles can be stated either positively or negatively:

". . . because I feel really happy."
". . . because I think I really belong to this group."
". . . because my reputation is damaged with the rest of the employees."
". . . because I can't cope with things."

In short, consequence statements inform others of the effects their behavior is having on us. These statements need to be honest, non-threatening expressions of our perceived reactions to their behaviors.

RECOGNIZE CONSEQUENCE STATEMENTS WORKSHEET

Label the following statements as "T" for tangible or "I" for intangible.

_____ 1. . . . because I have to spend money on a new television set.

_____ 2. . . . because my feelings are hurt.

_____ 3. . . . because my calculator doesn't work anymore, and I need it.

_____ 4. . . . because I was unable to complete the work on time.

_____ 5. . . . because I could be injured if we have an accident.

_____ 6. . . . because I have to spend three hours redoing the work.

_____ 7. . . . because I can't go as fast as you do.

_____ 8. . . . because I'm late for work and get docked for pay.

_____ 9. . . . because I'm embarrassed to say I don't know.

_____ 10. . . . because I get annoyed and aggravated.

_____ 11. . . . because that makes me look bad.

_____ 12. . . . because then people won't believe me.

_____ 13. . . . because I think you don't like me.

_____ 14. . . . because my standing in the community is lessened.

_____ 15. . . . because I lose my place and have to start over.

WRITING CONSEQUENCE STATEMENTS WORKSHEET

Provide tangible consequence statements for the following messages:

1. When you don't lock out the power on the machine, I feel concerned because I

_____

_____.

2. When you said that you would be moving on to a new job at the end of the week, I was worried because I

_____

_____.

3. When you start talking to me as you are walking into another room, I get upset because I

_____

_____.

4. When you talk to me when I'm on the phone with a customer, I feel frustrated because I

_____

_____.

5. When you cleaned the apartment, I was elated because I

_____

_____.

6. When you borrow my car and return it empty of gas, I'm aggravated because I

_____

_____.

7. When you offered to change work assignments with me, I was grateful because I

_____

_____.

8. When you poured the antifreeze in the oil fill spout, I was annoyed because I

_____

_____.

9. When you smoke cigarettes in our enclosed work area, I feel uncomfortable because I

_____

_____.

10. When you said I didn't need a whole new stereo system, I was relieved because I

_____

_____.

Impression Checks

Impression checks are responses to someone's verbal or nonverbal communication which share an impression of that person's message in an open-minded, non-evaluative way and which invite a response from the person.

As a communication tool, impression checks help the sender to verify assumptions or inferences that are made in response to another's words or actions. Impression checks provide a way to confirm what you're thinking about other people without always having to ask a question.

Clear impression checks should do four things:

1. State your impression or inference of another person; that is, what you think that individual is wanting, needing, thinking, feeling, or going to do. For example, "I get the impression you want some time to yourself.".
2. Present your impression in an open-minded or tentative way which suggests "I may be wrong," by using phrases such as, "It seems" or "It looks as if. . . "
3. Express your impressions in a non-evaluative manner. Not even the tone of your voice should imply that you're judging, belittling, or putting down the sender. Statements such as, "It looks like you really botched the computer program this time," make an evaluation of the sender and should be avoided.
4. Invite a response by using either a rising inflection at the end of your statement or by a very short question. Questions like, "Are you? Am I right? Is that it?" invite a response without taking attention away from the impression check. These very brief questions should just invite a response to verify the accuracy of the impression. Avoid a longer, more involved question that will open a whole new area of concern.

Now that you know what impression checks are, let's consider when you might use these tools. Let's suppose someone has said or done something which you don't completely understand. You have some idea of what the sender might be feeling, wanting, needing, or thinking, but you're not sure. At this point you may ask a question, or you may just pretend you know what's going on and not say anything. Sometimes questions will clear things up; other times you'll only get a vague response.

At times like this, impression checks give you another tool in your communication skills toolbox. They help to start conversations when you want to show some empathy for the other person or when you need clarification of some inference you have made. Impression checks have to be used with a curious, questioning tone of voice that communicates your interest and concern.

Impression checks encourage the other person to confirm your inferences or to show you where they are incorrect. Either way, this skill enables you to show that you are listening and that you care enough to try to understand the other person.

RECOGNIZE IMPRESSION CHECKS WORKSHEET

Some of the following statements effectively state an individual's impressions, while others do not. Place an "X" next to those statements that effectively state impressions.

_____ 1. Fran, it sure looks like you woke up on the wrong side of the bed.

_____ 2. By your frown, I get the idea that Wednesday will not be a good day for us to meet, right?

_____ 3. You're late again. What the hell's the matter with you?

_____ 4. Why are you always so rude?

_____ 5. I might be wrong, but I get the impression that you feel disappointed because you just flunked the test?

_____ 6. You seem disappointed to me. What did I do wrong?

_____ 7. I get the idea that you made another silly mistake.

_____ 8. What's got you so excited? You're not always this excited.

_____ 9. Shelby, I get the idea that you think I'm having trouble with this work, right?

_____ 10. Looks to me like you're thinking of quitting here and starting at Acme Engineering?

_____ 11. It seems to me that you should find an apartment closer to your job. Don't you agree?

_____ 12. I get the feeling you're looking forward to your vacation out West, right?

_____ 13. My impression is that you don't agree with the union's demand for a four-day workweek. Is this true?

_____ 14. I'm getting the idea that you're happy about Dale's promotion. Am I right?

_____ 15. It appears to me that you're being too hasty.

Rewrite those statements that you did not "X" so that they become effective impression checks.

WRITING IMPRESSION CHECKS WORKSHEET

Refer to the worksheet titled, "Writing Behavior Descriptions" on page 82. For each of the behavior descriptions, write an appropriate impression checking statement.

1. When you _____

   _____ it seems to me that _____

   _____ .

2. When you _____

   _____ I get the impression _____

   _____ .

3. When you _____

   _____ I sense that _____

   _____ .

4. When you _____

   _____ it looks like _____

   _____ .

5. When you _____

   _____ I thought that _____

   _____ .

6. When you _____

   _____ it appears as if _____

   _____ .

Request Statements

Being able to communicate through the use of behavior descriptions, impression checks, feeling messages, and consequence statements is necessary if others are to understand you better and react to you more positively. Combining behavior descriptions, feeling messages, and consequence statements will often get people to modify their actions in a way that reduces the concern at hand. For example, you tell a friend, "I feel irritated when you leave your clothes lying around the living room in our apartment because I have to spend my time and energy to put your clothes where they belong." This may be the first time that your roommate has come to know that such behavior is affecting you negatively. Your roommate may respond with, "Oh, I'm sorry; I didn't know that bothered you. You never said anything before, so I thought it was okay. Now that I know it irritates you, I'll make sure I put my clothes in my own room."

Getting people to modify their behavior is the goal, and if others change without having to be directly asked, great. However, sometimes people don't realize that their behavior is having a negative effect on you, even when you tell them, or they do not know how to relieve the irritation that you're experiencing.

In such situations, request statements are the next logical messages you will want to send. Requests are polite statements that directly and specifically ask someone to modify her behavior in a way that gets your needs met and that maintains the quality of the relationship. Requests may seek the permission of others for actions you want to perform, such as, "I would like to have off on Saturday the 18th." Or they may ask for help from others, such as, "Can you help me understand this diagram in the service manual?" Or they may ask for cooperation from others, such as, "Let's work toward a solution of the work schedule, one which meets all of our needs."

The essential parts of a request statement are as follows:

1. Requests should be direct. You must state directly what you need, want, or would like to see happen.
2. Requests must be specific. You need to tell others exactly what you are asking them to do.
3. Requests must allow for a freedom of response. You need to be open-minded enough to realize that people may say "no" to your request because they are unable or unwilling to do what you ask. You also need to listen to alternative suggestions from others that may meet both your needs as effectively as your original request.
4. Requests should be courteous and polite rather than sounding like demands. Remembering to include a **please** can make your request more welcomed.

Request statements are most helpful for interpersonal relationships when they directly ask the other, specifically express your needs, openly accept alternative suggestions, and actively encourage a freedom of response.

RECOGNIZE REQUEST STATEMENTS WORKSHEET

Place an "R" next to those statements listed below which make direct and specific requests. Those statements that are not specific and direct requests should be left blank.

_____ 1. Please hand me that 7/16-inch socket.

_____ 2. Thanks to your late arrival, we couldn't start the safety training on time.

_____ 3. Would you kindly return the insurance enrollment forms by Friday this week?

_____ 4. The RGB electric typewriter needs to have a semiannual cleaning.

_____ 5. I want you to go to Quality Plating to pick up the reconditioned parts that I have on order.

_____ 6. Since I've been putting in overtime at work, could you please help get supper on the table?

_____ 7. Employee to boss: "You know, it's been almost a year and a half since I had my last raise."

_____ 8. I'd like you to pick me up for work tomorrow because my car won't be repaired until Wednesday.

_____ 9. I want to talk to you about the low rating you gave me on my work evaluation last month.

_____ 10. Wouldn't it be a good idea to move on to the next item on the agenda? This meeting is running too long already.

_____ 11. I'd like you to let me know before you use that new numerical control machine so that I can see how it works.

_____ 12. What do you know about the settings on this new copier?

_____ 13. Can you help me file this batch of office equipment requests that came in this morning?

_____ 14. Would it be possible for you to change vacation days with me next week?

_____ 15. Why can't I have the same assignments as everybody else? I can do everything they can.

Now change the non-requests into requests.

CHAPTER 4 TOOL CHECK

Directions: Find the key words from this chapter to complete the following sentences.

1. Communication _____ should reveal a desire to improve relationships.
2. Others become _____ when you communicate with them in ways that attack or evaluate them.
3. _____ is a central attitude that will help you to communicate clearly, non-defensively, and assertively.
4. _____ is when we say nothing and let people "walk all over us."
5. It is best when _____ to realize that ultimately you are the best judge of your own behavior.
6. Specific versus general language will help you to communicate with _____.
7. Responding to criticism with _____ involves lashing out strongly at the critic.
8. _____ involves stating your concerns, feelings, impressions, consequences, and intentions.
9. _____ are problems to be solved.
10. An attitude that communicates that you are important and valued is one of _____.

CHAPTER 4 INTERACTIONS

INTERACTION #1—Sending Combined Assertion Messages

Combined assertion messages provide a way to share information in a conflict situation. They help us share valuable information about what happened, how we feel about the situation, how we are affected by the other person's behavior, what assumptions we have made, and what changes we would like to have happen. By sharing this information and listening to the other person's responses to combined assertion messages, we can discuss the conflict in a productive way. Preparing these messages takes practice.

Below is an example of ways to combine an assertion message. Refer to this example to see how to phrase your combined assertion messages.

COMBINED ASSERTION MESSAGE SAMPLE

The person who relieves you at work has demanding family responsibilities and is constantly coming in late. This person is your friend, so you don't want to tell the boss. Three times, however, you've missed some important engagements because you left work too late. You've mentioned something before in passing, but this person keeps showing up late, including right now.

Your ASSERTIVE OPTIONS include the following:

Behavior Descriptions: You came to work 25 minutes late today, and this is the third time in the past two weeks.
Feeling Messages: I feel perturbed that I have to stay late but also trapped because I think I can't do anything about it.
Consequence Statements: I have to miss some important engagements and spend my free time at work when I'd rather be somewhere else.
Impression Checks: I get the impression that your family responsibilities are making you late. Are they?
Request Statements: I would like to know how much longer this is going to continue and if there is some way I can be notified earlier when you can't be at work on time.
Sample Combined Assertive Statements:
When you came to work 25 minutes late today, and this is the third time in the past two weeks, I got the impression that your family responsibilities are making you late. I would like to know if there is some way I can be notified earlier when you can't be to work on time.
OR
When you came to work 25 minutes late today, and this is the third time in the past two weeks, I felt perturbed and also trapped because I have had to miss some important engagements.

COMBINED ASSERTION MESSAGE SUMMARY SHEET

Behavior descriptions should meet the following criteria:

1. Behavior descriptions should report only behaviors we can observe with our senses.

2. Behavior descriptions should exclude any evaluation of the behavior or statement of what we believe may be the feelings, motives, or intentions that prompted the behavior.

3. Behavior descriptions should be specific and tentative rather than general and absolute (i.e., avoid words like "always" and "never").

Feeling messages contain these elements:

1. Feeling messages include an "I" message which makes it clear to a receiver that you are claiming ownership of and accepting responsibility for the feelings you are expressing.

2. Feeling messages identify the precise feeling you are experiencing (e.g., hurt, annoyance, happiness, uncertainty, confidence, etc.).

Consequence statements report the effects of others' actions on us in tangible, concrete terms. Telling others how their behavior has had a real, lasting effects on our *time, money, work, possessions, and effectiveness or health and safety* shares our consequences with them. These tangible, concrete effects can be measured in terms of gains, savings, or losses. As such, they represent the most potent form of consequence by showing how someone's behavior affects us directly.

Impression checks should do four things:

1. Impression checks state your impression or inference of another person; that is, what you think that individual wants, needs, thinks, or is going to do.

2. Impression checks present your impression in an open-minded or tentative way which suggests "I may be wrong," by using phrases such as, "It seems" or "It looks as if. . . ."

3. Impression checks express your impressions in a non-evaluative manner. Not even the tone of your voice should imply that you're judging, belittling, or putting down the sender.

4. Impression checks invite a response by using either a rising inflection at the end of your statement or by very short questions like, "Are you? Am I right? Is that it?"

Request statements require the following three essential parts:

1. Request statements should be direct. You must state directly what you need, want, or would like to see happen.

2. Request statements must be specific. You need to tell others exactly what you are asking them to do.

3. Request statements must allow for a freedom of response. You need to be open-minded enough to realize that people may say "no" to your request because they are unable or unwilling to do what you ask. You also need to listen to alternative suggestions from others that may meet both your needs as effectively as your original request.

COMBINED ASSERTION MESSAGE PRACTICE

Following are four practice situations for combining assertion messages. Three conflicts have been provided, and in situation number four, space has been left for you to describe a conflict you've had or are having. For each situation, you are asked to be open-minded and think of both sides of the conflict. Then you are asked to construct several messages that show your assertive options in these situations.

Practice writing combined assertion statements for the following situation:

Situation #1

Ardon Caterers tell you that they will cater your wedding for $200.00, plus food. You provide most of the food, and Ardon gives you a bill for $1,000.00, which you feel is totally unreasonable. You pay only $500.00. Ardon calls to demand the rest of the money.

Write your assertive options below.

BEHAVIOR DESCRIPTION:

_____

_____

_____

FEELING MESSAGE:

_____

_____

_____

CONSEQUENCE STATEMENT:

_____

_____

_____

IMPRESSION CHECK:

_____

_____

_____

REQUEST STATEMENT:

_____

_____

_____

Combine three of your options from above to make a combined assertion statement.

COMBINED ASSERTION MESSAGE PRACTICE

Practice writing combined assertion statements for the following situation:

Situation #2

You're concerned about a co-worker at the company. You've become very good friends, but you notice that your friend has come to work intoxicated several times in the last few weeks since being denied a recent promotion. When you asked about this behavior, your friend yelled at you and told you to mind your own business. You believe this person needs your friendship more than ever.

Write your assertive options below.

BEHAVIOR DESCRIPTION:

_____

_____

_____

FEELING MESSAGE:

_____

_____

_____

CONSEQUENCE STATEMENT:

_____

_____

_____

IMPRESSION CHECK:

_____

_____

_____

REQUEST STATEMENT:

_____

_____

_____

Combine three of your options from above to make a combined assertion statement.

COMBINED ASSERTION MESSAGE PRACTICE

Practice writing combined assertion statements for the following situation:

Situation #3

Your employer had told you that your vacation request was approved. Two days before the vacation is to begin, you have heard through the grapevine that your vacation request is to be denied. You've already made extensive plans to travel and will lose money if you have to cancel. Your supervisor is now telling you about the denial of your time off.

Write your assertive options below.

BEHAVIOR DESCRIPTION:

_____

_____

_____

FEELING MESSAGE:

_____

_____

_____

CONSEQUENCE STATEMENT:

_____

_____

_____

IMPRESSION CHECK:

_____

_____

_____

REQUEST STATEMENT:

_____

_____

_____

Combine three of your options from above to make a combined assertion statement.

COMBINED ASSERTION MESSAGE PRACTICE

Practice writing combined assertion statements for a conflict that you have experienced at home, work, or school.

Situation #4

Your Conflict: _____

_____

_____

_____

_____

_____

Write your assertive options below.

BEHAVIOR DESCRIPTION:

_____

_____

_____

FEELING MESSAGE:

_____

_____

_____

CONSEQUENCE STATEMENT:

_____

_____

_____

IMPRESSION CHECK:

_____

_____

_____

REQUEST STATEMENT:

_____

_____

_____

Combine three of your options from above to make a combined assertion statement.

INTERACTION #2—Responding to Criticism

Communication, to be effective, must be conducted in an atmosphere where the participants feel "valued." Certainly, communicating with others who are critical, manipulative, inattentive, and closed-minded is frustrating and unproductive. Of course, some constructive criticism is necessary if we are to become aware of our shortcomings and find new and more effective ways of behaving.

When criticized we often find the need to justify our behavior.

Dealing with criticism and responding non-defensively may be one of the most difficult and challenging aspects of effective communication. The natural tendency to become defensive when we are criticized may result in a negative, upward spiral of defensiveness, which may provoke insults, put-downs, and hurt feelings.

Manuel Smith, in his book, *When I Say No, I Feel Guilty (1975),* suggests three specific communication techniques an employee can use to cope effectively with criticism. These three skills are "fogging", "negative assertion," and "negative inquiry." We will be using the following, descriptive labels: "acknowledging the criticism," "strongly agreeing with the criticism," and "clarifying the criticism."

Fogging or acknowledging

Fogging is a technique of calmly acknowledging unfair criticism without agreeing or disagreeing with it. The fogger is then allowed to make a judgment of what to do with the criticism: believe it, challenge it, or discard it. Fogging is based on the assumption that the individual is the ultimate judge of criticized behavior.

For example, to the boss who says, "Fran, your uniform is a mess." Fran might respond by saying, "Perhaps my uniform is too messy." This fogging response shows that Fran was listening and acknowledged the criticism without being defensive or without agreeing. Fran's indifferent, matter-of-fact tone of voice communicates the unspoken part of fogging: "I'll decide." Fogging then is a way of acknowledging the criticism without "buying" into it.

Negative assertion or strongly agreeing

Negative assertion is a technique where you agree with valid criticism without having to apologize or give excuses. This has the dual effect of allowing you to acknowledge your shortcomings and to reduce your critic's negative feelings. Negative assertion is based on the assumption that "to err is human," and the best way to deal with our mistakes is to strongly agree with the criticism.

For example, after you offered to pick Jan up from work, you completely forgot until an hour later. When you finally arrived, Jan said, "You forgot to pick me up. I nearly froze my toes off waiting for you." Rather than giving excuses, it might be best to say, "I did forget to pick you up. That's the dumbest thing I've done all week." This response strongly agrees with the criticism without offering excuses, placing blame, or becoming defensive. Negative assertion helps us accept our mistakes and learn from them.

Negative inquiry or clarifying

Negative inquiry is a technique requiring the active questioning of the critic for more specifics or for more criticism. The desired effect is that the criticism, if valid, will help you to improve, and if unfair, will exhaust your critic's concerns and thereby reduce defensiveness. The assumption behind negative inquiry is that through active questioning, you can determine if the criticism is valid or unfair. Your concerned, curious tone of voice should say, "I'm confused; I need more information." Questions such as, "What is it about my...? How does my... affect...? What specifically did I...? What else am I not doing effectively?" help the critics explain in greater detail the nature of the criticism and disclose their needs to you.

For example, the crew leader has just told you that your work is not up to company standards. You're confused and say, "What is it about my performance that is less than standard?" You may follow this question with, "Is there anything else that I'm not doing well on the job?" These kinds of questions will generate more open communication between you and your critic and will help you to decide whether the criticism is valid or unfair and whether you need to respond further with fogging or negative assertion.

Use the exercise that follows to practice these three techniques for dealing with criticism.

RESPONDING TO CRITICISM EXERCISE

For each of the following criticisms, determine if it is manipulative, valid, or vague criticism and then write your response according to the type of criticism that you have identified.

1. We give you people a uniform allowance, and you come to work looking like slobs. What do you do, spend it all on booze or dope? You're a disgrace to this company.

   Type of Criticism _____, Your response _____

   _____

   _____

   _____.

2. If you'd pay closer attention to me, I wouldn't have these hassles with inspection. I distinctly told you only one anchor hole goes in the JS708. The JA710 gets two anchor holes. Pay attention! Will ya?

   Type of Criticism _____, Your response _____

   _____

   _____

   _____.

3. If you keep bouncing those tanks around, we'll all get blown up. You don't have to be so damn careless around others. But then you don't care! You know it all.

Type of Criticism _____ , Your response _____

_____

_____

_____ .

4. Quality control just returned three more housings for rework. The machinery tolerances aren't close enough. You did all three jobs. What have you got to say this time?

Type of Criticism _____ , Your response _____

_____

_____

_____ .

5. You've been taking breaks that are too long this past week. We give each employee 10 minutes for break, and you were gone at least 15 minutes yesterday, Tuesday, and today. What's the story here, anyway?

Type of Criticism _____ , Your response _____

_____

_____

_____ .

6. Every time there's a rejection of your work, you blame it on the prints. It's always engineering's fault! Sometimes I wonder if you even know how to read those prints.

Type of Criticism _____ , Your response _____

_____

_____

_____ .

7. How come you always get the best machines to work on? You never get stuck with the relics that I have to use. How did you get such pull with the boss, anyway?

Type of Criticism _____ , Your response _____

_____

_____

_____ .

8. Your work is overrated. I don't think you're working at labor grade #7. The flaws in those last two orders are proof enough for me. You might think you're doing a great job, but you're just fooling yourself.

Type of Criticism _____ , Your response _____

_____

_____

_____ .

9. Maybe I deserve that bad evaluation; maybe I'm not perfect yet. But, what help have you been? You criticize without offering any help at all. You complain about my work but don't take time to show me how to improve. You're responsible too! Don't just blame me!

Type of Criticism _____, Your response _____

_____

_____

_____.

REFERENCES

Bach, G., & Goldberg, H. (1974). *Creative aggression.* Garden City, NY: Doubleday.

Bolton, R. (1979). *People skills: How to assert yourself, listen to others and resolve conflicts.* Englewood Cliffs, NJ: Prentice Hall.

Edelman, J., & M. B. Crain. (1994). *The tao of negotiation: How you can prevent, resolve, and transcend conflict in work and everyday life.* New York: Harperbusiness.

Filley, A. C. (1975). *Interpersonal conflict resolution.* Glenview, IL: Scott, Forseman.

Smith, M. (1975). *When I say no, I feel guilty: How to cope-using the skills of systematic assertive therapy.* New York: Dial Press.

Verderber R. F., & K. S. Verderber. (1998). *Inter-Act: Using interpersonal communication skills,* (8th ed.). Belmont, CA: Wadsworth.

CHAPTER 5
PRESENTATIONS BLUEPRINT

Identify Workplace Presentations

Preview Preparation Steps

Select Delivery Style

PRESENTATION TOOLS

State Central Ideas

Select Supporting Materials

Construct Outlines

Rehearse Delivery

TOOL CHECK

INTERACTIONS

Central Idea Exercise

Scrambled Outline Exercises

Informative Presentation Assignment

Persuasive Presentation Assignment

PRESENTATIONS BLUEPRINT

In today's workplace, the ability to communicate effectively is one of the most important skills employees can possess. Advances in computers and various other technologies have taken over tasks once performed by human workers, freeing them up to engage in face-to-face interactions with co-workers and customers more frequently. In addition, one's ability to communicate is often a top priority among employers seeking to hire employees. Adler and Marquardt-Elmhorst, in their book, *Communicating at Work*, cite a study which appeared in a January 1997 edition of the *Journal of Business Communications*. This study involved a survey of 500 managers from various businesses and industries, including manufacturing, retail, service, and finance, all of who were asked to rank their considerations when hiring individuals. At the top of their list was oral communication skills (Adler & Marquardt-Elmhorst, 2001, p. 3).

Once employees have been hired, the forms that their workplace communication can take are many and varied. They may include resolving a customer complaint, working collaboratively within a team, or asking for a raise. However, workplace communication is not limited to interpersonal (i.e., one-to-one) or group settings alone. Sometimes workers are expected to speak more formally by delivering presentations. Introducing a new product to a group of potential customers, making a proposal for on-site child care to a group of upper managers, or building company/community relations by addressing a local Rotary club are all examples of presentations employees might be called upon to make.

Not surprisingly, these kinds of presentations are more likely to intimidate workers than other forms of communication. "According to the book of lists, the fear of speaking in public is the number one fear of all fears. The fear of dying is number seven! Over 41% of people have some fear or anxiety dealing with speaking in front of groups" (*www.ljlseminars.com/anxiety.htm*).

It is because of this prevalent fear of public speaking that an organization like Toastmasters International has become so popular. Toastmasters clubs meet in most major cities of the United States at different times and locations during the week and offer a supportive and affordable way for those interested to practice their public speaking skills. In *The Toastmasters International Guide to Successful Speaking*, authors Slutsky and Aun state that "Over 3 million people have gone through the Toastmasters program. Clubs generally meet weekly. There are currently over 170,000 members of 8,189 clubs located in 55 different countries throughout the world, and the organization is still growing" (Slutsky & Aun, 1997, p. x). They also point out, "Some clubs meet inside an organization and are distinguished as corporate clubs, including IBM, Apple Computers, AT&T, Bank of America, Coca-Cola Co., Disneyland, Eastman Kodak, Hewlett Packard Co., Kraft, Inc., Rockwell International, Levi Strauss & Co., the United States Armed Forces, and hundreds of others" (Slutsky & Aun, 1997, p. xi).

Slutsky and Aun go on to point out, "There is perhaps no greater skill that can help you build your career or business better than effective public speaking. Whether you're speaking to a small committee of ten decision makers or an arena filled with 10,000 future leaders, knowing how to persuasively present your point of view can make the difference between merely surviving or thriving in a vastly competitive environment" (Slutsky & Aun, 1997, p. 1).

So that you may be among those who "thrive" rather than merely "survive" within your careers, the rest of this chapter will provide you with the framework you need to hone your own presentation skills. This information will include a discussion of the types and purposes of workplace presentations, a preview of the steps in preparation, and a selection of an appropriate delivery style.

Identify Workplace Presentations

Workplace presentations can take a variety of forms. Stop and consider for a moment the various opportunities you may have to speak before a group of people at work. Perhaps you are a member of a union and have occasion to voice your opinion at a meeting addressing recent contract negotiations. Maybe you've been asked to say a few words at a retirement dinner for a co-worker. Possibly you're in line for a promotion and have to convince a panel of managers that you are the best candidate for the position. Imagine that you have been asked to conduct part of a plant tour for a group of school children from the community. Or maybe as a senior member of your department you have been asked to provide some job training for a small group of newly hired employees. As these examples show, workplace presentations need not take the form of a "lecture" to a full auditorium of listeners. In fact, most public speaking that goes on in the workplace is part of day-to-day operations and more likely involves speaking to relatively small groups of people rather than to hundreds.

However, even given the range of speaking opportunities, most workplace presentations fall into two general categories: **informative** and **persuasive.** Let's take a moment to examine each of them.

Informative presentations are intended to increase the level of knowledge and understanding among listeners. One purpose of informative presentations may be to instruct the audience. For example, when a speaker takes the listeners through a step-by-step process in order to teach them how to use the new company voicemail system, he or she is being instructive. Informative presentations can also describe something. Presenting the layout of a new addition to the plant, outlining the features of an upcoming automobile prototype, or helping listeners to envision a proposed landscape plan for the company would all require detailed description. Finally, informative presentations can provide explanations that typically clarify how something works, is constructed, or performs. Employees who make presentations to new customers, for example, will frequently need to explain their product in terms of its function, construction, and performance.

Persuasive presentations are designed to influence audience beliefs, opinions, or behaviors. They generally take the form of convincing, reinforcing, or actuating. When a speaker attempts to convince an audience, he or she seeks to have the listeners adopt a particular point of view. For instance, members of a workplace team may try to convince management that the existing performance evaluation system isn't working as effectively as it should. In order to accomplish their objective, the team would need to present plenty of sound evidence, along with logical reasoning. Reinforcing involves strengthening an existing belief an audience is already presumed to have. A union president, for example, may reinforce the belief among members that they deserve a wage increase for the quality of work they produce. Last, actuating presentations seek to move the audience to take action. In other words, these speakers want the audience to "do something." A worker may urge co-workers to contribute a portion of their time to a community food pantry. A team leader may motivate the other members on the team to take a more active role in problem-solving discussions. A manager may encourage his or her subordinates to improve their quality of customer service.

Preview Preparation Steps

Mentioned earlier was the anxiety that speaking before a group can evoke. In fact, this anxiety can be so great that individuals will go to unbelievable lengths to avoid such speaking opportunities, often undermining their chances of job advancement. While we will address the topic of speaker anxiety in the tools section of this chapter, it may help to remember that one of the best ways to minimize nervousness is to be well prepared. In his article, "Overcoming Speaking Anxiety in Meetings & Presentations," author Lenny Laskowski (1996) states, "To reduce your fear, you need to make sure you properly and thoroughly prepare yourself before you speak. Proper preparation and rehearsal can help to reduce this fear by about 75%" (*www.ljlseminars.com/ anxiety.htm*). Given the importance of sound preparation not only to reduce nervousness but also to increase speaker effectiveness, let's examine the steps involved in the preparation process.

1. **Determine the General Purpose.** Before undertaking any speech presentation, you must know your overall objective. As discussed previously, general purposes can be classified as informative or persuasive. Keep in mind, too, that these purposes can be subdivided to identify your goal more precisely. In other words, you may intend to inform your audience but must then go one step further to decide if you will instruct, describe, or explain. The same approach is true if your general purpose is to persuade.

2. **Determine the Specific Purpose.** Once you have determined your general purpose, you need to formulate your specific purpose. Essentially, the specific purpose identifies the desired audience response at the end of the presentation. In other words, what do you want the audience to have achieved once your speech is over? Keep in mind that for most audience members, the greatest concern they have when listening to a presentation is, "What is in this message for me?" "How will this information be of value to me?" Consequently, a specific purpose statement might be phrased something like this: "At the end of my instructions, my listeners will be able to complete the monthly inventory online in less than one hour." Or, "At the end of my sales presentation, my customers will be able to identify three features that make our rust-resistant paint better than our competitor's."

3. **Analyze the Audience.** This step involves taking a closer look at the composition of your audience. First there are the obvious features of your listeners, sometimes referred to as their **demographics.** These demographic features include measurable characteristics such as age, race, gender, occupation, education, and so on. But in addition, there are other non-demographic considerations just as important, if not more so. These considerations include some of the following: Why is the audience there? How much do they know about your subject? What are their attitudes about that subject? Knowing as much as possible about your non-demographic will enable you to select supporting materials, organize your ideas, design appropriate visuals, and deliver your presentation in a way most suited to meet their needs.

4. **Identify the Central Idea.** Think of the central idea as the core or foundation of your presentation. A central idea states, in a single sentence, the essence of the speech. It needs to be clear, concise, and focused for the audience. So important is this central idea that the effectiveness of the entire

presentation is largely dependent upon it. It tells the audience what the speech is all about. Here is an example: "Our XK1500 rust-resistant paint outshines our competitor's." Or consider this example: "The online monthly inventory can be completed in half the time by following four simple steps."

5. **Identify the Main Points.** Once the central idea has been written, you can determine the main points for the body of the presentation. For most speeches, you will want to limit the number of your main points to three and certainly no more than five. Three seems to be a number of points most listeners can easily remember. More than five main points decreases the possibility of your audience retaining the information. Just like the central idea, main points should be stated in sentence form, contain only one idea per point, be expressed in parallel form and establish a direct connection with the central idea. Parallel form means that the points should follow a uniform grammatical structure. This example will illustrate three main points that meet all of these criteria: **(Central Idea): Quality customer service includes three primary goals**.

Main Point 1: Quality customer service includes treating the customer with respect.

Main Point 2: Quality customer service includes listening to customer needs.

Main Point 3: Quality customer service includes providing customer satisfaction.

6. **Gather Supporting Material.** After you have determined your main points, you are now ready to develop those points with factual information and evidence. The best place to begin your search is with yourself. In other words, how much do you already know about each point from your own experience? Next, you might want to interview other experienced co-workers to see what additional information they can provide. Of course, don't forget to check company resources such as annual reports, product catalogs, and so on. Finally, library and Internet searches can yield valuable supporting materials. Be aware, too, that including visual aids enhances verbal supporting materials. Charts, graphs, models, and computer-generated graphics are some of the ways speakers can incorporate visual support.

7. **Organize the Outline.** Now that you have assembled your supporting materials, you are ready to construct an outline. An outline provides the framework for putting all of your information together in a logical sequence. While outlines can take a variety of forms, depending upon the nature of your subject and purpose, generally outlines consist of three primary parts: the introduction, the body, and the conclusion. The introduction captures your audience's attention and identifies the nature and purpose of your presentation. The body provides the verbal and visual supporting information and evidence to make your presentation clear and convincing. The conclusion brings closure to the presentation by providing a summary and appropriate closing comments.

8. **Rehearse the Presentation.** After the outline has been completed, you are now ready to rehearse the presentation. Sufficient rehearsal is necessary for you to become comfortable with the information you will soon be

delivering to a live audience. As you practice, you will find yourself becoming less dependent on your outline and more conversational in your delivery. With this added comfort comes increased confidence, and confidence is the key to a truly effective presentation. In the tools section, you will learn more about the specifics for rehearsing the speech.

Select Delivery Style

The final consideration in public speaking is determining your style of delivery. Even if you have spent hours preparing your presentation, unless you have selected the appropriate style of delivery, your speech may not be as effective as you'd like it to be. Following are the four styles you should be familiar with.

1. **Manuscript.** As the name implies, manuscript deliveries are read word-for-word off the printed page. To avoid nervousness, some speakers think that if they write out their entire speech and then read it, they will be less likely to make a mistake. While their perception may be true on the one hand, on the other hand, they run the risk of delivering a dull, lifeless presentation. Audiences easily become bored by speakers reading to them with little or no eye contact and spontaneity. On occasion, a speaker may need to read a quote or cite some important data exactly as it is written to ensure accuracy, but to read an entire speech should be avoided at all costs.

2. **Memorized.** To reduce the tendency to read the speech, as with manuscript style, some speakers think it is a good idea to memorize the speech instead. They feel memorization will free them of the dependence upon their notes. However, even without notes, speakers who memorize their speech still tend to sound stilted and artificial. In addition, speakers may actually increase their anxiety by worrying about the possibility of forgetting the information they had memorized. While you may choose to memorize a short quote or brief fact or two, committing the whole speech to memory is not the best choice of delivery styles.

3. **Extemporaneous.** This style is the most versatile of all the styles. It requires the speaker to be thoroughly prepared and well rehearsed, but the speaker delivers the speech in a conversational style with little reliance on notes. With this delivery, the audience feels as if you are speaking to them directly and personally. Obviously, for speakers to use this style, they must have a sound grasp of their subject matter and have practiced sufficiently so they can speak with ease. By far, extemporaneous speaking is the most effective delivery style.

4. **Impromptu.** As you probably already know, impromptu speaking involves speaking unexpectedly or off-the-cuff. Your manager may ask you to voice your opinion at a meeting; you may need to introduce yourself and to share some of your background with a group of new employees; at a company banquet, you may be asked to "say a few words." These are just some of the instances that require an impromptu delivery. While it is never a good idea to use the impromptu style for a presentation that demands conscientious prior preparation, it can be a versatile style to cultivate in the situations previously described. If you find yourself in an impromptu setting, consider doing the following: state your point concisely, offer any necessary information to clarify your point, and make a brief statement to indicate closure.

PRESENTATION TOOLS

State Central Ideas

One of the most important elements of an effective presentation is the central idea, sometimes called the thesis statement. As was previously explained, the central idea expresses the theme of the speech in a single sentence. This central idea appears in the introduction of the speech and prepares the audience for what is to come in the body of the speech. In addition to preparing the audience, the central idea also helps you, the speaker, to develop and organize the presentation. It serves as a focal point for selecting supporting materials, designing visual aids, and structuring an outline.

In order to create a clear, concise central idea, keep in mind the following criteria:

1. A central idea must be expressed as a sentence. In other words, central ideas cannot be stated as phrases or titles of a speech. Consider the following example: "How to Handle Customer Complaints." This is a phrase that could also serve as the title of a speech. However, it does not represent a sentence and is, therefore, not a central idea. Revised to form a central idea, it might sound something like this: "Handling customer complaints requires strong communication skills." As you can see in the latter example, the focus of the speech is much clearer. The audience now knows that the presentation will address the communication skills needed to handle customer complaints skillfully. In addition, central ideas should not be expressed as questions: "How can you handle customer complaints better?" Questions such as this one might be used to arouse audience interest in the introduction of the speech, but like phrases or titles, questions do not set the stage for the specific information that is to follow.

2. In addition to being expressed as sentences, central ideas should contain only one key idea. "Laptop computers are a convenience for business travelers, and they are also quite affordable." This example contains two key ideas. It attempts to address not only the convenience but also the affordability of laptops. Speakers will do better to confine their presentation to a single key idea. In this case, the speaker could eliminate the part about laptops' cost and deal solely with their convenience. If, however, the speaker really wanted to cover both issues, the speaker could rephrase the central idea to read: "Laptop computers offer several advantages for business travelers." With this revision, the central idea still has only one key idea, the advantages. Then in the body of the speech, the speaker might include among those advantages convenience and affordability.

3. As you might have already observed from the previous examples, central ideas consist of two parts: a subject and a focus. The subject of a central idea represents who or what the speech is about. "Handling customer complaints requires strong communication skills" is a speech whose subject is handling customer complaints. The focus, however, represents the key idea of the speech. In other words, what does the speaker wish to emphasize about the subject? With this example, the focus is on strong communication skills. The focus allows both speaker and audience to determine the main points in the body of the speech. Given this particular focus, one could safely assume that the rest of the speech will discuss the communication

skills that employees need to handle customer complaints. It is also important that subjects and focuses be neither too general nor too specific. Consider this example: "Technological advances in the workplace have changed the way workers work." This central idea has a subject (technological advances) and a focus (changed the way workers work) that are both too general and, therefore, lack direction for both the speaker and the audience. Consider this improved version: "E-mail systems have revolutionized the way workers communicate with each other." Notice that both the subject and the focus have been sharpened. Now the audience and the speaker are clear about what technological advancement will be discussed, namely e-mail, and they are also clear about the change e-mail systems have brought to workers, namely how they communicate with one another. In contrast, a central idea that is too specific leaves the speaker with no place to go. Take this example: "The view function on e-mail allows workers to look at a document without actually opening it." While this statement may be true, there is little more that a speaker can say about this function.

4. Finally, the central idea is generally stated in both the introduction of the speech as well as in the conclusion. In the introduction, the speaker first attempts to capture listener interest and then states the central idea so his/her audience knows what to expect in the body of the presentation. The central idea is stated once again in the conclusion for two reasons. First, such restatement reinforces the importance of the information the speaker has just shared with the audience. In addition, listeners remember most what they hear last. Including the central idea in the closing remarks helps to ensure that remembrance.

Select Supporting Materials

In order to deliver an effective presentation, whether informative or persuasive, make sure that you include adequate supporting materials. Supporting materials are of two types: verbal and visual. In both cases, their function is to make the information more interesting, more easily understood, and more believable. When searching for appropriate supports, speakers should begin by inventorying their own level of knowledge. In other words, ask yourself, "How much do I already know about my topic based upon personal experience?" In most instances, you will discover that you have a variety of facts, examples, stories, and so on that you can incorporate into a presentation. In addition, you may also need to seek outside resources in the form of company files, annual reports, product information, and so on. Regardless of their source, however, supporting materials fall into several general categories. We will examine the categories of verbal supports first.

1. **Explanations.** This form of verbal support defines, analyzes, or describes. Definitions involve clarifying technical or complex terms that may not be familiar to the audience. If you have occasion, for instance, to provide on-the-job training for a group of new employees, you will probably have to familiarize them with the jargon that is used among more experienced workers. Analyses break down complex processes or concepts into their component parts to ensure understanding. If an experienced nurse is instructing a group of nursing assistants about how to take a blood pressure, the nurse would have to explain that process step-by-step. Descriptions provide detailed pictures for an audience by explaining how something looks, sounds, feels, smells, or tastes. A company sales representative would likely use descriptions when in-

troducing a new line of orthopedic mattresses to potential retailers, explaining the construction, appearance, and feel of the mattresses.

2. **Examples.** Examples are typical instances used to clarify a point. They work particularly well when used in groups of two or more. A health care professional speaking to a community group about the value of regular aerobic exercise might suggest walking, biking, or dancing as suitable choices. An interior designer speaking to several customers about window treatments may mention mini blinds, pleated shades, or sheers as possibilities. Offering a variety of examples helps to ensure audience understanding of the information being presented.

3. **Statistics.** Statistics are numerical facts that show relationships. For instance, if a speaker attempts to convince a group of managers that sales have been steadily increasing over the last quarter, the speaker would probably use statistics to prove the point. Statistics can be highly convincing forms of evidence, but to use them effectively, you need to follow certain guidelines. To begin, always cite the source of your statistics, including the date. Statistics have much more credibility when the audience knows how they were obtained. Next, display them visually if you can. Reading off a list of statistics is less effective than presenting them on a graph or chart where your listeners can actually see the information. Also, it is better to round your statistics off if possible. Instead of saying "We had 2,962 in attendance at the annual convention," consider saying "We had close to 3,000 attending the annual convention." Such rounding off makes the figures more memorable. Finally, even though statistics can be persuasive forms of support, don't overdo them. Inundating your listeners with lists of statistics decreases their impact.

4. **Illustrations.** These verbal supports take the form of short stories or anecdotes. They can be factual, or they can be hypothetical. Factual stories report incidents that have actually occurred. If a speaker relays an experience that involved satisfying a difficult customer, the experience would obviously be factual. However, hypothetical stories are imaginary but believable. If that same speaker wanted the audience to think about how they would respond to a difficult customer, the speaker might first create an imaginary scenario for the audience to reflect upon. Illustrations can be highly effective forms of captivating audience interest for the beginning of your presentation. Most listeners enjoy a well-timed story in the context of a speech.

5. **Testimony.** Quotes from experts in a given field constitute testimonials. A company's nurse practitioner might promote a seminar on worker safety by using a quote from the Surgeon General on work-related injuries. A union officer might quote an expert on labor negotiations when speaking to a group of co-workers about a contract dispute. If you decide to use testimonials, be sure your choice meets the following criteria. First, the person you are quoting should, in fact, be a legitimate expert. Second, it is helpful if the audience is familiar with the expert. If not, you should share the speaker's credentials. The audience doesn't need to know the expert personally, but should be aware of his/her expertise. Finally, make certain you quote or paraphrase the expert accurately.

6. **Comparisons.** Comparisons attempt to show similarities between objects, ideas, or concepts. Typically, if a speaker is introducing the audience to new or unfamiliar information, the speaker will use comparisons by linking the new to something the audience is already familiar with. For example, a

speaker who is training co-workers to use new computer software may compare it to software they are currently using. A sales rep may show potential customers how a new piece of machinery compare to an older model. Both of these are examples of literal comparisons. They show how items of the same class are alike. Consumer's Reports compares products in order to help readers make purchasing decisions. Speakers can also use figurative comparisons when they attempt to explain an unknown concept in terms of a more familiar one. The human heart is like a fuel pump in a car, or the hard drive of a computer is like a phone directory. These figurative comparisons help listeners understand new concepts.

Supporting materials that develop a presentation are not only verbal but may be visual as well. The inclusion of visual aids enables the audience to "see" what the speaker is talking about. By coupling verbal and visual support, speakers can powerfully reinforce the information they are presenting. For example, a speaker who is trying to persuade co-workers to contribute to the United Way Campaign may use statistics to illustrate how the funds are allocated among various social agencies. However, if that same speaker uses a pie chart to visually divide the funds, the listeners have a more memorable picture of the figures.

Visuals can be used in a variety of forms. Those forms include some of the following: objects and models, charts and graphs, lists and tables, photographs and diagrams. The media for presenting these visuals can be equally diverse. They include flip charts and poster boards, transparencies, slides, videotapes, computer-generated graphics, and handout materials.

Deciding on the type of visual and the choice of media for presentation is dependent upon several factors. First, what is the nature of your subject? Highly complex information, for example, might demand the use of slides coupled with handout materials the audience can take with them at the conclusion of the presentation. Simpler, more straightforward information might be easily presented on a flip chart. Second, what is the audience's level of sophistication? Audiences that are accustomed to hearing professional speakers may come to expect a PowerPoint presentation. Other audiences may be easily accommodated with the use of poster boards. Third, where will the presentation take place? A large lecture hall might necessitate the use of computerized displays or transparencies. A small meeting room might be suitable for objects and models that the audience can examine up close. Finally, what purpose is the visual intended to serve? If the visual is intended to provide step-by-step instruction of some process workers need to follow, a videotape that can be viewed again at a later date might work well. If, however, the visual is intended to record information from an audience brainstorming session, a flip chart or white board may suffice.

Regardless of a speaker's choice of visual, however, certain guidelines must be followed in order to maximize the visual's effectiveness.

1. Make sure the visual is large enough for the entire audience to see.
2. Keep the visual simple by resisting the temptation to cram too much information onto a single visual.
3. Create "eye appeal" by using colors, fonts, and graphics in imaginative ways.
4. Have a definite purpose in mind for using the visual.
5. Introduce the visual, explain it, then put it away.
6. Be certain you have the necessary equipment available and in working order before the presentation.
7. Practice the speech using the visuals.

Construct Outlines

After you have selected the most appropriate verbal and visual supports for a presentation, your next task is to organize your information in outline form. Outlines can be constructed in several ways, but we will examine the most basic and versatile outline form that should serve you well for your workplace presentations. This outline consists of three major parts: the introduction, the body, and the conclusion. Let's look more closely at each part.

The Introduction. The introduction acts as a preview for the remainder of the speech. The speaker should begin by capturing the audience's attention. Creating interest can be accomplished in several different ways. The speaker may cite some startling facts, tell a brief story, ask a rhetorical question, use a quotation, refer to the audience and/or the occasion, or include appropriate humor. Whatever device the speaker chooses, the goal is the same—to motivate the audience to listen. Second, listeners need to know how the information that follows will be of value to them. The speaker should try to show some tangible gain, such as saving of time or money, enhancing health or safety, or making more informed decisions. Third, the speaker must state the central idea or thesis. A well-written central idea communicates the theme of the speech in a single sentence and lets the audience know what the speaker hopes to accomplish. Finally, the speaker needs to preview the main points that will be developed in the body of the speech. As was stated earlier in this chapter, speakers should limit their main points to about three, and generally not more than five. Once these three steps have been accomplished, the speaker is ready to move on to the body of the outline.

The Body. The body of the outline contains the speaker's choice of main points, along with the necessary verbal supports. These main points should be expressed as parallel sentences, and each main point should be developed by at least three **different** verbal supports. In other words, resist the temptation to use three testimonials for a main point. Instead, consider using one explanation, some examples, and perhaps a testimonial, or a comparison. Varying the choice of verbal supports not only makes the information more interesting but more easily understood as well.

It is also important for a speaker to make a smooth connection between one main point and the next. This connection is made largely by the use of **transitions**—words or phrases that create a bridge between ideas. You've undoubtedly heard speakers say "first, next, then" to signal movement from one thought to another. Other examples of transitions include "in addition," "consequently," "therefore," "however," "finally," and so on. Beside the use of these common transitions, speakers may comment on how one main point relates to the next one. For instance, a speaker might say, "Now that you understand the importance of proper lifting techniques, we will examine those techniques one step at a time." Transitions can be used not only in the body but throughout the entire speech as well. In fact, they exist in all of the necessary parts of the outline.

Finally, speakers must make sure that the main points in the body of their presentation are logically organized. Numerous patterns of organization can be used to give presentations a coherent structure. Some of the most common patterns of organization are:

Chronological. Chronological patterns organize information in a time sequence. Typically, this pattern is used when the speaker is delivering a set of instructions, explaining a series of events that happened over time, or retracing history.

Topical. Topical patterns divide information into logical categories or groupings. A design consultant might discuss office furniture options as being traditional, contemporary, or eclectic. An insurance representative might explain to company employees the various choices of health care coverage: traditional major medical, PPO, HMO, or self-insured.

Spatial. Spatial patterns organize ideas on the basis of physical location or how something is put together. A presentation delivered to company stockholders might discuss net profits from plants located on the East Coast, in the Midwest, and on the West Coast. An employee conducting a plant tour will likely discuss the layout of the various departments within the company. A speaker introducing a new piece of machinery to a group of workers might describe the machinery in terms of its component parts and their relationship to each other.

Cause/Effect. Cause/effect patterns show the audience what might happen as the result of a specific cause or set of causes. A work team might report to management what they see as the possible effects of a proposed employee assistance program. This pattern can also examine a particular effect and suggest the causes that may have precipitated it. For instance, a worker in a department meeting might suggest possible reasons for increased absenteeism.

Problem/Solution. Problem/solution patterns typically include the following parts: a discussion of a problem, along with its possible causes and effects; and a proposed solution and its potential benefits. A work team, for example, might address the problems posed by inadequate training of new employees in the area of handling customer complaints. The team might then present their findings to a group of managers, coupled with suggested solutions and the benefits inherent in those solutions.

The Conclusion. The final part of the outline is the conclusion. This section contains three major parts: a summary of the main points, a restatement of the central idea, and appropriate closing remarks. Although the conclusion represents the final portion of a presentation, do not underestimate its importance. The conclusion gives the speaker a chance to review his/her key information one final time, as well as an opportunity to close the presentation memorably. Interestingly, some of the most noteworthy lines in famous speeches have occurred in the conclusion. After the speaker has reviewed the main points and central idea, the speaker can then end with a quotation, a brief illustration, a provocative question, a humorous anecdote, or refer back to an attention-getter used in the introduction. Most importantly, speakers should be brief and to the point, not allowing the conclusion to drag on. In addition, no new information should be introduced in this final portion of the speech.

Below is a skeletal outline form representing the various parts just discussed.

   I. Introduction
      A. Attention getter
      B. Need for information

C. Central idea
D. Preview of main points
II. Body
  A. First main point
    1. Verbal support
    2. Verbal support
    3. Verbal support
    Transition
  B. Second main point
    1. Verbal support
    2. Verbal support
    3. Verbal support
    Transition
  C. Third main point
    1. Verbal support
    2. Verbal support
    3. Verbal support
III. Conclusion
  A. Review main points
  B. Restate central idea
  C. Close memorably

Rehearse Delivery

After the outline has been completed, the speaker is ready to rehearse the delivery. As mentioned earlier, the most versatile form of delivery is the extemporaneous style. This style of speaking is carefully prepared and well rehearsed but delivered conversationally. To ensure an extemporaneous presentation, several guidelines should be followed.

Develop a speaking outline. Avoid speaking directly from the detailed outline you prepared. This type of outline is an excellent way to solidify your thoughts and to make sure you are expressing your ideas clearly and specifically. However, speaking from this outline can tempt you to read the information with little audience eye contact. Instead, consider constructing a speaker's outline, note cards, or a map. A speaker's outline is an abbreviated form of the detailed outline you prepared. It may contain your central idea and main points, along with some key words and phrases to remind you of what you want to say. In other words, this outline serves mainly as a memory jogger and not as a complete transcript of your speech. Such an abbreviated outline will discourage you from becoming overly dependent upon your notes and force you to speak more directly to your listeners.

If you choose to prepare note cards instead, remember some of these tips: number them sequentially; keep the information on each card as brief as possible; write legibly or type them; use boldfacing, underlining, or colored highlighting to make key information stand out; practice your delivery with the note cards; use them as unobtrusively as possible.

If you choose to prepare a map for your speaking notes, you will be designing a visual representation of your information. Maps can look like a solar system, with main points orbiting around a central idea, or they may resemble an organizational chart with boxed information arranged in a linear pattern. Refer to the first page of each chapter in this text to see how maps are used to introduce key topics.

Practice out loud. Once you have prepared a speaker's outline, a set of note cards, or a map, you can actually practice delivering your speech. Effective practice involves going over your entire speech several times out loud. Some speakers make the mistake of simply reading their notes silently. Practicing aloud, however, gives you the opportunity to develop a conversational style and to incorporate effective use of eye contact, gestures, posture, and facial expressions.

Practice in front of an audience. Friends, family, and co-workers are often willing to lend an ear and offer constructive feedback as you rehearse. Videotaping can be another excellent tool to help you review strengths and weaknesses in your delivery. In addition, if you are able, try to schedule at least one rehearsal in the room where you will be delivering your presentation. Be sure any audiovisual equipment you need to use is available and in good working order. Also, practice your speech with the visuals you intend to use with your audience.

Pay attention to your voice. In terms of voice, speak loudly and clearly enough to be heard by the entire audience. Establish a rate of speech that is neither too fast nor too slow. Make use of vocal variety and appropriate pauses to avoid a monotone delivery. Be sure to pronounce words correctly and to enunciate distinctly. Watch out for what are sometimes called "non-fluencies." Non-fluencies are the "ums," "ahs," and "you knows," that can disrupt a delivery and make the speaker seem unsure of him- or herself.

Pay attention to your body. Remember that you speak not only with your voice but with your body as well. Be sure to stand tall, with weight evenly distributed on both feet, assuming a posture that conveys confidence. Gesture naturally as you would in less formal conversation, and avoid nervous fidgeting. Moving about during your presentation is fine, as long as you avoid pacing back and forth. Also make certain you look at your audience frequently. A good rule of thumb is to look at one listener for four to five seconds; then shift your gaze to another listener for the same approximate time. Continue this pattern throughout your speech, making eye contact with as many members of the audience as you are able. This technique will establish rapport with your audience and also put you at ease.

Cope with nervousness. In order to be fully at ease with an audience, you must also give some consideration to coping with nervousness. Five suggestions can help you minimize speaker anxiety before you actually address your audience. First, be well prepared. Some experts say that nervousness can be reduced by 75 perent with sufficient preparation and practice. Second, accept that some tension before a presentation is natural. In fact, it represents a heightened sense of awareness that can be used to add life and energy to your speech. Third, consider practicing visualization. Sit comfortably in a chair and relax your body. Then mentally role-play your presentation, envisioning yourself as being confident and successful. The key to this kind of visualization is to make your mental imagery as vivid as possible. In other words, picture the room you will be speaking in, imagine what you will be wearing, see the audience in your mind's eye, and so on. Fourth, have a strong introduction. Many speakers find that when they get off to a good start, much of their nervousness dissipates within the first few minutes of the presentation. Finally, practice positive self talk several days before the actual delivery. When you find yourself feeling apprehensive about the upcoming presentation, remind yourself that you are well prepared, that you have a valuable message to share with the audience, and that you have the capacity to speak with sincerity and enthusiasm.

By following these guidelines for stating your central idea, selecting your supporting materials, constructing your outlines, and rehearsing your delivery, both you and your audience are likely to enjoy a polished presentation.

CHAPTER 5 TOOL CHECK

Directions: Use the key words from this chapter to complete the sentences below.

1. Two types of general purposes for a speech include _____ and _____.

2. When seeking to persuade an audience, a speaker can convince, _____, or _____.

3. The desired audience response the speaker is seeking is referred to as the _____ _____.

4. The _____ of an audience consists of factors such as age, race, gender, occupation, and education.

5. The two parts of a central idea are the _____ and the _____.

6. A verbal support that includes definition, description, and analysis is called _____.

7. Cite the source, round them off, and display them visually are guidelines for using _____ in a presentation.

8. Use of expert opinion as a verbal support is called _____.

9. Chronological order organizes information according to _____.

10. A delivery that is well prepared and delivered conversationally is called _____.

CHAPTER 5 INTERACTIONS

INTERACTION #1—Central Idea Exercise

The central idea or thesis is the controlling idea that identifies the essence of your speech. It contains two parts: the **subject** and the **focus.** The subject states who or what the speech is about, and the focus states what information about the subject will be emphasized. Consider this central idea: "Behavior-based job interviews require careful preparation." The subject is **behavior-based job interviews,** and the focus is on the **careful preparation** required. You may find it helpful to remember that the focus states the main points that will be developed in the body of the speech. Note, too, that central ideas are always expressed as complete sentences rather than as questions or phrases.

As a preliminary step to formulating your central idea, you should determine your **specific purpose.** A specific purpose statement represents what you want your audience to have accomplished after they have listened to your presentation. In other words, identify what you want your audience to know, understand, or do by the end of your speech. Given the central idea on behavior-based job interviewing stated previously, your specific purpose statement might sound something like this: **At the end of my speech, I want my audience to prepare for behavior-based interview questions.** Unlike the central idea, you do not actually share your specific purpose with the audience. The specific purpose simply acts as a guide for you in determining the desired outcome of your speech.

Finally, you will need to determine the main points that will develop your central idea and help you accomplish your specific purpose. Try to limit your speech to three main points. These main points should meet the following criteria:

1. Be expressed as complete sentences.

2. Contain only one key idea per point.

3. Develop the central idea.

4. Be stated in parallel form.

For example, the central idea on behavior-based job interviewing might include these three main points:

A. Behavior-based interview responses include a challenge from your past experience.
B. Behavior-based interview responses include an action that met the challenge.
C. Behavior-based interview responses include the results that occurred from the action.

Part A
Directions: For each of the central ideas below, underline the subject once and the focus twice.

1. New cars can be purchased with a number of expensive options.

2. Keeping physically fit takes continuous effort.

3. Many healthful benefits are provided by organic fruits and vegetables.

4. Whoever smokes cigarettes is asking for trouble.

5. The variety of disposable products available to consumers is mind-boggling.

Part B
Directions: Rewrite the following phrases or questions so they become central ideas.

1. How can you become a better student?

2. The high cost of building your own home.

3. Are you aware of the benefits of regular aerobic exercise?

4. How television violence affects young children.

5. Buying a used car wisely.

Part C
Directions: Choose three central ideas from **Part A** or **Part B,** and do the following:

1. Write the central idea.

2. Write a specific purpose statement.

3. Write three main points for the central idea.

Central Idea #1 _____

    Specific Purpose _____

    Main Point A _____

    Main Point B _____

    Main Point C _____

Central Idea #2 _____

    Specific Purpose _____

    Main Point A _____

    Main Point B _____

    Main Point C _____

Central Idea #3 _____

    Specific Purpose _____

    Main Point A _____

    Main Point B _____

    Main Point C _____

INTERACTION #2—Scrambled Outline #1

Directions: Unscramble the outline below by placing the correct numbers in the blanks provided below the scrambled information.

1. Engaging in physical activity can be a powerful stress reducer.

2. Your physical and mental health can be jeopardized if you don't manage stress.

3. Meditation is another great stressbuster.

4. Last year alone, an estimated $1.6 million in health care costs were the result of stress-related illnesses.

5. Just remember the words of Dr. Martin Shoreland: "Beat stress before it beats you!"

6. You can reduce stress in your life by following a few simple guidelines.

7. Finally, laughter is a great way to minimize stress in your life.

8. As you can see, physical activity, meditation, and laughter all help keep stress at bay.

9. If you keep these suggestions in mind, you, too, can reduce stress in your life.

10. These guidelines include the following: physical activity, meditation, and laughter.

  I. Introduction
    A. _____ (attention-getter)
    B. _____ (need for information)
    C. _____ (central idea)
    D. _____ (preview of main points)

 II. Body
    A. _____ (first main point)
    B. _____ (second main point)
    C. _____ (third main point)

III. Conclusion
    A. _____ (review of main points)
    B. _____ (restatement of central idea)
    C. _____ (closing remarks)

Scrambled Outline #2

Directions: Refer back to the scrambled outline exercise on stress reduction just completed. In the blanks on this worksheet, record the three main points of the outline next to the letters **A, B,** and **C.**
Then examine the various verbal supports that follow and decide which verbal supports go with which main points. Record the numbers of the verbal supports under the appropriate main points. Finally, once you have decided where each of the verbal supports belongs in the outline, label the type of verbal support (**explanation, example, illustration, statistics, testimony, comparison**) in the blanks provided.

Verbal Supports

1. Walking, biking, and swimming can all be good choices.

2. Listen to this story about how Norman Cousins reduced stress by watching funny movies.

3. According to Dr. Thomas Hansen, "Focusing on a peaceful scene can produce deep relaxation."

4. When you get your body moving, the following result: adrenaline is reduced, muscle tension is eased, and physiological symptoms of stress become more manageable.

5. Looking at the humorous side of a stressful situation is very much like seeing a glass half full rather than half empty.

6. In a study done at the University of Wisconsin School of Medicine, college students who exercised three to four times a week for at least 30 minutes reported a 70 percent reduction in their stress levels.

7. This process involves getting into a comfortable position, progressively relaxing all muscles, slowing down breathing, and mentally repeating a word like "Peace."

8. In the words of stand-up comic Jess Benton, "A good belly laugh can give you a whole new perspective on life."

9. Yoga, Zen, and meditation offer mental techniques to slow down racing thoughts and improve concentration.

A. **First Main Point** _____
   1. _____ **Type of Support:** _____
   2. _____ **Type of Support:** _____
   3. _____ **Type of Support:** _____

B. **Second Main Point** _____
   1. _____ **Type of Support:** _____
   2. _____ **Type of Support:** _____
   3. _____ **Type of Support:** _____

C. **Third Main Point** _____
   1. _____ **Type of Support:** _____
   2. _____ **Type of Support:** _____
   3. _____ **Type of Support:** _____

INTERACTION #3—Informative Presentation Assignment

Directions: The goal of this assignment is to prepare and present an effective **5- to 7-minute** informative speech in which you will do one of the following: **explain how to do something, explain how to make something, or explain how something works.**

Here are some examples of topics that would be appropriate for the three approaches listed above.

How to do something:	Establish a good credit rating
	Reduce stress
	Start a regular aerobic exercise program
How to make something:	Build a backyard bird feeder
	Construct a resume
	Design an organic vegetable garden
How something works:	A cellular phone
	The human heart
	Aromatherapy

In order to complete this assignment, you must meet the following objectives:

1. **Analyze** your audience.

2. **Select** a topic that is appropriate to the setting and composition of the audience.

3. **Gather** supporting material from at least three outside authoritative sources.

4. **Construct** a typed outline that clearly organizes your main ideas and supporting details.

5. **Include** at least three different verbal supports for each main point in your outline.

6. **Prepare** a visual aid that enhances your speech.

7. **Practice** your speech by videotaping it.

8. **Present** your speech to your audience using effective verbal and nonverbal strategies.

Let's briefly discuss some of these objectives. To begin, it is most important that you select a topic that meets the requirements of this assignment and that will be of interest to your audience. While it's a good idea to choose a topic you already know something about, you are also being asked to supplement your personal knowledge with information from three outside authoritative sources, such as books, magazines, newspapers, the Internet, and so on. Including authoritative sources enhances your credibility and confidence as a speaker. Be sure to cite your sources on a separate reference page. Below is a sample reference page.

Adler, R., & Elmhorst, J. (2005). *Communicating at work* 8th edition. New York: McGraw Hill.

Pellman, S. J. (2004, May). Managing your time. *International Business*, pp. 16–19.

Seniors return to school. (2005, January 17). *Princeton Gazette*, p. 21.

Writing research papers: A step-by-step procedure. (1995). Retrieved October 29, 2004, from the World Wide Web: *owl.english.purdue.edu/Files/94.html*.

In addition, you'll want to make sure you include three different verbal supports for each main point in your outline. Keep in mind that these supports consist of the following: **explanation, example, illustration, statistics, testimony, comparison.**

The complete sentence outline and reference page you submit must be typed. On this outline, all of the sections marked with capital letters (A, B, C) must appear as complete sentences. The subsections marked with numbers and lowercase letters (1, 2, 3, a, b, c) may have only short phrases or key words.

Your speech will be clearer and more interesting if you use visual aids. You may choose visuals from among the following: **posters, overhead transparencies, computer-generated graphics, models, charts, slides, and videotapes.**

Finally, you are encouraged to practice your speech by videotaping it. Viewing yourself on tape is an excellent way to polish both the delivery and the content of your speech.

With a positive attitude and a bit of hard work, this assignment should prove to be enjoyable for both you and your classmates. Good luck!

Informative Presentation Evaluation Form

Preparation (25 pts.) _____   **Comments:**

Uses logical outline designed to aid delivery

Includes reference page with three outside authoritative sources

Conforms to the time limit

Introduction (10 pts.) _____

Begins with effective attention-getter

Relates speech topic to audience's needs/interests

Emphasizes central idea

Previews main points

Body (50 pts.) _____

Presents clear, parallel main points

Organizes main points logically

Uses main points that all support central idea

Uses at least three different verbal supports for each main point

     explanation

     examples

     statistics

     illustration

     testimony

     comparison/contrast

Cites sources in speech

Employs at least one effective visual aid

Uses specific and vivid language

Uses smooth transitions between points

Conclusion (5 pts.) _____

Re-emphasizes central idea

Reviews main points

Closes memorably

Delivery (10 pts.) _____

Appears poised, confident, without distracting gestures

Maintains eye contact with audience

Speaks in fluent, conversational manner

INTERACTION #4—Persuasive Presentation Assignment

Directions: The goal of this assignment is to prepare and present a **5- to 7- minute** persuasive speech in which you will attempt to **convince, reinforce, or motivate** your audience. Select a topic that is of interest and concern to you as well as to your listeners. Try, if you are able, to choose a topic that is in some way related to workplace issues.

Here are some examples of topics that might be appropriate:

Speech to Convince: Attitude makes the difference in effective job performance.
Rising health care costs threaten employee insurance coverage.
Flex time has many advantages for single-parent families.

Speech to Reinforce: Time management skills can reduce workplace stress.
Good customer service is critical to company success.
Open-door policies foster effective workplace communication.

Speech to Motivate: Get involved in a Big Brother/Big Sister program.
Practice on-the-job safety to reduce work-related injuries.
Sign up for "Lunch & Learn" to upgrade your computer skills.

In order to complete this assignment, you must meet the following objectives:

1. **Analyze** your audience.

2. **Select** a persuasive topic that convinces, reinforces, or motivates.

3. **Gather** supporting material from at least three authoritative sources.

4. **Construct** a typed outline that organizes your main ideas and supporting evidence and a reference page that lists your sources.

5. **Include** at least three different verbal supports for each of your main points.

6. **Prepare** a visual aid that enhances your speech.

7. **Practice** your speech by videotaping it or rehearsing in front of a live audience.

8. **Present** your speech using effective verbal and nonverbal strategies.

Persuasive Presentation Evaluation Form

Preparation (25 pts.) _____   **Comments:**

Uses logical outline designed to aid delivery

Includes reference page with three outside authoritative sources

Conforms to the time limit

Introduction (10 pts.) _____

Begins with effective attention-getter

Relates speech topic to audience's needs/interests

Emphasizes central idea

Previews main points

Body (50 pts.) _____

Presents clear, parallel main points

Organizes main points logically

Uses main points that all support central idea

Uses at least three different verbal supports for each main point

 explanation

 examples

 statistics

 illustration

 testimony

 comparison/contrast

Cites sources in speech

Employs at least one effective visual aid

Uses specific and vivid language

Uses smooth transitions between points

Conclusion (5 pts.) _____

Re-emphasizes central idea

Reviews main points

Closes memorably

Delivery (10 pts.) _____

Appears poised, confident, without distracting gestures

Maintains eye contact with audience

Speaks in fluent, conversational manner

REFERENCES

Adler, R. B., & Marquardt-Elmhorst, J. (2001). *Communicating at work.* New York: McGraw-Hill.

Laskowski, L. (1996). Overcoming speaking anxiety in meetings & presentations. Retrieved June 11, 2001, from the World Wide Web: *www.ljlseminars.com/anxiety.htm.*

Slutsky, J., & Aun, M. (1997). *The Toastmasters international guide to successful speaking.* Chicago, IL: Dearborn Financial Publishing.

CHAPTER 6
TEAMWORK BLUEPRINT

Identify Benefits of Workplace Teams

Analyze Effective Teams

Recognize Stages of Team Development

Identify Positive Participation Skills

TEAMWORK TOOLS

Organize the Team

Accept Member and Leader Responsibilities

Employ a Problem-Solving Approach

Communicate Team Progress

TOOL CHECK

INTERACTIONS

Participation Style Self-Analysis

Team Article Review

Self-Analysis of Teamwork

A Tropical Island Exercise

Interview a Work Team

TEAMWORK BLUEPRINT

According to an Internet article entitled "New Teams in the Workplace," "Teamwork. . . an idea as American as the hot dog or baseball. . . will be the compelling theme of the 21st century. The people who succeed will be those who get high marks in 'works and plays well with others.' And the successful organizations of the future will be customer-focused, team-based organizations" (Parker, 2000).

The movement toward self-directed work teams in American business and industry gained increasing popularity in the early 1980s with the philosophy of W. Edwards Deming and the emergence of TQM (Total Quality Management). TQM was an effort on the part of management to involve teams of workers in the process of continuous improvement. In other words, workplace teams played an integral role in seeking new and better ways to produce a product or provide a service for the benefit of the company and the customer alike.

The use of workplace teams has continued to grow since that time, and the trend appears to be continuing. A number of studies seem to support this prediction. For example, "It is estimated that in 1995 only 17% of employees in the United States were working in teams" (Roberts, 2001). However, according to a 1998 study done by Beyerlein and Harris, 80 percent of companies with more than 100 employees reported 50 percent of their employees were participating in at least one team (Yancey, 2001).

More recent than TQM, Six Sigma has provided a methodology for ensuring quality. In particular, this method "strives for near perfection" by "eliminating defects (driving towards six standard deviations between the mean and the nearest specification limit) in any process—from manufacturing to transactional and from product to service" (Six Sigma, 2000–2003).

For example, "General Electric, one of the most successful companies implementing Six Sigma, has estimated benefits on the order of $10 billion during the first five years of implementation" (Six Sigma, 2000–2003).

In addition, while most teams in today's workplace interact face-to-face, computer technology has provided a medium for team members to interact in ways that transcend both time and space. These work groups are often referred to as virtual teams. Computerized discussion groups via e-mail provide an opportunity for virtual teams to collaborate across the globe. While this technology is unlikely to replace the personal contact that face-to-face teams represent, it does offer a new dimension for working collaboratively, a dimension that requires not only teambuilding skills but technical skills as well.

The viability of workplace teams should not really come as a surprise to any one of us. After all, human beings are "social animals" who tend in general to gravitate toward groups. We play sports in groups, worship in groups, and seek social interaction in groups. And it seems that even if companies do not establish formal work groups or teams, individual workers themselves often create quite powerful informal groups within their company's formal structure. One such classic example of the impact that informal groups or teams can have within an organization comes from a study done in the mid-1920s and early 1930s at Western Electric's Hawthorne plant. In this study, "researchers studied three small groups of men who wired switchboard equipment to determine what kind of effect a piece-rate pay system would have on their performance. In the piece-rate system implemented, the workers were paid by the number of switchboard banks they wired. In the time period in which this study was conducted, it was common practice for managers to lower the rate of pay per piece if the workers produced at a level that was beyond what they wanted to pay for them.

The researchers found that the workers, who were unaware that they were being watched, set up their own rules and regulations regarding productivity. In an effort to ensure that their pay per piece would not be reduced, the workers set a productivity goal that was just below what the company expected of them. Most of the workers in the study followed the group because they did not want their pay lowered. Those who tried to undermine the efforts of the group by working too hard or 'slacking off' were coerced into going along with the group through corporal punishment or banishment by group members. The members of this informal group were so good at hiding what they were doing that their supervisors and managers never noticed what was going on (Roberts, 2001). This rather dramatic, although not necessarily uncommon, example illustrates the power that work groups or teams can exert within an organization.

Given the likelihood that work teams are here to stay and that they possess the resourcefulness to exert powerful influence in the workplace, we would do well to examine our own abilities to function as effective team players. The sections that follow cover the benefits and characteristics of effective workplace teams, the stages of development teams go through, the skills required of both members and leaders, and the ways to manage team conflicts.

Identify Benefits of Workplace Teams

Given the increased utilization of teams in the workplace, it seems safe to assume that companies must find them to be of value. Some of the benefits companies hope to realize by implementing teams are identified in the article, "New Teams in the Workplace." Author Glenn Parker states that, "teams have been at the core of organizational efforts" to achieve the following objectives:

"Reduce the time it takes to bring a new product to market."

"Provide quality customer service and speedy turnaround time on customer requests."

"Collaborate with business partners around the world."

"Reengineer the design of work processes."

"Improve the quality of products and services."

"Increase sales and improve after sales support."

"Reduce cross-functional competition and 'turf' conflicts."

(Parker, 2000)

Regardless of the type of organization using self-directed work teams, there seems to be a consensus about the benefits. For one, morale among workers tends to be higher and absenteeism is less of a problem. These benefits are likely the result of a greater sense of empowerment that team members enjoy. Second, customer satisfaction increases since teams focus on ways to improve the quality of the goods and services they provide. Third, decisions can be made more quickly and problems addressed at the source, in part because teams often have the luxury of giving their attention to a single issue. But these benefits are largely realized when a team is functioning effectively. The next section discusses the characteristics of effective workplace teams.

Analyze Effective Teams

Before examining the factors that contribute to an effective team, whether that team is one in which members function face-to-face or one that interacts by way of computer networks, one should first define the word "team." A team is a collection of interdependent individuals who work together, generally over a period of time, in order to achieve a common goal. Teams are sometimes referred to as committees or task forces in certain organizations. But regardless of how these groups are labeled, their function remains essentially the same. In some instances, a team may be organized to address a specific concern within the workplace, and when that concern has been satisfactorily addressed, the team is disbanded. One company, for example, was planning on switching insurance carriers. A team was formed to explore other potential carriers and to weigh the pros and cons of these alternative carriers in terms of premiums, types of coverage, lists of providers, and so on. After these comparisons were made, the team presented their findings to management, along with their recommendations. Once management had reached a decision, the team was no longer necessary. In other cases, however, a team's objective may be ongoing. Consider a company team whose function is to plan semi-annual in-service training for employees. This team is likely to operate on a permanent basis.

Regardless of whether a team functions for a short period of time or over an extended period of time, the factors that enhance its performance remain the same. Following are some of these factors:

1. **Clear goals.** In order for a team to function optimally, the members have to operate on the basis of clearly defined goals. In certain instances, a team may be given a specific goal or series of goals before they even begin work. The perviously mentioned team that was assigned to assess alternative insurance carriers on the basis of set criteria (i.e., premiums, types of coverage, etc.) represented a team with goals already defined for them. However, some teams might have less tangible goals presented to them and have greater responsibility in establishing their priorities. A team that is directed to examine ways of increasing company sales as its primary goal may have to identify a series of preliminary goals first. Team members may decide that their first objective is to design a market survey to assess the current needs of their customers. After the survey has been designed, they may need to determine how the survey will be administered and the results tabulated, and so on. In this latter instance, members need to be very clear on the preliminary goals they need to attain before they can achieve their overall objective.

2. **Capable team members.** In addition to having clearly defined goals, team members must be capable. Generally, team members should possess sufficient technical expertise in their respective fields so that they can make meaningful contributions to the group. Many companies see to it that teams are comprised of members from various departments in order to broaden the base of technical knowledge. Also, team members should be good problem solvers and critical thinkers. Much that goes on within a workplace team involves careful analysis of data and decision making, so the ability to think critically and solve problems logically are indispensable skills for all participants. In addition, members must have good communication skills. The success of any team endeavor is largely dependent upon the members' abilities to voice their ideas clearly and concisely and to listen objectively to opposing points of view. Finally, for members to be truly capable, they need to receive training in the teamwork process.

Sometimes overly zealous companies who are eager to implement strategies like TQM (Total Quality Management) or Six Sigma assign their employees to teams and expect them to perform without any prior instruction. It should not be surprising when, under such circumstances, teams experience less than satisfactory results.

3. **Commitment to excellence.** For a team to be truly successful, members must be committed to achieving excellence. In large part, this commitment stems from members' beliefs that the goals they are working to achieve are worthwhile and will in some measure contribute to overall company, employee, and customer satisfaction. As a result of this commitment, members are more willing to put the team's interests above their own personal interests and to engage in the process of continually evaluating their effectiveness, both as individuals and as a team.

4. **Outside recognition.** If a team is operating effectively, members can derive great personal satisfaction from the work they are accomplishing. However, such personal satisfaction is often not sufficient to keep the team highly motivated and productive. What members also need is some form of outside recognition, usually from company management. Consider, for example, a worker who is doing his job superbly but gets little or no recognition from the boss. Contrast this situation with one where another worker is doing an equally outstanding job but receives acknowledgement and appreciation from the boss. Which of the two workers is most likely to sustain his quality of work? Most would probably say the latter. The same principle holds true in a team setting. Teams that receive management recognition tend to feel that the work they are doing is of greater value than teams that receive no recognition at all. In addition, this recognition can occur when management actually implements the ideas a team has generated or acts upon a decision a team has made.

5. **Collaborative climate.** A climate or atmosphere most conducive to productive teamwork is one in which members have an established rapport with one another. This type of environment results when trust has been established among the members and they feel free to share information openly and honestly. Another factor that enhances the climate occurs when members feel valued. Feelings of value result when individual members are listened to, respected, and acknowledged for their contributions by other members on the team. Finally, a collaborative climate develops when members experience interdependence. Members need to know, for example, that they can count on one another to get the job done. They also need to have worked out a system of conflict resolution strategies so that problems can be worked out while relationships remain intact. Keep in mind too that a collaborative climate is not only fostered within the team but must be supported by the culture of the organization itself. In other words, management from the top down must be committed to promoting an environment that makes teamwork possible.

Recognize Stages of Team Development

Like most interpersonal relationships that develop over time, so too do team members develop a working relationship among themselves over time. Beth Camp, in her book *Effective Workplace Writing* (1997), discusses five stages of what she calls the "life cycle" of any work group or team. The first stage is the **form** stage. In this stage, team members become organized, identify the strengths and weaknesses of the group, define their task, establish meeting times, and so on. The second stage is the **norm** stage. This stage involves clarifying goals, determining norms for the meetings, fine-tuning team tasks, assigning who will do what by when, and setting standards for the work that will be produced. Stage three is the **work** stage. The primary purpose of this stage is for the team to begin substantive work on their goals. This stage involves gathering information to complete the task and beginning to evaluate team performance as the work proceeds. Stage four is called the **storm** stage. Since conflict is an inevitable part of team interaction, the members now begin to resolve any disagreements that may occur over performance, the quality of work produced, or the deadlines that have been established. The final stage is the **perform** stage. At this point, the team has completed its assigned task and is ready to present the work to the intended audience (p. 14).

During this entire developmental process, we can observe two distinct phenomena occurring. First, we can observe the actual work that is being accomplished by the team members. This work follows a pattern of identifying tasks, assigning work to individual members, gathering the necessary information, evaluating and refining the work, and then producing the final product. But in addition to the work that is being accomplished, we can observe a second phenomenon occurring—the development of relationships among the team members. As the team begins working together, they develop a rapport among themselves. This rapport is critical to the success of the team, since it provides a climate in which the members can work harmoniously and productively. The next section examines some of the specific skills that enhance this type of climate.

Identify Positive Participation Skills

Most of us have probably experienced the satisfaction that comes from working with others whose company we enjoy. Working relationships that are supportive and nurturing make our jobs easier, increase our level of creativity, and energize our performance. This same principle holds true in a team setting. Teams where members feel a genuine sense of belonging are much more likely to be productive than teams where members feel a lack of connection to one another. In order for a team to maximize its productivity, members must possess attitudes and exhibit behavior that fosters the kind of climate we have been describing. Below is a list of the factors that enable team members to be positive participants.

1. **Accountability.** One of the most important qualities team members can possess is a sense of accountability. To be accountable means to be responsible. Team members need to be clear on their responsibilities to the group and to assure one another that they can be counted on to fulfill those responsibilities.

2. **Trustworthiness.** Members must also exhibit that they are worthy of trust. In part, trustworthiness results when members are accountable. However, in addition, trust is built when members are open and honest with each other, when they honor confidences, and when they refuse to participate in gossip about other members of their team.

3. **Spirit of Cooperation.** For any team or group to be successful, the members must be cooperative. Teams are often comprised of diverse individuals with conflicting points of view, and cooperation is generated when members are willing to be flexible, open-minded, and able to compromise when necessary.

4. **Respectfulness.** Along with cooperation, team members must have respect for each other. Although members may be very different from one another, each member deserves to be treated with respect. Respect is evidenced when participants are given the opportunity to voice their views and are listened to fairly, when differences among members are celebrated for the richness they bring to the group, and when all members demonstrate courtesy in their interactions with fellow team members.

5. **Enthusiasm.** When team members approach their work with interest and enthusiasm, they set in motion an energy that keeps them focused and on track. Enthusiasm also stimulates creativity and makes whatever work the team must address more enjoyable.

6. **Willingness to Resolve Conflicts.** Even among the most amiable teams, conflict is likely to occur from time to time. These conflicts can range from disagreements about the work being done to differences of opinion that seem irreconcilable. Regardless of the source of the conflict, however, effective teams have a variety of strategies for working through conflicts while keeping relationships intact.

TEAMWORK TOOLS

Up to this point, we have been discussing fundamental principles and ideas that underlie teamwork. Now we are ready to explore some specific tools for implementing workplace teams. This section will focus on four primary "tools." First, we'll examine the process of organizing a work team; second, we'll determine the leader's and members' responsibilities; third, we'll employ a problem-solving strategy for resolving team conflicts; and finally, we'll review a strategy for recording the team's progress in the form of meeting minutes.

Organize the Team

Let's begin by identifying how a work team might be organized. Prior to such organization, a company must have determined the need for the existence of a team approach. This need is frequently the result of a shift in management philosophy that seeks to involve all employees in the process of continuous improvement so that customers may be served well, workers may experience greater satisfaction, and management may realize higher levels of productivity. In addition, a company must ensure that adequate time, resources, and support will be provided so that teams can function as optimally as possible. Once these preliminary considerations have been addressed, the team organizational process can begin.

The first step in the team organization process involves **recruiting** members. Ideally, recruitment should be voluntary, if at all possible, to ensure interest among the members. A second approach is to allow workers to choose from a variety of teams being organized so they do not feel compelled to participate without any available options. Next, an ideal number of participants on a team is either five or seven. This odd number eliminates the possibility of tie votes. Also, this number reasonably assures a fair representation of varied points of view and reduces the manageability problems that are more likely to occur with larger groups of participants. Finally, recruitment efforts should encourage diversity among members, both personally and professionally. For example, members representing several departments would be more desirable than all members from the same department. Likewise, a mix of men and women, along with participants from different racial, ethnic, and cultural backgrounds, would enhance the team as well.

The second step in team organization is **training** the members. As mentioned earlier, workers who have never been team participants before cannot be expected to perform ideally without some prior instruction. To begin, all members need to understand the company's philosophy and goals and should be shown how the team's various efforts will support that philosophy and those goals. Second, members should be offered suggestions for maximizing their productivity within the team. These suggestions might involve discussion of member responsibilities, available styles of leadership, strategies for managing conflict, and so on. Next, each team needs to be given clear direction as to its purpose. Those purposes reveal the work the team needs to accomplish, such as developing an ad campaign for a new product, designing a customer feedback form, or evaluating several lines of computer software the company is considering purchasing. Finally, some companies provide "ongoing" training for team members to continually fine-tune their participation skills. Other companies will assign a mentor to each team so that if problems and concerns arise during the team's work, a mentor can step in and provide whatever assistance might be necessary.

The third step in team organization is **identifying roles.** Once a team has been assembled and the members trained, it is now time for the team to determine the roles that each member will play. Some teams elect to have members assume very specific roles. For example, one member might be assigned to record meeting minutes; another may serve as timekeeper; a third member may be responsible for reserving meeting rooms and facilities. Sometimes these roles are maintained for the duration of the team. Other times the roles may rotate among members. In addition to these kinds of functional roles, individual members may be expected to conduct research, seek information, meet with other company teams, and report back at their next meeting in order to facilitate decision making.

The fourth step in team organization is **selecting a meeting format.** At this step, the team must decide how often they will meet, when they will meet, and how long they will meet in order to accomplish their assigned task. In addition, they need to determine whether or not it will be necessary for them to follow a strict agenda, to be governed by *Robert's Rules of Order,* and so on.

The fifth step in team organization is **determining a team assessment method.** For any team to be successful, the members need to periodically take stock of how they are doing. Some teams may choose to develop a simple assessment form that members can complete anonymously. This form can include criteria to assess the quality of the work, the effectiveness of the meetings, and the nature of the personal interactions. Some teams do a quick check of their performance by having members write on a three-by-five note card one example of something the team is doing well (such as staying on schedule with their work) and one example of something that could be improved (such as being more careful not to interrupt other members when they are making a contribution to the discussion). Other teams whose members value their openness with each other may simply take time to periodically voice their personal assessment of team performance. Regardless of which method is selected, teams should also determine the frequency of these assessments. For a team that will be functioning for only a short period of time, these assessments might be conducted every meeting or two in some brief form. For teams that are ongoing, every few weeks may be sufficient.

The sixth step in team organization is **identifying methods of conflict resolution.** It is very important for teams to acknowledge in the early stages of their work that conflict is an inevitable part of group interaction. They also need to recognize that these conflicts can be substantive (i.e., dealing with the nature of the team's work) or personal (i.e., dealing with how the members interact with each other). In addition, members should appreciate that there are a variety of conflict resolution strategies that they can choose from, depending upon the circumstances. For example, if members are finding it difficult to reach a decision on a matter they are discussing, they may choose an approach which involves defining the problem, analyzing the problem, brainstorming for a list of solutions, evaluating the solutions, and so on. (Note: This reflective approach will be explained more fully later in the chapter). If the conflict involves personalities, the team may decide to have the concerned member or members schedule a private meeting with a team mentor.

Accept Member and Leader Responsibilities

Once the team has been organized, participants need to be aware of their individual responsibilities. As already discussed, all members must exhibit positive participation skills. In this section, we will explore the tasks faced by members and leaders in more specific detail. Let's look at the responsibilities of members first.

To begin, members need to **attend** meetings regularly and **be on time.** When a member is absent, extra time may be required by other members and/or the leader to inform the absent member about what took place during her absence. In addition, when members are late for meetings, they may delay available work time while others wait for them to arrive or cause disruption of a meeting that may have already begun.

Next, members should come to meetings **prepared.** Preparation requires members to review the agenda prior to the meeting so they are familiar with the topics to be addressed. Also, they should come to the meeting with any previously assigned work completed so they are ready to make productive contributions to the discussion.

In addition, members need to stay **involved** during the course of the meeting. Involvement means that members remain alert, interested, and eager to volunteer their ideas to the discussion. They should also seek clarification by raising questions when necessary and encourage more reticent members of the team to make contributions of their own.

Finally, members need to **adhere** to the meeting protocol established by the team. For example, if a policy has been established that each member can speak only once until each other member of the team has had the chance to speak one time as well, members need to honor this limitation. Or perhaps the team has opted to follow *Robert's Rules of Order.* In such a case, members need to be familiar with these rules so the meeting can run more smoothly.

In order for meetings to run smoothly, some type of **leadership** is generally needed. Some teams function with a designated leader, whereas other teams function by having members share leadership responsibilities among themselves. Neither of these approaches is necessarily better than the other, so teams need to decide which approach works best for their purposes, goals, and personalities. However, whether leadership roles are designated or shared, certain responsibilities remain constant.

First, leaders normally **set meeting agendas** and see to it that these agendas are distributed to members in advance of the meeting. These meeting agendas typically include when and where the meeting will take place, what topics will be discussed and the order in which they will be discussed, how much time will be allotted for each topic, and who will be attending the meeting.

Second, leaders **encourage participation.** To do so, leaders often raise questions to initiate discussion, call on specific members to make contributions, and draw out members who tend to be more hesitant to speak in the group. In addition, leaders make sure that all members are given equal opportunity to voice their ideas and opinions freely and without censure.

Third, leaders **keep the discussion on track.** In order to accomplish this responsibility, leaders make sure that members stick to the agenda and may appoint a timekeeper to assure that all agenda items are covered during the meeting. If the discussion strays from the topic at hand, leaders need to adeptly steer the discussion back in the right direction to avoid wasting valuable time.

Fourth, leaders **clarify and summarize** frequently. During the course of discussion, many different ideas and viewpoints may be voiced. A skillful leader is able to paraphrase this information to verify understanding for the group and to provide a smooth transition to the next topic of discussion.

Fifth, leaders **facilitate problem solving.** Much of the work that takes place within a workplace team involves problem solving. Successful leaders are able to lead the team through a logical, systematic sequence of steps that ensure satisfactory resolution to the problems the team is facing.

Sixth, leaders **bring closure** to the meeting. A skillful leader is able to wrap up the meeting with a quick summary of the team's accomplishments, to identify what issues still need to be addressed, and to set the next meeting time so members can plan their schedules accordingly.

Employ a Problem-Solving Approach

How a team decides to solve problems is largely dependent upon the nature of the problem as well as the type of relationships the team members have with each other. While a variety of strategies are available for problem solving, we will examine one of the most versatile methods of problem solving, the **reflective approach.** This approach requires the full participation of all members and involves an attempt to reach a consensus. The seven steps of this process are not new. In fact, they have been in use for more than half a century and were originally developed by John Dewey.

The first step is to **define the problem.** Before members can even think about resolutions, they need to have a clear understanding of the problem they are facing. For example, if a team has been asked to develop an employee training program for new computer software to streamline the monthly inventory, the members clearly have a two-part problem: What is the best instructional method to provide this training? And what specific information needs to be included in the training?

The second step is to **analyze the problem.** This step demands that team members explore the problem in greater depth to determine its scope. Oftentimes, this step requires some outside research or investigation before the problem can be explored from all angles. In the case of the software training program previously discussed, team members may discover that this new software is somewhat challenging to use for those with little or no computer background. They might also determine that a significant number of senior employees are resistant to computerizing the inventory process when they have been doing it by hand for so many years. Both these issues need to be considered when the team moves on to a discussion of possible solutions to the problem.

The third step is to **establish criteria for a solution.** Here the team needs to prepare a list of requirements that a solution must meet. For instance, the software training must be done outside normal working hours; certain cost restraints of the training must be kept in view; follow-up support must be made available after the training for employees that need it; instructional provisions must be made to accommodate employees with little or no computer background; the approach selected must be persuasive enough to "win" over those employees resistant to change, and so on.

The fourth step is to **consider possible solutions.** This step is where "brainstorming" takes place, and team members are able to exercise their creativity. The goal of brainstorming is to generate as many solutions as possible, keeping in mind the criteria that was established in step three. As members suggest solutions, they can be written down or recorded on audiotape. It is important that all solutions volunteered by members be acknowledged without any criticism or evaluation at this point. Members will have time to reflect on the viability of proposed solutions in the next step. You will note that the software training program we have been working with involves a two-part problem (i.e., what instructional method to use and what information to include in the training). Consequently, when considering possible solutions, members would do well to create two separate brainstormed lists, one for each part of the problem. Or, they may even want to cycle through this seven-step process entirely with one part of the problem only and then return to the start of the cycle for the second part of the problem.

The fifth step is to **select a solution.** Now the team members are ready to examine the solutions generated in step four. To begin, they need to weigh each suggestion on the basis of the criteria cited in step three. For example, if one suggestion proposes that the company use videotapes to train the employees, the team might collectively decide that a hands-on approach would be better for all trainees, especially those with little or no computer experience. In addition, the team might decide that two or more of the proposed solutions be combined. So, the team may opt to combine the suggestion for a hands-on approach (suggestion one) along with the use of a "buddy system" (suggestion two) so that employees with less computer experience are paired up with a more experienced employee for hands-on training.

The sixth step is to **implement the solution.** This step occurs only after the team has a detailed plan for putting their proposed solution or combination of solutions into effect. In some cases, the team itself will actually implement the plan, assigning specific tasks to individual team members, establishing timelines for implementation, and so on. However, with the computer software training, this team will more likely be expected to submit their detailed plan to management for implementation.

The seventh and final step is **follow-up on the solution.** This step requires either the team or management to evaluate the success of the solution after it has been implemented. Employee feedback forms would be an excellent way to assess employee satisfaction in response to the software training. Based on these responses, the team or management could make adjustments in the training, if necessary, to ensure even greater success in the future.

Communicate Team Progress

One final tool that teams need is a way of keeping records of their work as it progresses. Since most teams will meet routinely until they have reached their goals, they will want to document what takes place at each meeting for the benefit of themselves and, perhaps, for those outside the group, such as management or even other teams.

The primary vehicle for this kind of communication is meeting minutes. This form of communication typically keeps record of the following information: the date, place, and time of the meeting; a list of members present and sometimes those absent; a list of topics that were discussed; a brief description of decisions made and/or follow-up actions required; the date of the next meeting; the time the meeting adjourned; and a signature of the member who prepared the minutes.

Sometimes teams will appoint an official recorder to take meeting minutes. In other instances, this duty will be rotated among the members. After the meeting, the recorder will usually type the minutes on the computer, print copies for all who need them, and then distribute them for review. Some teams will have a laptop computer available during the meeting so that the recorder can enter the minutes into the computer.

Whoever prepares the minutes should keep them clear, concise, accurate, and easy to read. Typically, boldface headings are used to separate key issues the team discussed. The information is single spaced within paragraphs and double-spaced between them.

The best way to understand a typical format for meeting minutes is to examine the sample that follows.

WELLNESS TEAM MEETING ←
December 5, 2004
Conference Center Room B

MEMBERS PRESENT:
Sara Alby
Jeff Bogart
Randy Carter
Sue Frazier
Martin Peterson
Karen Olson
Robert Wilson

The meeting of the Wellness Team began at 9:45 A.M. and was chaired by Karen Olson. The agenda was reviewed, and members agreed to the time allotments for each topic of discussion.

Company Health Fair: Robert Wilson reported that the company health fair would take place on April 14, 2005, in the Conference Center Auditorium. He stated that employees, their families, and the community would have access to a variety of free screenings including blood pressure, cholesterol, vision and hearing, etc. Local area health care providers are also being scheduled to do 30-minute presentations at various intervals during the course of the fair. To date, Dr. Richard Weber, a local chiropractor, has volunteered to discuss proper lifting techniques to reduce back injuries. Nurse practitioner Sandy Christel has agreed to speak on ways to relieve workplace stress. Tom Kendall, a fitness trainer, will talk about getting in shape for the summer. Robert informed the team that he would let them know more about community organizations that would have booths at the fair by the next meeting.

Stress Management Speaker: Sue Frazier reported that the stress management speaker who spoke to employees last month was well received. One hundred ten employees attended the lunch hour presentation. Feedback forms indicated that employees would welcome more special programs like this in the future. Sue asked the team to think about other topics of interest for such programs and to bring back ideas for the next meeting.

Hazardous Waste Disposal: Randy Carter reported that the State has issued new guidelines for disposal of hazardous industrial waste. He said that those guidelines are available in the Health and Safety Office for employees who need copies for their departments.

Smoking Cessation Classes: Sara Alby reported that March 15th is the company "Smoke Out" Day. All smokers are encouraged to quit for a day. Those who are interested in remaining smoke free can sign up for a series of three smoking cessation classes offered by the public health department. These classes are free to all employees, and the first class will take place in Conference Center Room C from 4:00–5:00 P.M. beginning March 15th. The participants will decide on subsequent class meetings.

NEXT MEETING:

The next meeting is scheduled for 9:45 A.M. in Conference Center Room A on January 10, 2005.

Meeting Adjourned at 11:00 A.M.

Respectfully Submitted,

Jeff Bogart

CHAPTER 6 TOOL CHECK

Directions: Use the key words from this chapter to complete the sentences below.

1. Factors that can enhance team performance include clear goals, capable team members, commitment to excellence, _____, and _____.
2. The seven-step problem-solving strategy based on the ideas of John Dewey is sometimes referred to as the _____ approach.
3. _____ _____ enable teams to keep a written record of the work that takes place at each meeting.
4. Positive participation skills required of team members include accountability, trustworthiness, cooperation, respectfulness, _____, and _____.
5. Some of the responsibilities that team leaders have include _____, _____, and _____.
6. Some of the responsibilities that team members have include _____, _____, and _____.
7. An increased popularity of workplace teams occurred with the emergence of TQM or T_____, Q_____, M_____.
8. After a team has been organized and its members recruited, the next step in the team organization process involves _____.
9. The fourth stage in team development in which members attempt to work through conflicts they are experiencing is called the _____ stage.
10. Two benefits of workplace teams include _____ and _____.

CHAPTER 6 INTERACTIONS

INTERACTION #1—Participation Style Self-Analysis

As you might imagine, workplace teams can be comprised of many diverse individuals. This diversity can be related to one's position within the company, educational background, gender, race, ethnicity, and so on. But in addition, team members can also represent different styles of participation. Those among you who have participated in any kind of group or team setting know that some members like to "take charge." Others prefer to sit back and watch things happen. Some are outstanding critical thinkers who carefully scrutinize all the ideas that are generated in the group. Others are socially outgoing and good at maintaining group harmony. The list of these participation styles is probably endless, and all of these styles can offer valuable contributions to the effectiveness of the group or team.

This self-analysis exercise is designed to have you, as well as your team members, determine your predominant participation style. Knowing your own style and those of your teammates can enable the entire team to capitalize on one another's strengths and compensate for one another's weaknesses.

To complete this self-analysis, read the groups of statements that follow. For each group, select the characteristic that most applies to you by checking the H, A, O, or M. While more than one characteristic may apply, choose the one that comes closest to describing your behavior in a group.

When you are finished with the self-analysis, tally your score and read the explanation of what your score says about your participation style. Finally, take some time for all of your team members to share their results with one another.

When getting started with a team:

1. It's most important to get to know my teammates. _____ H

2. It's most important to have a clear vision of the team's purpose. _____ A

3. It's most important to have the team set up a work schedule. _____ O

4. It's most important to get down to business as quickly as possible. _____ M

When working together with a team:

1. It's most important that we all get along with each other. _____ H

2. It's most important that we think logically before making decisions. _____ A

3. It's most important that we use our time wisely. _____ O

4. It's most important that we remain enthusiastic about our work. _____ M

When considering ideas with a team:

1. It's most important that all members have a chance to share ideas. _____ H

2. It's most important that all ideas are subject to critical thinking. _____ A

3. It's most important that we use a systematic order of discussion. _____ O

4. It's most important that we foster creative ideas. _____ M

When handling conflicts with a team:

1. It's most important that we resolve those conflicts harmoniously. _____ H

2. It's most important that we consider all the facts first. _____ A

3. It's most important that we follow a problem-solving strategy. _____ O

4. It's most important that we resolve conflicts quickly. _____ M

When attempting to feel personal satisfaction with a team:

1. It's important to have established positive relationships with members. _____ H

2. It's important to have done our work with careful attention to detail. _____ A

3. It's important to have done our work in an orderly, time-efficient way. _____ O

4. It's important to feel energized by our accomplishments. _____ M

Now that you have completed the self-analysis, tally the number of times you chose each of the various answers:

H _____   A _____   O _____   M _____

Most of you should have a predominant score in one of these four categories. Read on for a description of these participation styles.

H= Harmonizers. This group of participants tends to be outgoing and to thrive on developing satisfying interpersonal relationships. Consequently, harmonizers are eager to establish rapport with their teammates, maintain harmony within the group, encourage all members to share their ideas, and resolve conflicts amicably. However, the harmonizers' tendency to be very sociable can sidetrack them from the work that needs to be accomplished. In addition, their gregarious nature may put some members off, especially those who are more reserved by nature.

A= Analyzers. This group of participants is represented by those who are logical, critical thinkers. Analyzers want to know what the team is expected to do and pride themselves on their ability to think clearly and logically. They also tend to be attentive to detail and prefer to solve problems by carefully considering all of the facts. Due to their analytical nature, these individuals may appear to be cold and distant, especially to harmonizers. Also, their linear way of thinking may be frustrating to those team members who are more creative thinkers.

O= Organizers. This group of participants is characterized by those who are highly efficient. They prefer to operate on a set schedule, using time wisely. Therefore, they feel most productive when meetings are conducted in an orderly, predictable fashion. They also like to solve problems systematically. Organizers are also good at keeping the team "on track" by sticking to the set agenda. Because of their highly efficient nature, organizers may become impatient with those who take a more relaxed approach to their work. In addition, they may lack needed flexibility when it comes to adjusting meeting schedules or agendas.

M= Motivators. This group of participants is highly enthusiastic, energetic, and eager to work! Motivators are also creative thinkers and innovators. They are always on the lookout for doing things in new and better ways. When it comes to conflicts, motivators want to resolve them quickly in order to return to the task at hand. However, due to their somewhat overly zealous nature, motivators may be impulsive in their decision making. Also, their high energy might be agitating to others on the team who are more low-key.

INTERACTION #2—Self-Analysis of Teamwork

Directions: After you have worked for a period of time with an actual workplace team or in a team with your classmates, take a few moments to reflect on your experience by completing the evaluation form below. Rank the statements as follows: **1=Yes; 2=Partially; 3=No.** When you have completed the form, follow the directions at the bottom of the form to tabulate your score and to determine your score's value.

1. The team was clear about their intended purpose (i.e., what they were expected to accomplish).	1	2	3
2. The team encouraged open discussion about how the work should be divided so that all members were satisfied.	1	2	3
3. The team established a work schedule so all members knew what they were expected to do and by when.	1	2	3
4. All of the members came prepared for the work that needed to be done each time they met so the time was used productively.	1	2	3
5. The team found a style of leadership that all members were comfortable with, whether that leadership was provided by one member or shared among the members.	1	2	3
6. The team was able to work out any conflicts that may have occurred among members so that they never lost sight of their goal.	1	2	3
7. All members were respectful of others on the team.	1	2	3
8. All members were willing to help one another whenever necessary.	1	2	3
9. At the completion of their task, the team felt confident about all of the work they had accomplished.	1	2	3
10. The members seemed personally satisfied with their team experience.	1	2	3

Scoring Key:

10–12: Excellent

13–15: Good

16–21: Average

22 or more: Needs Improvement

INTERACTION #3—A Tropical Island Exercise

Directions: Read the following situation and take about five minutes to rank the supplies in terms of their importance for your survival. Number 1 would be the most critical supply, number 2 the second most critical, and so on through number 15, the least critical. Record your answers in the column marked **Yours.** Complete this portion of the exercise first; then wait for further directions from your instructor.

Situation: You have been marooned on a tropical island after a shipwreck. You are alone and have no idea when a rescue might occur. You have nothing with you except a backpack that includes the following items. Rank these items in the order that seems most crucial for survival.

1. one change of clothes   Yours _____   Group's _____

2. pocket knife   Yours _____   Group's _____

3. pack of matches   Yours _____   Group's _____

4. one blanket   Yours _____   Group's _____

5. two oranges   Yours _____   Group's _____

6. tube of sunscreen   Yours _____   Group's _____

7. 1 qt. bottled water   Yours _____   Group's _____

8. the Holy Bible   Yours _____   Group's _____

9. flashlight   Yours _____   Group's _____

10. bar of soap   Yours _____   Group's _____

11. toothbrush   Yours _____   Group's _____

12. bottle of aspirin   Yours _____   Group's _____

13. ballpoint pen   Yours _____   Group's _____

14. manicure scissors   Yours _____   Group's _____

15. baseball hat   Yours _____   Group's _____

Note: Now that you have completed ranking these supplies, join with three to four others to compare your choices and to discuss the rationale for making the choices you each did. Then see if you can reach a consensus of how to rank the items, and record the group's choices in the appropriate blanks. To the right of each supply, write a brief reason for your group's choice.

The last step in this exercise is to take a few minutes to answer the following questions:

1. Which set of rankings do you feel is more accurate, yours or the group's? Why?

2. Why do you think you were individually asked to rank the supplies before getting into groups?

3. What were some of the skills you needed to reach a consensus within your group?

INTERACTION #4—Interview a Work Team

Whether or not you have already had experience as a workplace team participant, it can be enlightening to discover how other teams function. This activity is designed to help you gather information from an existing workplace team and to identify some of the ways in which members work together to achieve their goals.

Date _____

Name of Company _____

Team Name _____

Members' Names _____

1. What is the purpose of your team?

2. How was the team formed? (i.e., were members assigned, or did they volunteer to participate?)

3. What kind of diversity is represented among your team members? (i.e., different positions within the company, different racial and/or ethnic groups, etc.)

4. What kind of team building training did your members receive?

5. Does your team have a designated leader, or is leadership shared among the members?

6. Aside from the role of leader, do members hold any other roles? (i.e., recorder of minutes, timekeeper, etc.)

7. How frequently does your team meet?

8. How are meetings conducted? (i.e., by following an agenda, using *Robert's Rules of Order,* etc.)

9. How are team conflicts resolved?

10. How would you rate overall member satisfaction with the team experience?

INTERACTION #5—Team Article Review

Directions: Find a two- to three-page magazine article on some facet of teamwork. You can use *The Reader's Guide to Periodical Literature* found in your school or community library or various search engines on the Internet to locate such articles.

Make a copy of the article of your choice; read it carefully, noting the purpose and supporting facts; then prepare a typed summary of the article's contents and a personal reaction to it.

After sharing your summary and reaction with the class, turn it in to your instructor, along with a copy of the article.

Article Title: _____

Publication Title: _____

Date of Publication: _____

Author: _____

Summary:

Reaction:

REFERENCES

Camp, B. (1997). *Effective workplace writing*. Chicago: Irwin Mirror Press.

Parker, G. (January 5, 2000) New teams in the workplace, reprinted from *U.S.1*. Retrieved June 14, 2001, from the World Wide Web: *www.glennparker.com/Freebees/new-teams.html*.

Roberts, S. (2001). Assessing organizational readiness for work teams. Retrieved June 14, 2001, from the World Wide Web: *www.workteams.unt.edu/reports/Roberts.html*.

Six Sigma. (2000–2003). Six Sigma–What is Six Sigma? Retrieved November 24, 2003, from the World Wide Web: *www.isixsigma.com/sixsigma/six_sigma.asp*.

Yancey, M. (2001). Work teams: Three models of effectiveness. Retrieved June 14, 2001, from the World Wide Web: *www.workteams.unt.edu/reports/Yancey.html*.

CHAPTER 7
JOB SEARCH BLUEPRINT

Recognize Employment Trends

Define the Job Search

Identify the Components of the Job Search

Identify the Need for a Job Search

JOB SEARCH TOOLS

Analyze Yourself

Investigate Your Career

Identify Sources of Job Leads

Interests and Achievements Inventory

TOOL CHECK

Job Leads Exercise

INTERACTIONS

Skills Inventory

Values Inventory

RIASEC Self-Assessment

Occupational Survey Assignment

JOB SEARCH BLUEPRINT

Thinking about what you want out of life and getting a job that is compatible with those needs is a difficult and time-consuming process. Unless you're willing to work, work, work, you may as well resign yourself to boring jobs with insufficient reward. Thinking about what you want from life and employment is no simple task. Richard Bolles (1999), noted career expert, maintains that the first three to five days of job hunting should be spent at home doing career/self exploration "homework." Knowing yourself through self-assessment is another important employability skill.

Likewise, the process of finding employment takes considerable time and effort. University of Wisconsin-Milwaukee's Career Development Center advises job searchers that finding the "perfect job" can take 6 to 18 months. However, the average time it takes to find employment varies from field to field. For example, health care professionals may find employment in weeks, while information technology personnel may take considerably longer. You can benefit by using this time to research prospects that are compatible with your interests and needs.

Chapter 7 discusses employment trends, defines the job search, and identifies needs for and the components of the job search. In addition, job search tools are presented for analyzing yourself, investigating your career, and identifying sources of job leads. Finally, interactions present activities to apply the skills addressed in this chapter. Although this preliminary work may seem time consuming and unnecessary, careful planning can make the difference between a successful job search and one destined for frustration and disappointment.

Recognize Employment Trends

Whether you are new to the job search or are changing careers, one truth remains certain: employment trends continue to change. In our fast-paced, dynamic economy, today's "hot jobs" can quickly become tomorrow's layoffs. Different sectors of our diverse workforce have experienced booms with labor shortages—unlimited opportunity, only to collapse a few years later as jobs were exported or labor demands shifted. These dynamic changes require the need to make adjustments in your career plans and to be prepared for the opportunities that the future can provide.

CareerPerfect.com reports that the U.S. Department of Labor, Bureau of Labor Statistics, has predicted that for the period through 2008, the number of workers in the labor force will expand with a projected increase of 12 to 14 percent (*careerperfect.com,* 2001).

Ball State University's Career Center summarizes the U.S. Bureau of Labor Statistics' findings by predicting 149 million workers will be employed in the year 2006. Ball State further asserts that, "Service-producing industries will account for virtually all of the job growth. Only construction will add jobs in the goods-producing sector, offsetting declines in manufacturing and mining. Manufacturing's share of total jobs is expected to decline, as a decrease of 350,000 manufacturing jobs is projected. Manufacturing is expected to maintain its share of total output, as productivity in this sector is projected to increase. Precision production, craft and repair occupations and operators, fabricators, and laborers are projected to grow much more slowly than the average due to continuing advances in technology, changes in production methods, and the overall decline in manufacturing employment" (Ball State University, 2001).

The United States Department of Labor, in *Futurework: Trends and Challenges for Work in the 21st Century,* notes the shift of employment in America's "postindustrial" economy. "This shift from agricultural to manufacturing was followed by a second major shift from manufacturing to services . . . . Though manufacturing's share of total employment has declined, it still accounts for about 30 percent of total gross domestic product today, as it has for the last three decades" (U.S. Department of Labor, 2001).

Chapter 8 of *Futurework* addresses the needs of workers in tomorrow's workforce, citing three concerns:

1. Opportunity for lifelong economic security through skilled use of technology.
2. Balance of work with caring for families through flexible schedules, childcare, health and pension benefits.
3. Safe and fair workplaces, free from health hazards, discrimination, and unfair employment practices (U.S. Department of Labor, 2001).

The Department of Labor further notes that, "Changes in technology, particularly in computers and telecommunications, have virtually transformed whole industries and occupations."

In Chapter 7, Implications for Workplace Change, *Futurework* cites the following changing skill content of jobs in manufacturing:

Skills requirements have increased for many jobs in the U.S. economy, but a closer examination reveals a more complex relationship between technology and job content. Consider the change in machine shops from manually operated machine tools, such as lathes and drilling machines, to computer programmed machine tools. . . . The machine-tool operator of today is more likely to insert a programmed diskette into a control module than set measurement devices manually. The computer program itself is likely to have been written by a programmer, not by a machine-tool operator on the shop floor. Though it might appear that machine-shop workers' skill requirements have decreased, some workers may exercise discretion over the programmed tool. In fact, some jobs in the machine shop have been "de-skilled" while others have been redesigned to require formal education in new, abstract skills such as use of programming languages (U.S. Department of Labor, 2001).

"Demand for higher-skilled employees is a 50-year trend that has become increasingly important. Where strength and manual dexterity used to be enough to ensure employment and a comfortable standard of living, more jobs now and in the future will require verbal and mathematical, as well as, organizational and interpersonal skills. Emerging technologies, globalization, and information revolution are also increasing demand for high-tech skills . . . There are few working Americans who will not face the need for supplementary skills to remain competitive in their existing jobs" (U.S. Department of Labor, 2001).

The knowledge and skills required to meet the needs of this evolving workplace demand that employees of the future become lifelong learners. The Department of Labor advises that, "The majority of jobs created today, while requiring less than an associate's degree, will require other cognitive and communication skills. Continued technological change will increase the number of occupations that require at least some technical skills. Lifelong learning will grow in importance."

Whether the trends in your field show an increased demand for your skills or decrease in growth of the industry, your chances of landing a job and succeeding in the workplace are, to a great extent, determined by how you approach the job search process and by the preparations you make to match your qualifications to the positions available in the labor market.

Define the Job Search

According to John J. Marcus in his book, *The Complete Job Interview Handbook (1994),* "It has been estimated that during any given month, over 13,000,000 Americans are in the job market, because they are unemployed, want to change companies, or want to make a complete career change"(p. xiii). You can see from these statistics that searching for a job can be highly competitive. In addition, the search can be very time consuming. As a result, some job seekers give up looking and remain in their current job or jump at the first offer. A successful job search requires patience, persistence, and careful planning. Without these qualities, job seekers may find their search disappointing or misguided.

A job search can be defined as a systematic process, requiring personal initiative that results in securing satisfying job leads. This process is accomplished in three steps.

Identify the Components of the Job Search

The first step required when choosing a career is analyzing yourself. In fact, many noted career experts maintain that 90 percent of finding a job involves knowing what you want from a career. The process of knowing yourself is not an easy one. You know your name, age, height, weight, and so on. But this process requires more than an awareness of your vital statistics. This self-analysis includes thinking about what you want out of life (goals), what's important to you (values), what you enjoy doing (interests), and what abilities you have to offer a prospective employer (skills and achievements).

With this expanded understanding of yourself, you can begin to investigate those careers that have the greatest appeal. When investigating a career, consider the type of work, the job outlook, the training, the potential for advancement, and the salary, benefits, and working conditions in your area and around the country.

After you have completed an investigation of your career, the next component of the job search blueprint is identifying sources of job leads. Finding the right job in today's economy can challenge the most talented and skilled worker. However, becoming familiar with the sources of job leads will make your job search more efficient.

The strategies you employ in your job search may be as varied as the shopping techniques you use to buy a car. Suppose you were buying a car, and you knew just what style and options you wanted. You'd probably start looking for leads by checking the newspaper ads, visiting dealers, attending auto shows, checking the Internet, reading auto shoppers' catalogs, and asking friends and family. You may know from experience that all of these leads can be productive, and some will be more productive than others.

One placement specialist advises that the chance of finding a job increases as the number of job leads increases. Others suggest that you zero in on one job and develop leads that will result in getting that job. Still others believe that your best chances come from the back door approach of "interviewing for information" to tap the hidden job market. Regardless of which method you choose, job leads are essential for finding the right place of employment to put your skills to work.

Identify the Need for a Job Search

A successful job search will increase the likelihood you will find a career that is compatible with your goals, values, interests, and skills. Generally, the more consistent these factors are with your work, the greater the degree of employment satisfaction. If you begin work at age 20 and work 40 hours per week for 50 weeks per year until 65, you will log 90,000 hours at work. Almost one-third of your life will be spent in employment, and you may as well choose a career that you will enjoy.

Unfortunately, 80 percent of all workers label themselves as underemployed, that is, doing work that does not use their full potential. Most likely, they have haphazardly chosen careers, taking jobs that happened to open up, rather than carefully planning for their future.

You may feel that exploring career choices is a waste of time because you've already chosen a career and may be near completion of a technical program. Keep in mind that the average American will make seven occupation or job changes in life, and with the modernization of our society, chances are that the future holds even more change. Gone are the days of the lifelong, single-job worker.

JOB SEARCH TOOLS

Three tools can contribute to a thoughtful job search: analyzing yourself, investigating your career, and identifying sources of job leads.

Analyze Yourself

Self-analysis is especially important as you begin your job search. Just as any salesperson needs to know the product or service she is selling in order to be effective, you need to know your strengths as an employee to sell yourself to an employer. In fact, interviewers are likely to ask you personal questions that directly relate to knowing yourself, such as, "Give me some specific examples of special skills that set you apart from other applicants," or they may ask questions that search the depth of your self-analysis, such as, "Describe a time when you had a difficult problem to solve and the steps that you went through to solve it."

Discovering "who you are" can be simplified by asking yourself whether you prefer to work with people, information, or machines, since most occupations require a greater emphasis in one of these areas. For example, an auto mechanic and an administrative assistant may work primarily with machines and information, whereas the hospitality manager or medical assistant may work mainly with people. This general perspective provides a valuable way to begin the process of self-exploration. John Holland, Ph.D. has developed a RIASEC model for typing the kinds of work that match people's interests.

This RIASEC model involves typecasting yourself according to the following categories:

REALISTIC:	Having athletic or mechanical ability.
INVESTIGATIVE:	Preferring to observe, learn, analyze, and solve problems.
ARTISTIC:	Having intuition, imagination, and/or creativity.
SOCIAL:	Preferring to work with people to train/cure.
ENTERPRISING:	Working with people but for economic gain.
CLERICAL:	Working with numbers, data, and following instructions.

How would you describe yourself?

Uh...well...size ten feet umm...egg shaped head and type A positive blood.

Knowing yourself involves more than an awareness of your vital statistics.

Holland believes that ranking the types most typical of you gives an important indication of your personality. Questionnaires have been developed by John Holland to help identify your personality type. One such questionnaire is *The Self-Directed Search* that can be used with *The Occupations Finder* to determine your most appropriate career choices using the RIASEC categories. Many school counselors use this system or can direct you in finding these resources. An online version of *The Self-Directed Search* can be found at *www.self-directed-search.com*. A report, a list of occupations, and fields of study that match your interests are provided for a modest charge. Similar online resources are provided by *http://myfuture.com*, where both interest and personality tests are available. Another helpful site is *www.personalitytype.com/index.html* that provides a personality inventory based on the work of Carl Jung and Katharine Briggs and Isabel Briggs-Myers, creators of the Myers-Briggs personality assessment. This website offers a brief online quiz to help you determine your personality type. Following the quiz is a list of careers that match your personality type. For more complete information on matching your career to your personality, you may want to read *Do What You Are* by Paul D. Tieger and Barbara Barron-Tieger.

Finally, self-analysis inventories are provided in the Interactions section of this chapter to help you answer the questions, "Who am I, what kind of work do I want, and what kind of work can I do?" You will begin by identifying your interests, listing your achievements, defining your skills, and identifying your values. With this information, you can begin to find out about occupations that are compatible with your personality.

Investigate Your Career

When exploring the type of work included in a career, pay attention to the duties performed, the tools and resources used, and the areas of specialization available. Investigating the job outlook for a career can give you a clue as to what you can expect in the future. For example, "Employment in the steel industry is expected to decline by about 22 percent over the 2000-10 period, primarily due to increased use of labor-saving technologies and machinery" (*www.bls.gov/oco/cg/cgs014.htm*). In contrast, the job outlook for registered nurses is expected to increase faster than average, at a rate of 21 to 35 percent (*www.bls.gov/oco/ocos083.htm*).

Resources available in most libraries (when read) provide
valuable information when considering employment.

Training includes the formal education, work experience, certification, or licensure. While some careers, such as nursing and dental hygiene, require completion of both degrees and state board exams, other careers, such as building-cleaning workers, may need no formal training at all. However, most careers require some form of preparation or certification of skill development.

Advancement represents the potential for growth and diversification within a career field. Automotive service technicians may, for instance, start as trainees, mechanic's helpers, or lube workers. After several years of experience, they can become journey level technicians who perform more difficult types of services and repairs. After still further training, experience, and certification, the trainees may become master mechanics who perform the most sophisticated repairs, such as electrical troubleshooting, engine overhaul, or transmission rebuilding.

Salary includes weekly or monthly pay, incentives or bonuses, overtime, or shift premiums. Keep in mind, however, that starting wages may be considerably less than regular full-time pay. Starting pay for beginning police officers in 2000, for example, was $31,410, while police lieutenants made $47,750 and police chiefs earned $62,640 (*www.bls.gov/oco/ocos160.htm#earnings*). Several websites offer salary information for careers by zip-coded areas around the United States. Refer to Salary.com at the following address: *www.salary.com/salary/layoutscripts/sall_display.asp.* In addition to salary, benefits to consider include health, dental and life insurance, retirement programs, and profit sharing. Sometimes these added benefits offset a lower starting salary and produce a more attractive total compensation package.

Working conditions are a final consideration when investigating your career. These conditions include a variety of factors: length of workweek, physical location of the work, exposure to hazardous materials, physical demands of tasks, and size of the employer. You can see, for example, how the working conditions of an accountant would differ from those of a police officer or a welder. An awareness of these conditions can help you determine how comfortable you will be in your career choice.

Several resources can help you find the kind of information you are seeking when investigating your career. The most readily accessible are found in your local or school library. Books, magazines, and newspaper articles can provide background information about your career. Some libraries offer videotaped career biographies presenting detailed interviews with employees doing the work you are interested in pursuing.

The Internet offers any number of search engines that will allow you to research your career. By simply typing in a job title or occupation, you may access job listings, professional organizations, employers, educational institutions that provide training, and even links to other professionals in the field.

Community and technical colleges generally house placement/workforce development centers that can offer a wealth of career information. Such centers are familiar with the local economy and employment opportunities. These centers provide career counseling, assessment, training, and even placement to users.

Interviewing professionals in the field is another good way to obtain up-to-date information about your career. The Interactions section of this chapter includes a Career Path Interview where you can find out how others have entered the field, the challenges and rewards of the job, the future direction of the industry, and information about others the interviewee thought excelled in the career.

Finally, after deciding what type of work you desire, you should locate the online *Occupational Outlook Handbook (www.bls.gov/oco/ocos).* This resource provides an alphabetized listing of jobs, along with the information you will find helpful when investigating your career. An Occupation Survey Assignment is provided in the interaction section of this chapter to give you practice in using this resource.

Identify Sources of Job Leads

Seven basic types of leads should be considered when looking for your ideal job: personal contacts, school placement services, private agencies, newspaper classified ads, trade journals, online resources, and the hidden job market. Let's look at each.

Personal contacts are by far your best source of productive job leads. The importance of these contacts lies in the fact that employers prefer to hire someone who is known rather than take a chance on a stranger. Even if you know someone who knows someone who knows someone else, you're still regarded as an acquaintance. The people you especially want to become acquainted with are workers in the area of your desired occupation. This preference for hiring friends and those known to other workers is one major reason why 80 percent of jobs are never advertised. This lends credibility to the statement, "It's not what you know, but who you know."

How do you tap into the system of people who are known in the industry? One of the most effective ways is through your family and friends. Another is through churches, clubs, organizations, or groups to which you belong. The places where you spend your time and money may also be sources of job leads.

Let it be known to as many people as possible that you want to work at a specific job. If you obtain any leads from these people, follow up on the leads immediately. Make contact with the prospective employer even if the job does not exactly meet your requirements. This contact may result in a link to the position you desire because those who are hiring know others who are also hiring.

Take time out of your active life to tell folks about yourself, your career plans, your abilities, and your need for a job. Emphasize your training and skills. Be positive and enthusiastic about work. Talk up a full-time job and settling down. Sound serious about applying your skills and learning more. You can't sit back and expect to tap into this system. Family and friends won't go looking for jobs for you, but they will help if you make your needs known. By talking with these people, you'll have a chance to find out more about yourself and your field while practicing your interviewing skills. No guarantee exists that this or any other system will land you a job, but by using these contacts, you become assertive. You look interested and eager; family and friends will continue to talk you up when they see the effort you're putting forth.

Another source of leads is the school placement office, which provides excellent contact for many graduates. Placement counselors who know the program offerings of your school are also familiar with the employment needs of local businesses and industries that hire graduates. In addition, many placement departments provide services such as job boards, graduate referrals, mailing lists, resume writing and typing, campus interviews, and specialized career counseling. Stop at your school placement office, find out what services they offer, and register for those you need.

Private agencies are a third source that help secure employment. Many are specialized for particular occupational areas. Some require payment from the applicant, some from the employer, and some collect from both. Most require a contract of some sort. Fees may range from 50 to 120 percent of your first month's earnings. Agencies are worth contacting to see what jobs are available. You'll find the yellow pages helpful for the names, addresses, and phone numbers of agencies in your area.

Another source to consider is that old standby, the Sunday paper. The ads are neatly classified for all to see; some employers use this source exclusively. If the statistics are accurate, however, only 20 percent of available jobs are listed in the want ads. But don't dismiss ads; your job may be there. The secret to using the classified ads is in knowing how to read them.

Three kinds of ads appear in the paper: open, blind, and spot. Open ads provide the most information about the position. They identify the firm, the position, even the wage range. You respond directly to the person identified in the ad. Blind ads provide limited information about the job or list only the position and the requirements. They ask the applicant to respond to a box number or the newspaper. This technique helps the employer screen applicants and discourage the casual job seeker. Employers place blind ads in newspapers, at times, to survey the potential workforce in a given occupation. The employer may not even have a position available. Remember, employers take a box number and use blind ads so they don't have to respond to applicants. Employment agencies place spot ads to promote positions they have listed and to develop a list of potential workers to place in the future. These ads may offer several positions and wage ranges, but such ads do not identify the employer. When you use the classified ads, read them faithfully, and respond immediately to new ads. Be prepared to send a resume and letter of application quickly in response to new ads.

Don't overlook another source, trade journals, which offer specialized job opportunities for technicians and professionals. Firms usually seek experienced people among the ranks of those who are active in a specific field. Both open and blind ads appear in these journals. Respond to these ads as you would those in the newspaper.

Online resources have mushroomed in the past few years, with most of the major search engines providing employment advertisements and offering help in preparing and posting resumes. America's Career *Infonet* offers a complete career resource library online at *www.acinet.org/acinet/library.htm.* Adquest, America's Job Bank, Job Quest, Monster Board, and many more private agencies offer online job leads and other services. Corporations also have online posting of available career opportunities.

Finally, the "Hidden Job Market," which Richard Irish (1987) writes about in his book *Go Hire Yourself an Employer,* becomes available to the applicant who seeks leads through interviewing for information. Applicants, particularly students, make contacts with those actively employed in their chosen field, question these professionals, and discuss the future of the occupation. Irish suggests the applicants approach employers and supervisors in their field, not to seek employment but to seek information.

Prior to graduation, students can conduct career path interviews with professionals to obtain a realistic view of their occupation and, more importantly, to make contacts for later when they will be seeking employment. These interviews involve asking a series of questions ranging from, "How did you get started in this business?" to "What changes do you see occurring in this field in the next 10 years?" Any of these leads may result in employment; all have worked for applicants in the past. Try not to limit yourself to only one source of job leads. Be persistent and optimistic about finding new leads and a new job.

CHAPTER 7 TOOL CHECK

Directions: Find the key words from the preceding chapter to complete the following sentences.

1. _____ is a systematic process requiring personal initiative that results in securing satisfying job leads.
2. The first step required when choosing a career is analyzing _____.
3. _____ percent of all workers label themselves as underemployed.
4. According to the RIASEC Model, someone who possesses athletic or mechanical abilities is labeled _____.
5. The _____ Handbook is a resource for investigating your career.
6. _____ are by far your best source of productive job leads.
7. Private employment agencies may charge between _____ and _____ percent of your first month's earnings.
8. _____ ads provide limited information about the job and ask applicants to respond to a box number rather than a company name.
9. Publications that offer specialized job opportunities for technicians and professionals are called _____ journals.
10. By interviewing those actively employed in a chosen field, applicants tap into the _____ job market.

CHAPTER 7 INTERACTIONS

INTERACTION #1—Interests and Achievments Inventory

Professional angler? Professional wine taster? Professional billiards player? Sound like the kind of job you would like to have? Though most of us can't get paid for doing what we enjoy most, a few people are fortunate and creative enough to find ways to turn active interests into full-time careers.

The majority of us have to be content with finding careers that give us the flexibility to engage our interests, either indirectly on the job or directly off the job. In fact, there is a logical connection between our degree of career satisfaction and the degree to which we are allowed to participate in our areas of active interest.

Obviously, the auto mechanic who enjoys working on cars, both as a hobby and for a living, will experience a high degree of worker satisfaction. The secretary who likes international travel but who does not have enough time off to do so will be resentful about having chosen a field that gives minimal opportunity for personal enjoyment. Employees need to choose occupations that enable them to pursue their interests.

Many employers ask about interests in job interview situations. Questions frequently asked about interests include the following: How do you spend your free time? How do you spend vacations? What are your hobbies? What did you like about school or past jobs? All these questions are ways of finding out about your interests and providing interviewers with a clear picture of those you do well.

How you spend your free time gives some clue as to what you're interested in. When identifying your interests, consider hobbies, enjoyable aspects of past or present jobs, classes taken that were enjoyable, people you're with and activities you do together, topics you like to talk about or listen to, achievements, and volunteer activities.

Complete the Interest Inventory that follows to help you to identify your interests and patterns in those interests. Use this information to help choose a career that will give you maximum opportunity to pursue your interests. Review this inventory before a job interview so you will be able to answer employer questions regarding your personal interests.

INTERESTS INVENTORY WORKSHEET

List your 10 most important interests, then complete the following questionnaire related to those interests.

MY MOST IMPORTANT INTERESTS ARE:

1. _____

_____

2. _____

_____

3. _____

_____

4. _____

_____

5. _____

_____

6. _____

_____

7. _____

_____

8. _____

_____

9. _____

_____

10. _____

_____

Interests Summary

What patterns can you see in the interests that you've identified?

1. Consider the following: alone or with others, indoors or outdoors, seasonal or year-round, relaxing and passive or tense and active, cooperative or competitive, inexpensive or expensive, equipment required or not, and so on.

2. Would you be willing to change professions if you could not pursue your interests? Why or why not?

3. To what extent do you believe your chosen occupation will allow you to participate in your identified interests? What might you do to increase the chances of participating in your interest areas?

4. If an employer asked, "What do you do during your free time?" how would you respond?

Interests Discussion

Purpose: This exercise is designed to help you prepare for interviewing by developing valuable skills in talking about your interests and giving specific examples.

This exercise also requires you to apply some listening skills from the previous unit.

Interests

In groups of four, have students rotate through the following roles:

1. **Student #1** (who is oldest of the group) begins by sharing at least five interests from the list on the Interest Inventory Worksheet and a summary of answers to at least two items on the Interests Summary.

2. **Student #2** (who is the second oldest of the group) asks clarifying questions to gain a better understanding of the first student's report.

3. **Student #3** (who is the third oldest of the group) must paraphrase and summarize the conversation between students #1 and #2.

4. **Student #4** (the remaining youngest student) provides an assessment of how well student #3 summarized the discussion.

After this round, roles change, and student #2 presents at least five interests and two answers from the Interests Summary. Student #3 asks the questions, after which student #4 summarizes, and student #1 critiques the paraphrase.

Roles continue to change until each student has presented at least five interests and two answers.

Achievements Exercise

When your accomplishments are not national headlines, you may find it hard to get excited about what you have done. Even though you consider yourself a good technician, you might get uncomfortably modest about your achievements.

The worksheet that follows is designed to help you review your accomplishments and become confident when talking about them. First, you'll be asked to review the successes that you have had in different areas of your life. Next, you'll participate in an exercise talking about those achievements. Both are designed to prepare you for an interviewer's questions so that you may better sell yourself.

The first step in this process is to review your accomplishments. Richard Irish, in his book, *Go Hire Yourself an Employer,* suggests that this exercise should take three days. We hope to do it in less time, but it may take some time and effort to recall those moments in your life when you felt fulfilled.

Recount the sense of satisfaction that usually follows an accomplishment. Try to recall what you did when you have experienced feelings of pride, satisfaction, or fulfillment. List 10 of these achievements on the following worksheet. Use these questions as starters if you need to:

- Have you been successful in team sports, bands, clubs, and so on?
- Have you earned honors at school or work? Have you written any articles for publication?
- Have you participated in competition of some sort?
- What have you rebuilt, made, or repaired?
- Do you have any inventions?
- Do you work well with a variety of people?
- What work have you done that you are most proud of?
- Are you a person that people count on to organize or expedite a project?
- Have you done any risky yet successful adventures (skydiving, mountain climbing, solo singing, etc.)?
- Have you done anything very few people can say that they've done?
- Have you raised any animals or trained pets?
- Have you made public presentations before a group of people?

ACHIEVEMENTS INVENTORY WORKSHEET

List your top 10 achievements. Be specific, and give concrete examples.

MY PERSONAL ACHIEVEMENTS

1. _____
   _____

2. _____
   _____

3. _____
   _____

4. _____
   _____

5. _____
   _____

6. _____
   _____

7. _____
   _____

8. _____
   _____

9. _____
   _____

10. _____
    _____

PERSONALITY TRAITS WORKSHEET

Now that you have your list, look for trends or themes that show personality traits like, "I am eager, co-operative, creative, dependable, and so on." Determine five personality traits that you have, and find at least one example from your list of achievements to support each trait. This information will be shared with the class or in small groups. It may sound like this: *"I'm inventive; one of my inventions is a release for a compound bow. It enables the shooter to release the string more comfortably and with greater accuracy. I've also invented my own tree stand."*

If you can't come up with five personality traits, you'll have to read your entire list of achievements to the class and have the class offer five traits that suit you.

This exercise is intended to prepare you for talking about yourself so that you can both describe yourself to the employer and give concrete examples of your successes.

MY PERSONALITY TRAIT; EXAMPLE FROM MY LIST OF ACHIEVEMENTS

1. _____ ; _____

   _____

   _____

2. _____ ; _____

   _____

   _____

3. _____ ; _____

   _____

   _____

4. _____ ; _____

   _____

   _____

5. _____ ; _____

   _____

   _____

Achievements Discussion

Purpose: This exercise is designed to help you prepare for interviewing by developing valuable skills in talking about your achievements and giving specific examples.

    This exercise also requires you to apply some listening skills from the previous unit.

Achievements

Work in groups of four to review the results of the Achievements Inventory and the Personality Traits Worksheet. Each student should present five specific qualities and for each a specific example that clearly depicts that trait. Follow the rotation described below:

1. **Student #1** (the youngest in the group) begins by stating, "I'm _____, for example, I _____." This is done five times, one for each answer on the Personality Traits Worksheet. Pause after each item to allow the others to respond.

2. **Student #2** (the second youngest in the group) will ask clarifying questions to get a better picture of the example being presented.

3. **Student #3** (the next youngest in the group) will summarize what has been shared.

4. **Student #4** (the old timer) will critique the presentation, the questions, and the paraphrase.

INTERACTION #2—Skills Inventory

To decide what type of work you want, you must examine yourself and ask, "What do I have to offer an employer?" That is, what skills, assets, and/or attributes do you possess that an employer might desire in a candidate for a particular position? After all, an employer's main concern is what you have to offer as an employee.

Three categories of skills must be examined to have an accurate and complete answer to the above questions. First, what *technical* skills do you have to offer? These job-related skills include those you've learned and practiced in past jobs or in an educational setting. Some examples might include reading blueprints, operating a computer, or using a word processor. Keep in mind that just because you've acquired these job-related skills through years of training and experience, they do not guarantee you employment.

Personal skills are related to what others say and like about you. These skills deal with your ability to get along with others: co-workers, supervisors, customers, employers, and so on. Some examples might be that you are friendly, cooperative, and helpful.

Finally, *life* skills play an important role in an employer's hiring decisions. Though not formally a part of the job requirements, life skills set you apart from other applicants. Examples of these life skills include an ability to coach a softball team, to raise children, or to plant a garden. Hobbies and outside activities are typical ways of developing these skills. The skills gained through these experiences say something about your ability to organize people and materials, relate to others, and express your creativity.

Many applicants have the appropriate technical skills. The skills that distinguish one candidate from another are personal and life skills. For example, a travel agency may hire you over other applicants because you speak foreign languages, especially if the agency makes many international reservations. In this sense, personal and life skills may be more important in getting a job than are your technical skills.

The following assignments are designed to help you identify all three types of your skills: technical, personal, and life.

TECHNICAL SKILLS WORKSHEET

List five dominant, work-related skills that you've attained at this point in your training. Give an example of something you've done that clearly demonstrates you have this skill. (If you get stuck, you may want to use the checklist of 250 verbs that follows in the life skills area.)

Example: Designed; Designed a safe, economical storage system for preserving computer software.

SKILL   **CONCRETE EXAMPLE**

1. _____, _____

   _____, _____

   _____, _____

2. _____, _____

   _____, _____

   _____, _____

3. _____, _____

   _____, _____

   _____, _____

4. _____, _____

   _____, _____

   _____, _____

5. _____, _____

   _____, _____

   _____, _____

PERSONAL SKILLS WORKSHEET

The following list contains adjectives related to personal skills. Circle 10 adjectives that describe you. Then underline five that most clearly show "who you are." Give a specific example of why you would describe yourself in this way. Write your answers in the right-hand column.

Accepting	Honest	Example: Calm; Fire started in the kitchen of our house, and I calmly put it out.
Adaptable	Idealistic	
Alert	Independent	1. _____, _____
Ambitious	Initiative	_____
Assertive	Intelligent	
Attractive	Likable	
Brave	Lively	2. _____, _____
Calm	Logical	_____
Carefree	Loyal	
Caring	Mature	3. _____, _____
Commitment to grow	Modest	
Confident	Open-minded	_____
Conscientious	Optimistic	4. _____, _____
Content	Organized	
Cooperative	Outgoing	_____
Critical	Patient	5. _____, _____
Curious	Perceptive	
Decision-maker	Poised	_____
Dependable	Polite	
Determined	Precise	
Dignified	Progressive	
Diplomatic	Proud	
Disciplined	Realistic	
Dynamic	Reflective	
Efficient	Resourceful	
Emotionally stable	Respectable	
Empathetic	Self-control	
Energetic	Sensitive	
Enthusiastic	Spontaneous	
Expressive	Strong	
Fair	Tactful	
Firm	Tidy	
Friendly	Trustworthy	
Generous	Understanding	
Gentle	Versatile	
Giving	Warm	
Good judge	Wise	
Happy	Witty	
Helpful	Zestful	

LIFE SKILLS WORKSHEET

Listed below are some verbs of various life skills complied by R. N. Bolles in his booklet, "Your Career." Underline the 10 which are your best and most enjoyed. When you're done, circle the five verbs that you feel best describe you. Write your circled words at the end of this listing, and include a real example of something you've done that shows you clearly have this skill.

Achieved	Devised	Inspired	Printed
Acted	Diagnosed	Installed	Problem-Solved
Adapted	Directed	Instituted	Processed
Addressed	Discovered	Instructed	Produced
Administered	Displayed	Integrated	Programmed
Advised	Disproved	Interpreted	Protected
Analyzed	Distributed	Interviewed	Promoted
Anticipated	Diverted	Invented	Provided
Arbitrated	Empathized	Inventoried	Publicized
Arranged	Enforced	Investigated	Purchased
Ascertained	Established	Judged	Questioned
Assembled	Estimated	Kept	Raised
Assessed	Evaluated	Lead	Read
Attained	Examined	Learned	Realized
Audited	Expanded	Manipulated	Reasoned
Budgeted	Experimented	Mediated	Received
Built	Explained	Memorized	Reconciled
Calculated	Expressed	Mentored	Recorded
Charted	Extracted	Met	Recruited
Checked	Filed	Modeled	Reduced
Classified	Financed	Monitored	Rehabilitated
Coached	Fixed	Motivated	Related
Collected	Followed	Navigated	Resolved
Communicated	Formulated	Negotiated	Responded
Compiled	Founded	Observed	Restored
Completed	Gathered	Obtained	Retrieved
Composed	Gave	Offered	Reviewed
Computed	Generated	Operated	Risked
Conceptualized	Got	Ordered	Sang
Conducted	Guided	Organized	Scheduled
Conserved	Had responsibility for	Originated	Selected
Consolidated	Handled	Oversaw	Sensed
Constructed	Headed	Painted	Separated
Controlled	Hypothesized	Perceived	Served
Coordinated	Identified	Performed	Set
Copied	Illustrated	Persuaded	Setup
Counseled	Imagined	Photographed	Sewed
Defined	Implemented	Piloted	Shaped
Delivered	Improved	Planned	Shared
Designed	Improvised	Played	Showed
Detailed	Increased	Predicted	Sketched
Detected	Influenced	Prepared	Sold
Determined	Informed	Prescribed	Solved
Developed	Inspected	Presented	Sorted

Spoke	Systematized	Transcribed	Umpired
Studied	Talked	Translated	Understood
Summarized	Taught	Traveled	Undertook
Supervised	Team-Built	Treated	Unified
Supplied	Tended	Trouble-Shot	United
Symbolized	Tested & Proved	Tutored	Used
Synergized	Told	Typed	Utilized
Synthesized	Trained		

Example: Painted; Painted the complete interior and exterior of my parents' home in two weeks during the summer. Received many compliments.

SKILL   **CONCRETE EXAMPLE**

1. _____ ; _____

_____

_____

2. _____ ; _____

_____

_____

3. _____ ; _____

_____

_____

4. _____ ; _____

_____

_____

5. _____ ; _____

_____

_____

INTERACTION #3—Values Inventory

Like many people, you probably have never thought about what you value most. Yet values play a strong role in the decisions you make about your everyday life. Related to career decisions, your values play an essential role in career choices and career satisfaction.

Your values are those standards of good/bad and right/wrong by which you make personal judgments. Values are a matter of degree, with some values being more important than others. Values are usually long lasting and can be very specifically identified. When you become more aware of the unseen forces that guide your life, you can make more conscious and effective decisions as to which direction you plan to pursue.

For example, if you value security in a job position, you would probably not like a job that is seasonal or that fluctuates with economic conditions. However, if you value high financial rewards, taking a good paying seasonal job (such as working in a winter resort) would probably bring a significant degree of satisfaction.

The following activity will help you know what you value and how to rank those values so you can begin seeking a career that is consistent with your values. Remember, the greater the degree of compatibility of values with the occupation, the greater the level of job satisfaction.

Work Values Rating Sheet Inventory

The following list describes "satisfiers" that people obtain from their occupation. Rate the degree to which each of these satisfiers is important to you using the following scale.

5 - VERY IMPORTANT

4 - MOSTLY IMPORTANT

3 - NEITHER IMPORTANT NOR UNIMPORTANT

2 - MOSTLY UNIMPORTANT

1 - NOT IMPORTANT AT ALL

Rating	Work Value	Description
_____	1. Financial Reward	A good salary, and/or healthy benefits and/or perks.
_____	2. Flexibility/Variation	Opportunity to do different tasks; not the same thing day in and out.
_____	3. Creativity	Opportunity to use your imagination to solve problems or initiate new ideas.
_____	4. Security	The knowledge of future employment no matter what the economic conditions.
_____	5. Excitement/Challenge	Intellectually and/or physically demanding, yet also stimulating.
_____	6. Relationships	Opportunity to work with friendly people in a setting which emphasizes the value of people and encourages friendships.
_____	7. Independence	Opportunity to work on your own in as many ways as possible, being your own boss.
_____	8. Helping Others/Society	Working for the betterment of the lives of those who are in some way disadvantaged.

_____ 9. Advancement Potential

The opportunity to move up within the company to better positions.

_____ 10. Status/Recognition

Being seen as a leader in the community and others seeking your advice.

_____ 11. Sense of Accomplishment

Feeling proud about the end product and feeling you've accomplished something meaningful.

_____ 12. Responsibility/Power

Making important decisions and being accountable for success/failure.

_____ 13. Location of Employment

Situated in an area you feel comfortable with and providing you with an opportunity to enjoy your kind of life.

_____ 14. Physical/Psychological Health

An environment relatively free from danger to one's physical health and/or mental state.

_____ 15. Growth Potential

Opportunity to learn new things and expand one's level of awareness and abilities.

_____ 16. Time Off

Work the standard hours with sufficient time off during the week and for vacations.

_____ 17. Precision

Desire work requiring exactness and accuracy in whatever job tasks are given.

_____ 18. Competitiveness

Opportunity to have work matched against that of others.

_____ 19. Cooperation

Work in an environment where working together is important.

_____ 20. Family Happiness

Work provides well being to you and your loved ones.

_____ 21. Inner Harmony

A feeling of oneness, happiness, and contentment.

_____ 22. Integrity

An opportunity to maintain your own personal standards and values.

_____ 23. Loyalty

Demonstrating long-term commitment to a product or a company.

_____ 24. Order

Working in an environment where things are done in a set way without deviation.

_____ 25. Pleasure

Work provides much enjoyment and happiness.

_____ 26. Wisdom

Work includes opportunities to learn and grow in knowledge.

WORK VALUES SUMMARY WORKSHEET

Review the values identified in the previous exercise by completing the following worksheet. List your three most important values in the category called "essential." These values are absolutely important to you and must exist if you are to take a job. The next category is the "bonus" values, those three values that are not essential but are important to career and job satisfaction. Finally, list the "avoidance" values, those three values that would significantly reduce job satisfaction. When finished, answer the questions that follow relative to work values.

Work Value Essentials:

1.

2.

3.

Work Value Bonuses:

1.

2.

3.

Work Values to Avoid:

1.

2.

3.

Answer the discussion questions on the following page.

Work Values Discussion

1. What makes the three "essential" values you selected most important to you?

2. How does the occupational area you've chosen enable you to meet these essential values?

3. If your current occupation will not allow you to meet those important values, would you be able to gain them in another occupation? If so, what kind of occupations do you imagine would be most compatible with your values?

4. If an employer asked, "What do you value most in a job?" what would you say?

5. What other values come to mind when you think of what makes work rewarding?

INTERACTION #4—RIASEC Self-Assessment

Completing the RIASEC Self-Assessment referred to earlier in this chapter is one way to gain additional information about yourself. One way to access this assessment is through your school's career center or community workforce development center. The assessment is also available online for a nominal fee at the following address: *www.self-directed-search.com*.

After completing the RIASEC Self-Assessment, share the results with your instructor.

INTERACTION #5—Occupational Survey Assignment

Preparing for a satisfying career involves more than simply learning the technical skills required for a specific occupation. Job satisfaction is also dependent upon a more comprehensive knowledge of such factors as the working conditions, opportunities for advancement, future job prospects, and so on, which encompass your occupational field of interest.

An excellent resource for discovering this type of career information is the *Occupational Outlook Handbook,* published by the U.S. Department of Labor's Bureau of Labor Statistics. Your school and local community libraries should have copies of this publication.

The *Occupational Outlook Handbook* contains information about a variety of careers, grouped into six occupational areas: technicians, specialty professions, construction, mechanics and repairers, transportation and material handling, and service occupations. Within each occupational grouping, specific occupations are identified. The information provided for each occupation is listed under the following subheadings:

1. NATURE OF THE WORK	Gives a brief description of the tasks done as part of this occupation.
2. WORKING CONDITIONS	Lists the kinds of circumstances under which one can expect to work.
3. EMPLOYMENT	Accounts for the number of workers in the field.
4. TRAINING AND QUALIFICATIONS	Stipulates the amount of education and related experiences necessary to enter the field.
5. ADVANCEMENT	Indicates advancement opportunities and procedures.
6. OUTLOOK	Provides general information about the number of positions available and where in the United States they can be found.
7. EARNINGS	Suggests a range and average for workers who enter the field.
8. RELATED OCCUPATIONS	Identifies occupations which are similar and might be considered.
9. SOURCES OF ADDITIONAL INFORMATION	Provides a list of resources containing more information.

Occupational Outlook Exercise

Locate copies of the *Wisconsin Career Information Service Occupation Handbook* and the *Occupational Outlook Handbook* to complete the following worksheet.

Your occupation: _____

I. Nature of the Work
   A. Briefly describe the duties you are responsible for on your job.

II. Working Conditions
   A. Describe the physical setting in which you work.

   B. Does your job involve any safety hazards? If so, what are they?

   C. How many hours per week can you expect to put in on your job?

   D. Are you required to join any type of labor organization such as a union?

   E. How many workers are currently employed in your occupation nationwide?

      • In what particular areas of the country are job opportunities in your field most likely to be found?

III. Required Qualifications
   A. What kind of educational background are you required to have?

   B. What specific kinds of technical skills must you acquire for the job?

   C. Identify any on-the-job training that will be needed.

IV. Employment Outlook
   A. What rate of future employment is expected in your occupation?

V. Earnings and Benefits
   A. What is the average hourly and/or annual starting salary?

   B. What kinds of salary increases might you expect?

   C. What are the possibilities for promotion or advancement on the job?

   D. What fringe benefits are part of the job? (health and life insurance, sick leave, paid vacations, etc.)

VI. Related Occupations
   A. List several occupations that are closely related to your occupation.

VII. Trade Publications
   A. List the titles of two trade publications that could supply you with additional occupational information.

INTERACTION #6—Job Leads Exercise

Complete the following assignment.

1. List three people that you know of who work in your chosen occupation.

2. Go to your school placement office. What services do they provide? How do you apply for these services?

3. Name three employment agencies in your local area that you would consider contacting for employment help.

4. Out of the Sunday newspaper, cut out an example of each of the following three employment advertisements.

   OPEN   BLIND   SPOT

5. List two trade journals for your field. Give examples of two types of jobs listed in the employment sections of those journals.

   JOURNAL NAME   EMPLOYMENT LISTING

6. Name three companies that you would really like to work for. Then list five questions you might ask if information interviewing.

   COMPANY NAMES (3)

   QUESTIONS YOU MIGHT ASK (5)

REFERENCES

Ball State University. Retrieved August 29, 2001, from World Wide Web: *www.bsu.edu.careers/ trends.htm.*

Bolles, R. N. (1999). *What color is your parachute?: A practical manual for job-hunters & career-changers.* Berkley, CA: Ten Speed Press.

Bolton, R. (1979). *People skills: How to assert yourself, listen to others and resolve conflicts.* Englewood Cliffs, NJ: Prentice Hall.

Career Perfect.com. Employment trends. Retrieved August 29, 2001, from World Wide Web: *www.careerperfect.com/CareerPerfect/topicEmploymentTrends.htm.*

Holland, J. (1996). *Self-directed search.* Port Huron, MI: Sigma Assessment.

Holland, J. (2001). *Self-directed search.* Retrieved August 29, 2001, from World Wide Web: *www.self-directed-search.com.*

Irish, R. K. (1987). *Go hire yourself an employer.* New York: Anchor Press.

Lindquist, V. R. (1988). *The Lindquist-Endicott Report.* Evanston, IL: Northwestern University.

My future. Career toolbox. Work interest quiz. Retrieved May 17, 2001, from World Wide Web: *www.myfuture.com/career/interest.html.*

Marcus, John J. (1994). *The Complete Job Interview Handbook.* New York, NY: HarperResource.

University of Wisconsin Milwaukee, Career Development Center. Job search guide. Retrieved September 9, 2001, from World Wide Web: *www.uwm.edu/CDC/jobsearch_guide.html.*

U.S. Department of Labor (2001). *Futurework.* Retrieved August 29, 2001, from World Wide Web: *www.dol.gov/asp/futurework/report/chapter1/main.htm.*

CHAPTER 8
WRITTEN COMMUNICATION BLUEPRINT

- Look Good on Paper
- Identify the Role of the Resume
- Examine Types of Job Letters
- Assess Application Forms

WRITTEN COMMUNICATION TOOLS

- Determine Resume Format
- Meet Requirements for Letters of Application
- Select Elements for Follow-up Letters
- Follow Guidelines for Application Forms

TOOL CHECK

INTERACTIONS

- Resume Assignment
- Letter of Application Assignment
- Follow-up Letter Assignment
- Application Form Assignment

WRITTEN COMMUNICATION BLUEPRINT

Despite the warning that we should not "judge a book by its cover," most of us tend to make judgments on the basis of appearances, from time to time. Whether you are looking for something to drive, somewhere to work, someplace to live, or someone to live with, chances are your decision will be based to a great extent on first impressions. Looking good on paper is just as important when preparing resumes, cover letters, or application forms. In fact, employers are likely to determine which applicants get the interviews, at least in part, on the basis of the applicants' written work.

"Often, (job) seekers have a few mistaken opinions about potential employers. They believe that employers are able to easily separate the qualified job applicants from the less qualified applicants. But this is likely not true. Sometimes there are from 30 to 300 resumes for the same job. So the interviewer first does a fast screening of all the resumes to eliminate as many as possible. The 'good' resumes usually make it through the screening process. Many times the best job candidate is screened out due to a poor resume" (How to Write, 2002).

Most readers of application letters and resumes are busy people who are looking for individuals that can help solve problems. An employer may need to increase production, improve customer relations, or provide quality assurance. As a result of these needs, employers look for information in your written communication that shows you have the qualifications they seek. However, unless your qualifications look good on paper, you may not be among those chosen for an interview. According to Jo Allen, in her book *Writing in the Workplace* (1998), "On average, most readers of resumes spend only forty-five seconds reviewing an application package" (p. 359). To make a positive impression in this short amount of time, your written communication must present your skills and abilities to your reader in a clear, concise, visually appealing manner.

Look Good on Paper

In order to increase your chances of looking good on paper, consider the following suggestions:

Consider your reader. Pay close attention to the ad or posting for the position; looking for the reader's name and title. In addition, note the qualifications for the opening to gain insight into the employer's needs. For example, in an advertisement for an auto-servicing technician, the employer may seek an individual with ASE certification in at least two areas, an associate degree in auto technology, two years of recent full-time work experience, and the ability to relate successfully with a diverse cultural staff.

Write clearly. Be specific when describing skills and accomplishments. For example, rather than claiming to be "well versed in word processing," say "proficient in Word and Word Perfect." Use strong, active verbs to show what you can do, such as, "constructed and set up computer-controlled wire processing machine," "designed schematics for troubleshooting hydraulic circuits."

Organize logically, generally moving from most important to least important. In other words, if you wish to emphasize your education, that information should come before your work experience.

Be concise. Limit your documents to one page. For your resume, use short phrases rather than complete sentences to annotate your listings. In a resume, for instance, instead of saying, "I have recently completed a two-year technical diploma in industrial maintenance," say, "Two-year diploma–Industrial Maintenance." Edit entries to include information most relevant to the position sought. Your letter of application and resume don't have to list all of your skills and abilities but rather should emphasize those most closely related to the position.

Design an appealing document. Use bulleted lists to help your reader spot key information quickly. Allow plenty of white space to balance information and to avoid overcrowding. Include boldfaced headings and font changes for emphasis. Select paper stock that has the feel of quality. Choose a neutral colored paper such as white, gray, or buff. Use graphics and colored fonts sparingly to avoid distraction.

The written communication associated with the employment process is most important because it presents you to a prospective employer and often determines whether or not you will be granted an interview. To look good on paper, you must carefully prepare your written communication through the following steps:

1. Gathering information for a personal inventory assembles your employment history, educational history, references, personal history, military history (if applicable) and your qualifications and skills.
2. Putting together a resume entails creating a one-page summary of your most desirable qualifications, as well as personal, educational, and experiential information.
3. Writing a letter of application requires composing a cover letter to be sent along with the resume that introduces you, identifies the position sought, highlights your qualifications, and requests an interview.
4. Filling out application forms ensures that neat, complete, accurate, and honest information will be provided on this most important document.
5. Writing follow-up letters provides a valuable contact that thanks the employer for the interview; makes some positive comment about the position, place, process, or product; reminds the interviewer that you are qualified and serious about the position; or indicates you are no longer available for the job. This important contact should be made whether you have been accepted, rejected, or are still waiting to find out about the position.

One way to look at the job-seeking process is as an advertising campaign. A campaign program first consists of having a saleable product (your qualifications), and second, of making frequent contact with the consumer (the employer), without being a pest! Notice how the steps in this employment process involve "making contact."

Identify the Role of the Resume

Resumes contain vivid personal descriptions of your experiences and abilities in brief sentence form. A well-constructed resume makes you "come to life" on the printed page. According to an article entitled "About Resumes," "A resume is a marketing tool that helps you sell yourself. An effective resume offers an organized snapshot of your employment, educational history, and skills. A single job opening can generate 500 resumes or even more in a depressed economy. Yours has to stand out" (About resumes, 2001).

Since writing a good resume may take from eight to ten hours of your time, you may be wondering if this time investment is worthwhile. So let's look at some of the benefits of carefully preparing a resume. First, this process gives you an opportunity to reflect on your qualifications. Just as product knowledge is required for an effective sales presentation, so, too, is self-knowledge necessary for an effective job search. Second, constructing a resume helps you prepare for the interview by reminding you of the accomplishments that you wish to share with an employer. In fact, many employers request a resume and use it as a source of questions during the interview. Also, a good resume serves as a reminder of you after the interview. Third, the information in your resume helps you complete job application forms. Although your resume is not as detailed as most application forms, some of the same information is included on both documents, making the transfer of that information easier. Finally, a good resume sets you apart from other applicants, especially those who have not taken the time to prepare one. With the changes and updates that you make as you grow in your career, your resume should be a "living document" that is modified over your lifetime.

The true function of the resume is to make you look good on paper so that an employer wants to see you in person.

Examine Types of Job Letters

Applicants who send resumes to prospective employers need a cover letter to accompany their resumes. These letters of application also provide an excellent opportunity for applicants to sell themselves by emphasizing qualifications and personality traits.

The letter of application is often the employer's first contact with the applicant; it provides a first impression that can enhance the chances for employment. As the first piece of work presented to the employer, this letter must be well written and effective. The letter of application seeks to accomplish three primary objectives: identifies the position you are seeking, summarizes qualifications related to that position, and requests an interview.

Generally, your resume and letter of application will be sent together to prospective employers. Rather than repeating information in both documents, consider balancing the information presented in each, so that they complement one another. Qualifications mentioned in the letter of application should not be repeated in the resume. This balance is far more effective than repetition. When skills are presented in the resume, the letter of application could mention the source of those skills, either work experience or training. This balance enhances the applicant's appeal far more than repeating information in both documents.

After the interview, many applicants who have written letters of application, prepared a resume, filled out application forms, and answered questions in an interview think they have finished selling themselves to prospective employers. They fully believe that they have done their part to find a job.

Unfortunately, the majority of applicants overlook a very important opportunity to follow up on all the prior work they have done. The "Thanks-for-the-Interview" letter may be the most important one they ever write, yet fewer than 10 percent of applicants send one. The follow-up letter says a lot about you. It says, "I care," "I am responsible," "I'm better qualified than the other applicants for these specific reasons." It also says, "I appreciate the time you spent with me, and I would like to work for your company." This follow-up or thanks-for-the-interview letter provides another contact with the employer. It sets you apart from the countless applicants who don't take the time or initiative to write one.

The extra effort you take in preparing these letters will certainly affect your standing in the eyes of the employer. Your correspondence will make you look good on paper.

Assess Application Forms

Unless you have sent a letter of application and resume, the application form is likely to be the first written work that you turn in to an employer. As such, applications are a representation of you and the quality of your work. Applications not only reveal your education and experience, but also show whether you can write without error, follow directions, and express yourself clearly and understandably.

It is also important to see the application as an official document expressing your desire for employment and to realize that it becomes part of your official employment file. Therefore, be sure to fill out the application in ink.

Read through the entire application form before filling in any information. Take a careful look at the layout and types of questions the application contains. These few minutes spent previewing the form will prevent unnecessary errors later.

Generally the applications that make the grade for employers meet three criteria. Accuracy and honesty are first. Employment officers believe that if you lie on an application, you would also lie on the job. Honesty is so important that nearly all applications have a disclaimer that allows the company to terminate your employment whenever dishonesty is discovered.

Second, applications should be complete. Applications are only helpful to an employer when they contain the information that employers are asking for. Some questions on the form may not pertain to you, such as military status (if you've never been in the service) or number of dependents (if you have none). Still, the employer wants to know that you saw the question. For those items that do not apply or those for which you don't have an answer, respond with N/A (Not Applicable) or a slash through the space.

Finally, the third standard for judging an application is clarity and neatness. For that reason, it is always best to print your answers (except where your legal signature is required at the bottom of the application). Take your time when filling out the application, and correct errors with a single slash through the error with the correction on the side.

WRITTEN COMMUNICATION TOOLS

Determine Resume Format

Resumes are advertisements that present applicants to employers and can be developed through any number of resources. For example, they can be created from scratch on a word processor or constructed by filling in blanks on any number of resume-generating programs. Microsoft Word and Corel's WordPerfect both provide templates for a variety of resume styles. In addition, free web resume templates are available through *Job Search Page.com* at the following address *www.jobsearchpage.com/templates.html*. Keep in mind, however, these templates are often limiting in terms of format and creativity. Finally, employment agencies and career centers will construct resumes from your data for a fee.

Regardless of the method employed to prepare a resume, all resumes require specific information. Complete, accurate resumes contain personal information, a summary of your qualifications, education, work experience, references, and other pertinent information such as licenses, certifications, awards, and so on.

1. Personal Information—Name, address, phone number, e-mail address (Note: Make sure your e-mail address sounds professional. For example, cutiepie@aol.com may be fine for e-mailing your friends but not an employer).
2. Qualifications—Skills, competencies, or tasks that you feel qualified to perform on-the-job or that you have been trained to perform.
3. Education—Technical colleges, specialized training. Highlight relevant courses taken, degrees earned, academic honors, and extracurricular activities.
4. Employment Experience—Names, addresses, and phone numbers of current and former employers. Provide a brief description of the duties and responsibilities for each job listed.
5. Additional Qualifications—Hobbies, licenses, memberships in social or service organizations, honors, and awards. However, list only those that might help you land an interview.
6. References—Names, addresses, and phone numbers of references are generally listed on a separate page with your name, address, and phone number at the top.

The most challenging task you are faced with when preparing written communication is presenting your qualifications in a clear, meaningful, and interesting way that represents your uniqueness as a prospective employee. Pulling together pertinent information from your experiences can seem overwhelming; this task can be simplified considerably if you are well organized.

A tool that can assist you in organizing this information is the Personal Qualifications Inventory that requires you to list your job-related qualifications. This list will provide a foundation from which you can draw information to be incorporated into every contact with your prospective employer.

PERSONAL QUALIFICATIONS INVENTORY WORKSHEET

In the space provided, list your qualifications for the position you are seeking. Consider your skills and achievements, your education and training, and your work record and experience as the basis for these qualifications. Examples of what to include on your list might be as follows:

- Completed secretarial diploma program.
- Experienced using Microsoft Word.
- Outstanding work record with present employer; have not missed work in two years.

1. _____
   _____

2. _____
   _____

3. _____
   _____

4. _____
   _____

5. _____
   _____

6. _____
   _____

7. _____
   _____

8. _____
   _____

9. _____
   _____

10. _____
    _____

After you've completed the Personal Qualifications Inventory, you are ready to organize and develop your own personal resume. Of the many different styles of resumes that are used to present qualifications to employers, you want to select a style that provides vivid personal descriptions of your qualifications, experiences, and abilities with brief annotations. Such a choice makes you "come to life" on the printed page, rather than simply providing a list of facts about your background in a far less interesting manner.

Discussions with advisory committee members, program evaluators, and personnel managers reveal a preference for resumes that quickly communicate a candidate's qualifications, skills, and abilities. Two of the most common resume formats include the chronological resume and the functional resume. The chronological resume presents one's qualifications and experiences as they occurred over time, starting with the most recent. This format works best for experienced employees who are changing jobs. Those who have had less work experience or are recent graduates will find the functional resume a better choice to present their qualifications. Rather than organizing experiences by dates, the functional resume organizes qualifications based on skills and accomplishments. Given these two options, most applicants will find the blend of both styles found in the modified functional resume will work best. This combined style highlights skills and accomplishments, as well as the educational and/or work experiences that produced these qualifications.

On the following pages, you will discover how the modified functional resume meets the needs of employer and candidate alike. In a matter of minutes, your resume should announce who you are, what you want, and what you can do. Follow this information with documentation of where and when you gained these skills, and employers will be calling you with offers too good to pass up!

You may find the suggestions below helpful when creating your modified functional resume:

1. Prepare your resume and other written communication on a computer. Save the documents. The ease of revisions, the freedom to try different styles, and assistance of spell check make computer-prepared documents superior to any others.

2. Don't "date" your resume by including the day's date or your age.

3. Immediately following the heading, include a Career or Employment Objective that identifies the positions you're applying for and that reflects your current goal.

4. Beneath the Employment Objective, list your Qualifications, as illustrated on page 185.

5. Follow the Qualifications with either Education or Work Experience, depending upon which of the two you want to emphasize first for an employer.

6. Write short descriptions, using active verbs, to clarify the skills and experiences you've identified in the work and education sections. Your education and work experiences should be listed with the most recent first.

7. Provide additional information about "who you are" by listing honors you've received and professional organizations to which you belong.

8. Obtain three references. Generally choose two people who can discuss your technical skills and abilities and one person to serve as a character reference. It's a good idea if your references are individuals with varied backgrounds, such as a clergy, teacher, and former employer. These references should not be related to you.

9. Contact persons you want to use as references in order to obtain their permission. Not only is such contact a matter of common courtesy, but it also prepares your references for phone calls and/or letters from employers seeking information about you.

10. Limit your resume to one page. Busy employers or personnel managers may be unwilling to read resumes that are longer. If your resume absolutely must run longer than one page, it should be continued on a second page rather than on the backside of the first page. Include an appropriate heading in the top left-hand corner of the second page: Resume of Sandy Smith—Page Two.

11. Proofread your neatly printed resume for spelling and typographical errors. Have others double-check it for mistakes.

12. Make your resume visually appealing and easy to read. Balance the printed material with sufficient white space. Use underlining, capitalization, and boldface type and/or various fonts to make important information stand out.

13. Use a good quality, heavy bond paper of white or off-white, and avoid pastels or other unusually colored paper, as well as tissue-thin, erasable typing paper.

14. Duplicate quality copies of your resume. If you don't have access to a quality printer for your computer, find a print shop that can make professional copies rather than using the copy machine found in your local library. Professional duplication may cost you a few cents more per copy, but you can select the quality of paper you want for your copies.

Modified Functional Resume Format

Name
Street Address
City, State Zip
Phone Number
E-mail address

OBJECTIVE: Present your employment, work, or professional objective as a brief job title or position.

QUALIFICATIONS:
- List the skills, abilities, talents, or achievements that qualify you for this position.
- Bullet each capability for emphasis and easy reading.
- Add annotations to explain or clarify the entry.
- Group your qualifications to show your specialization in your field.
- Include numbers, percents, or amounts to show the impact or effects of your efforts.

EDUCATION: Note the most recent and relevant education related to the above qualifications. Include the address and the date of your completion of this schooling.

Consider adding the major courses or units of study for this program.

EXPERIENCE: Indicate your most recent employer, the address, your position, and duties. Include the dates of this employment.

Note previous employment as space and relevance allows. Try to show a solid work history with directly related or transferable skills highlighted for the reader.

Show advancements, promotions, or increased responsibility whenever possible. Use active verbs to express enthusiasm and drive. Create a positive picture of your skills and abilities.

REFERENCES: **Excellent references available!**

Sample Resume: Microsoft® Word Resume Wizard Template

ODIN O. O'NEIL

OBJECTIVE

Solar System Designer

QUALIFICATIONS

Designed and installed Passive Solar Systems

Certified by National Homebuilder's Association

Licensed Steam Fitter

EDUCATION

2003–2005   San Antonio Technical College
San Antonio, TX

Associate Degree HACR

Dean's List 3.85 GPA

WORK EXPERIENCE

2002 – 2003   Southwest Solar Inc.   St. Louis, MO

Solar Designer

Designed and installed solar systems in residential buildings.

Supervised 3-person crew in all aspects of construction from design to troubleshooting finished systems.

2001–2002   Organic Gardens   Mitchell, SD

Grower/harvester

Grew and harvested organic produce for CSA and local markets.

Excellent References Available.

1108 NORTH PINE STREET • CENTERVILLE, WI • 53313

PHONE 608–752–4309 • FAX 608–752–4309 • E-MAIL OONEIL@HOTMAIL.COM

Sample Resume: Microsoft® Word Resume from Scratch

TERRY ARAGON
3976 ELMBROOK COURT
MUNCIE, ARKANSAS 98654
(319) 871–0548

OBJECTIVE: **Appliance Service Repair**

QUALIFICATIONS:

- Excellent mechanical skills
- Experienced in troubleshooting circuit boards
- Three years' work for plumbing contractor
- Commercial Driver's License

EDUCATION:

Pleasant Valley Technical College   2002 – 2004
8234 Madison Avenue
Pleasant Valley, Arkansas 98965

Appliance Servicing (1 year Technical Diploma Program)
Entered to develop skills in appliance field. Courses taken
included Appliance Servicing (2 semesters), Appliance
Electronics, Industrial Communication, Applied Psychology, and
Industrial Mathematics (1 semester each). Dean's Honor List.

EMPLOYMENT:

Pleasant Valley Technical College   2002 to Present
8234 Madison Avenue
Pleasant Valley, Arkansas 98965
(319) 691–8765

Laboratory Assistant: Help students set up projects in
Commercial Refrigeration and Heating classes. Demonstrate
proper use of test instruments and gauges. Select proper tools for
students.

Little Rock Plumbing   1999 – 2002
Post Office Box 94
Little Rock, Arkansas 98756
(319) 987–6543

Laborer: Dug trenches, installed drain and fill lines, worked from
prints to measure placement of fixtures, soldered and cemented
fittings.

REFERENCES: Gladly furnished upon request.

Meet Requirements for Letters of Application

Typed in a standard business letter format, the letter of application includes the following parts:

Heading (your return address and the date);

Inside address (the name and mailing address of the employer);

Salutation (a formal acknowledgment of your reader, Dear Ms. Chang);

Body (three paragraphs are described in detail below);

Complimentary closing (a traditional ending for the letter such as Sincerely, or Yours truly);

Signature (type your name below the complimentary close with enough room above it for your signature);

Enclosure (below your typed name add the word "Enclosure" to remind your reader to look for your resume).

The heading includes your address and the date. You may include your phone number here, if you desire to do so. Many job seekers also include an e-mail address.

The inside address should include the recipient's full name and title, along with the business address. If you do not know your reader, call the company and ask for the person's name and the correct spelling. Chris Mueller could also be Kris Miller. It's also best to find out if that's Mr., Mrs., Ms., or Miss Miller.

Some problems may arise when addressing this letter if the letter is sent in response to a blind ad where the recipient is unknown. In such situations, include a subject line after the inside address. For instance, consider this example:

B433, c/o Journal Sentinel Inc.
333 West State Street
Post Office Box 2982
Milwaukee, WI 53201–2982

Subject: Quality Control Manager Position

Whenever possible, find out the name of the recipient in order to make the letter more personalized. Traditional salutations use Dear and the individual's name. Dear Mr. Smith: or Dear Dr. Jones.

The three paragraphs of the body are the most important part of the letter of application. The first paragraph identifies the specific position applied for and the source of the job lead. The second presents the primary qualifications for the position, and the final paragraph requests an interview.

Beginning the letter may be the most challenging part of writing it. Several stock introductions may be employed. Typically the letter should name the source of the job lead (the placement office, an instructor, a newspaper ad, or Internet posting), identify the specific job applied for, and express interest in the position.

The second paragraph in the body of the letter of application ought to answer the question, "Why should you be hired for this specific job?" The best way to answer this question is to present your strongest qualifications for the position. Relevant work experience and/or education could be mentioned. Each may be developed in a separate paragraph. Be certain to balance this information with the qualifications mentioned in your resume.

Discuss specific skills, concepts and procedures, equipment and machines, and abilities and talents that have been learned on other jobs or in your training. Be specific; use proper names and technical language to show the employer that you have valid qualifications for this position. Generally, students don't supply enough specific information about their abilities in these paragraphs. You can alert the employer to additional information that appears on your enclosed resume.

Think of a salesperson showing you a car. What happens if all that you are told is, "It's a good runner"? Are you convinced? Contrast that to the seller who talks about the mileage, the condition of the exhaust system, the sound of the engine, the quality of the tires, the recent paint job, and so on. In the same way "details" sell products, they also sell people. Be sure to include enough specific details about yourself in the body of the letter.

The final paragraph of the letter of application requests an interview to discuss your qualifications for the position. Make yourself available at the employer's convenience, and provide a phone number where you can be reached along with the hours most convenient for contacting you.

None of the paragraphs in the body needs to be long; three to five sentences will do. They should be typed, well written, and accurate in both spelling and punctuation. Use the form of a standard business letter, be clear, and above all, be neat. In addition, avoid too many "I" statements. Construct your sentences to appeal to the reader. For example, instead of saying, "I'm writing in response to your opening for a sales representative," say, "Your ad in the *Rocky Mountain Times* for a sales representative matches my qualifications." (See Example #1.) Saving this document on a computer makes revisions and updates very easy.

Review the format below to become familiar with the components of the letter of application. Note also the sample letters that follow the format.

Letter of Application Format

Street Address
City, State Zip   **HEADING**
Date
(Phone optional)
(E-mail address optional)

Mr./Ms. Name, Title
Company Name   **INSIDE ADDRESS**
Street Address
City, State Zip

Dear Mr./Ms. Name: **SALUTATION/ GREETING**

Your ad for. . . .

My present job at Generac. . . .   **BODY**

Please call to schedule an. . . .

Sincerely,   **COMPLIMENTARY CLOSE**

          SIGNATURE

Stew Dent   **TYPED NAME**

Enclosure

Review the samples that are provided on the following pages. Evaluate each using the previously discussed guidelines. Put yourself in the shoes of the employer, and ask yourself if this letter comes from a person you would like to talk to about a job.

Sample Letter of Application   **Sample #1**

234 Main Street
Hometown, Minnesota 51234
April 10, 2005

Mr. Joseph Smith, Manager
Acme Autoland
567 North State Avenue
St. Paul, Minnesota 59876

Dear Mr. Smith:

Your advertisement for an auto body repairman in the Sunday, April 3, 2003, edition of *The St. Paul Pioneer Press* caught my attention. Please accept this letter as my application for this position.

You may be interested to know that I am presently enrolled in the Auto Body Program at Hennepin County Technical College. This program includes skills development in rust repair, panel replacement and alignment, metal finishing, frame straightening, painting, and unibody construction and repair. All of these skills should be of value to you.

In addition, this program provides further preparation in related courses consisting of auto body welding, industrial math, communication, psychology, auto schematics, and auto body estimating. The training I'm receiving in these classes will enhance my ability to be a productive worker for your business.

Due to my interest in this field, I have in the past restored two collector's cars to showroom condition. I have been employed in the past at Joe's Service Station where I have learned the skills needed to restore these two vehicles. My enclosed resume presents greater detail about my previous job experience.

Could we arrange an interview at your convenience? You can reach me at (207) 789–5432 after 3:00 p.m. should you have any questions.

Sincerely,

Jan Richards

Jan Richards

Enclosure

Letter of Application   **Sample #2**

1684 West Colfax Avenue
Denver, Colorado 80267
May 23, 2005

Ms. Jean Wexler
Director of Personnel
Lance Manufacturing Company
309 Clyde Gallager Road
Arvada, Colorado 80003

Dear Ms. Wexler:

Your ad for the Payroll Clerk position posted on the Arvada Community College Job Board on May 21, 2005, looked interesting to me. Please consider my application for this position.

On May 12, 2005, I graduated from Red Rocks Community College with a Diploma in Accounting Services. You will find my training and hands-on experience in payroll procedures to be a plus for your organization. Currently, I am employed at Casa Bonita as a Swing Manager, and some of my responsibilities include auditing time cards and preparing payroll. You may also be interested to know that I have considerable experience working with taxes and interest computation through my employment at Aurora City Hall Treasurer's Office.

Enclosed is a resume so you can review my qualifications in more detail. Please feel free to contact me for an interview at your convenience. I may be reached at 637–4932 between 4–10 p.m. Monday through Friday. Thank you for your consideration.

Sincerely,

Chris Powell

Chris Powell

Enclosure: Resume

Select Elements for Follow-up Letters

Several types of follow-up letters can be used. Some will simply thank the employer for the interview. The content of these short letters should state your appreciation for the interview; explain what you liked about the position, place, process, or people; and express your enthusiasm about working for the firm.

Other follow-up letters accept a job offer. These letters should express your appreciation for the offer, your enthusiasm to start work, and your understanding of when and where the employer expects you to report for work.

Sample Follow-up Letter   **Sample #1**

387 Apple Lane
Newtown, Illinois 61433
April 9, 2005

Mr. Bob Marks
Director of Personnel
ABC Travel, Incorporated
3287 Westgate Avenue
Chicago, Illinois 60619

Dear Mr. Marks:

It was a pleasure to meet you yesterday and discuss with you my application for the
position of Travel Agent with ABC Travel, Incorporated. I especially appreciated the
opportunity to meet the other agents.

With my diploma in Travel Marketing and my strong organizational skills, I believe I
would be an asset to your firm.

I appreciate your consideration and look forward to hearing from you.

Sincerely,

Jo Morgan

Jo Morgan

Still other follow-up letters refuse job offers. When you are offered a job you
choose not to take, thank the employer for the interview, say something positive
about the company, and provide a brief explanation about your refusal.

Regardless of the interview's outcome—whether you are offered the position
or not; choose to accept the position or not; or even more importantly, have not yet
heard the interviewer's decision—you should send a follow-up letter in order to
show your appreciation, to remind the employer of your unique qualifications, and
to strengthen your position in the selection process. These brief letters need not fill
the page, but they should let the employer know you are grateful, regardless of the
outcome of the interview. Notice in the samples how the applicants express their
thanks and interest in the position in just a few short sentences.

Follow Guidelines for Application Forms

Whether or not you write a resume and letter of application, chances are you will
be required to complete an application form as well. For many companies, job application forms are used to screen candidates for interviews. However, some employers require candidates to complete an application when they come for an
interview.

According to Randall S. Hansen, Ph.D., "Many employers use applications as a
way of standardizing the information they obtain from all job-seekers, including some

---

Sample Follow-up Letter   **Sample #2**

903 Palm Drive
Miami, Florida 23984
June 28, 2005

Ms. Sandra Melendez
Director of Employment
Ace Corporation
11274 Orange Grove Road
Fort Lauderdale, Florida 24321

Dear Ms. Melendez:

Thank you for offering me the position of material handling technician at the Ace Corporation. I was impressed with the organization of your department and its commitment to quality robotic repair.

While my schedule at school does not permit me to accept the position at this time, I look forward to a future opportunity.

As you suggested, I will contact you when I finish my robotics training. If another position should occur that you think would fit my schedule before completion of my training, please feel free to contact me at (305) 783–9730.

Sincerely,

Carroll Rowe

Carroll Rowe

---

things that you would not normally put on your resume" (*www.quintcareers.com/ job_applications.html*). Unlike the resume and letter of application where you determine the content and focus, the application form solicits information from the employer's point of view.

Typically, employers request specific information, including personal information, position desired, education, employment experience, military service, references, health record, and any other information that is determined a legitimate condition of employment. Some of the following suggestions may be helpful to you when filling out an application.

1. Salary—Put "open" or "negotiable," or give a range (ex: $32,000 to 40,000) or state a figure based on research you have done.
2. Reason for leaving—Be honest; if fired from a previous job, write "let go" or "job ended" with the hope of having the opportunity to explain your situation.
3. Criminal record—If you were ever convicted of a felony (and you will know if you were), be honest and hope to explain how you have reformed. The question is not asking about "minor" traffic violations or misdemeanors.

Sample Follow-up Letter   **Sample #3**

3207 Birch Drive
Jefferson, WI 53549
April 9, 2005

Ms. Roberta Long
Director of Personnel
XYZ Manufacturing Company
1800 Main Street
West Allis, WI 53029

Dear Ms. Long:

It was a pleasure to meet you yesterday and discuss with you my application for the position of fabricator with your company. I especially appreciated the opportunity to meet the supervisor and other fabricators.

Although you said that you preferred to hire someone with more experience, I hope that you will consider my application in the future as I gain more familiarity with your processes and equipment.

I appreciate your consideration and look forward to hearing from you.

Sincerely,

Chris Morgan

Chris Morgan

---

4. Position desired—List the specific job for which you are applying (clerk-typist, travel agent, electronics technician, maintenance mechanic, etc.); avoid "anything available" answers.
5. Fine print—Be sure to read the fine print above the place for your signature and the day's date. Employers sometimes ask for authorization to do an extensive search into your past and present.
6. Signature—Don't forget to sign the application form; your signature verifies that all of the information is correct to the best of your knowledge.

Finally, keep in mind that the more flexible you appear on an application, the more attractive you will appear to an employer. This flexibility will be revealed in your willingness to work alternate shifts, be open to salary negotiation, be willing to travel, and so on.

CHAPTER 8 TOOL CHECK

Directions: Find the key words from the preceding chapter to complete the following sentences.

1. To increase your chances of looking good on paper, you should consider your reader, write clearly, and _____ and _____.
2. _____ contain vivid personal descriptions of your experiences and abilities in brief sentence form.
3. A letter of application identifies the position you are seeking, summarizes your qualifications, and _____.
4. The three standards for an application form include honesty and accuracy, completeness, and _____.
5. List at least three categories of information that are likely to be included in a resume: _____, _____, _____.
6. The _____ of a letter of application includes the reader's name, title, and address.
7. "Sincerely yours" or "Yours truly" are called _____.
8. Follow-up letters may accept a job offer, refuse a job offer, or _____.
9. Before filling in any information on an application form, you should _____ the entire form first.
10. Limit your resume to _____ page if possible.

CHAPTER 8 INTERACTIONS

This Written Communication Blueprint requires three writing projects: a resume, a letter of application, and a follow-up letter. Each should be computer printed on quality paper and prepared as if it would actually be mailed or delivered to an employer.

INTERACTION #1—Resume Assignment

Write a modified functional resume that includes the following sections: personal heading, employment objective, qualifications, employment, education, and reference. List qualifications that show what skills, competencies, talents, and abilities you have to offer an employer. Use strong active verbs to present your qualifications, and provide examples to validate your skills. Present your resume information with appropriate boldface and white space to balance the page(s). Eliminate all spelling, punctuation, and typing errors. Follow guidelines for the style of resume described in class. Submit a typed or printed copy of your finished resume for evaluation.

RESUME WORKSHEET

Read through the following worksheet, collect the information needed to complete the assignment, and fill in the blanks. Be as complete as possible. Do not use any abbreviations. Be sure to use as many action words as possible when describing job duties (see Life Skills Inventory page).

When finished, organize the information into a working resume that includes each category on the worksheet and highlights the qualifications that relate to your professional objective. Follow the previously mentioned assignment for your resume.

HEADING

(full name) _____

(street address) _____

(city, state, zip) _____

(area code, phone number) _____

(e-mail address) _____

EMPLOYMENT OBJECTIVE

_____

QUALIFICATIONS

_____

_____

_____

_____

_____

_____

_____

_____

_____

_____

EDUCATION

Most recent school name: _____

City, state: _____

Degree: _____

Program: _____

Graduated or Dates Attended: _____

Major Courses: _____

Acquired Skills: _____

_____

Grade Point Average: _____

Next most recent school name: _____

City, state: _____

Degree: _____

Program: _____

Graduated or Dates Attended: _____

Major Courses: _____

Acquired Skills: _____

_____

Grade Point Average: _____

WORK EXPERIENCE

Most recent employer: _____

Employer's address: _____

_____

Employer's Phone #: _____

Dates of employment: from _____ to _____

Job Title: _____

Specific job duties: _____

_____

_____

_____

Immediate Supervisor: _____

Next most recent employer: _____

Employer's address: _____

_____

Employer's Phone #: _____

Dates of employment: from _____ to _____

Job Title: _____

Specific job duties: _____

_____

_____

_____

Immediate Supervisor: _____

Next most recent employer: _____

Employer's address: _____

_____

Employer's Phone #: _____

Dates of employment: from _____ to _____

Job Title: _____

Specific job duties: _____

_____

_____

_____

Immediate Supervisor: _____

Next most recent employer: _____

Employer's address: _____

_____

Employer's Phone #: _____

Dates of employment: from _____ to _____

Job Title: _____

Specific job duties: _____

_____

_____

_____

Immediate Supervisor: _____

HONORS AND AWARDS and/or SCHOOL AND COMMUNITY ACTIVITIES

* _____

_____

* _____

_____

PROFESSIONAL AFFILIATIONS – CLUBS

* _____

_____

* _____

_____

REFERENCES

(name) _____

(position) _____

(company) _____

(address) _____

(city, state) _____

(zip code) _____

(phone) _____

(relationship to you) _____

• • • • • •

(name) _____

(position) _____

(company) _____

(address) _____

(city, state) _____

(zip code) _____

(phone) _____

(relationship to you) _____

• • • • • •

(name) _____

(position) _____

(company) _____

(address) _____

(city, state) _____

(zip code) _____

(phone) _____

(relationship to you) _____

INTERACTION #2—Letter of Application Assignment

Write a letter of application that presents you as an applicant for a specific job, identifies the source of your job lead, presents your strongest qualifications for the job, makes reference to your resume, and requests an interview. Be certain to follow a standard business letter format and eliminate all spelling and punctuation errors. Prepare this letter to balance information in your resume, not repeat the same qualifications. Present a letter that balances the white space of the page to provide a pleasing appearance.

INTERACTION #3—Follow-up Letter Assignment

Write a letter that would be appropriate to send to a prospective employer after a job interview. Include a thank you message and some positive comment about the interview, the company, or the people. Mention a strong qualification of yours and your interest in the firm. If appropriate, accept or reject a job offer. Balance the white space of this letter, correct all spelling and punctuation errors, and make a favorable impression with this letter.

INTERACTION #4—Application Form Assignment

Obtain an application form from a local employer. Complete the job application form, keeping in mind the suggestions discussed in this chapter. Submit the completed form to your instructor for evaluation.

REFERENCES

About resumes. Retrieved April 6, 2001, from the World Wide Web: *www.milwaukeetoday. webpoint.com/job/ar.htm.*

Allen, J. (1998). *Writing in the workplace.* Needham Heights, MA: Allyn & Bacon.

How to write a job-winning resume that puts yours on top. Retrieved July 17, 2002, from the World Wide Web: *www.majig.com/writing-a-resume/.*

Job Search Page.com Retrieved July 17, 2002, from the World Wide Web: *www.jobsearchpage.com/ templates.html.*

CHAPTER 9
INTERVIEWING BLUEPRINT

Determine Importance of the Interview

Identify Types of Interviews

Respond to Types of Interviewing Questions

Respond to Illegal Questions

INTERVIEWING TOOLS

Prepare for the Interview

Create a Positive Impression

Follow-up After the Interview

TOOL CHECK

INTERACTIONS

Interviewer's Plan Sheet

Applicant's Plan Sheet

Mock Interview Assignment

INTERVIEWING BLUEPRINT

Virtually everyone is interviewed before being hired. The interview is an opportunity to establish a relationship with an organization. The employer has reviewed applicants and selected you as a potential employee. Now that employer wants to get to know you, to see if you fit into the framework of the company, and to see what you have to contribute to the company's success. According to Connie Brown-Glaser and Barbara Steinberg-Smalley in their *Reader's Digest* article, "Four Minutes That Get You Hired" (August 1993), an interviewer decides whether or not to seriously consider you for the position in the first four minutes of the interview (pp. 129–132). Your clear understanding of the interview process will increase your chances of making a positive impression during those first crucial minutes. Chapter 9 provides information that will prepare you for the all-important interview. In the following pages you will learn about the importance of the interview, the types of interviews, and the types of interview questions. In addition, you will review the tools necessary for interview preparation, performance, and follow-up. Finally, you will have the opportunity to apply your understanding in practical interactions.

Determine Importance of the Interview

Barbara Holt, a tour guide for the San Francisco Performing Arts Center, recently told a group of visitors to the Center that when a position opens up with the symphony orchestra, anywhere from 200 to 500 applications might be received. From that number, the list is narrowed down to 100. Approximately 40 of those individuals will be invited to audition, with one performer being selected for the opening. While most of us will not be seeking symphony jobs with this level of competition, the fact remains that in today's workplace, company downsizing, a fluctuating economy, and technological advancements can all contribute to a more competitive job market in many career areas. Therefore, the way in which you approach an interview can be the determining factor that sets you apart from the other candidates.

The importance of the interview is based upon two factors. First, the interview provides a formal setting for the employer to get to know you—your skills, abilities, personality, and so on. Chances are if you made it to the interview stage, you are among those selected from a larger pool of applicants for serious consideration. The employer must have liked what he or she saw in your resume, letter of application, and application. Once all of the interviews are completed, the employer will most likely select the individual who interviewed the best. And exactly what are most employers looking for during this final screening process? According to Bob Goyer in an article entitled, "What Are Employers Looking For?" from *The Job Market* (1999), employers are seeking five qualities among applicants. These qualities include proven success, ambition, initiative, enthusiasm and high energy level, and ability to get along with others.

Second, the interview provides not only an opportunity to sell yourself to an employer, but it also gives you the chance to see if the company meets your expectations as well. During the course of the interview, you might have the opportunity to tour the facilities. Is the working environment clean, safe, and pleasant? You may meet future co-workers, supervisors, and staff and be able to assess your potential for establishing working relationships with them. Do they seem cordial, enthusiastic, and cooperative? Do you feel like you will fit in with them? You are certainly likely to discover more about the demands of the position itself. Are those demands consistent with your qualifications? Will you have room for advancement? Do the pace and volume of work offer a challenge for you?

As you can see, the interview is important because it provides both you and the employer with some valuable information about your future relationship with a company.

Identify Types of Interviews

There are as many different types of interviews as there are different interviewers and applicants. Generally, most job candidates will participate in one of two types of interviews: entry-level interviews or job-change interviews. Let us look at each of the types.

Entry-level interviews are most common for recent graduates. Applicants usually meet with a personnel manager or immediate supervisor to discuss the position. This type is typically conducted face-to-face with a question-answer format. Employers focus on discovering which candidates have the right mix of qualifications for the position.

Job-change interviews occur when an individual is changing jobs with a current employer or is moving to a new employer. Such interviews may be more demanding than the entry-level interviews, requiring the applicant to show examples of past work performances. The format for these interviews may be conducted one-on-one or with a panel of interviewers. In some instances, even role-playing is used for applicants to demonstrate qualifications in situations they will face on the job.

Respond to Types of Interviewing Questions

Two types of questions will challenge you during your interviews. The first type includes traditional questions that are broad-based and designed to solicit information about your skills and abilities. For example, you may be asked, "What kind of equipment can you operate?" "Did you hold any leadership positions while you were in school?" "What computer skills can you bring to this position?"

The second type includes behavior-based questions. These questions are based on the theory that your past performance is the best indicator of your future behavior. In order to give an employer evidence of past performance, applicants should describe a condition that they encountered in the past, the actions that they took, and the results that they achieved as a result of those actions. Interviewers may use behavior-based questions such as these:

> "Describe an instance on your last job when you had to think on your feet and get yourself out of a difficult situation."

> "Tell me about a time you went 'above and beyond' the call of duty on your last job."

> "Describe a day when you had multiple tasks to handle at work. How did you accomplish all that needed to be done?"

If you would like to learn more about "behavior-based" interviews, you may find the following websites helpful:

www.staffingworld.com/howtowin.htm
www.mrichampions.com/behaviorbsd.html

Respond to Illegal Questions

Despite laws designed to protect applicants from discrimination in the hiring process, some illegal practices continue to plague interviews. According to an article in *USA Today*, "Various federal, state, and local laws regulate the questions a prospective employer can ask you. An employer's questions—on the job application, in the interview, or during the testing process—must be related to the job for which you are applying. For the employer, the focus must be: 'What do I need to know to decide whether or not this person can perform the functions of this job?'" (Illegal interview questions (2001). While most application forms have been cleansed of illegal questions, these questions may come up during the course of an interview. Whether knowingly or just by accident, employers may ask questions that legally you are not bound to answer. Let us examine the types of illegal questions you might be asked and the various choices you have for responding to these questions.

Questions about national origin, disabilities, arrest record, marital/family status, age, race, religion, physical attributes, military background, and affiliations have the potential to be illegal if they are asked in a way that discriminates. For example, while it is illegal for an employer to ask you about your height and weight, an employer may ask if you are able to lift 75-pound packages as a part of the job. Likewise, if the job requires a security clearance, you may be asked about your arrest record.

Illegal and Legal Questions

Factor	Illegal Questions	Legal Questions
National Origin	Are you a U.S. citizen?	What languages do you speak fluently?
Disabilities	Do you have any handicaps?	Can you perform this job with reasonable accommodations?
Arrest Record	Have you ever been arrested?	Have you ever been convicted of auto theft?
Marital Status/Family	Are you married? Do you have any children?	Are you able to work overtime?
Age	How old are you?	Are you over 18 years of age?
Race	What is your race?	None!
Religion	What church do you belong to?	Are you able to work Saturday and/or Sunday shifts?
Physical Attributes	How tall are you?	Are you able to stand for eight hours?
Military Background	Were you honorably discharged?	What type of training did you receive in the military?
Affiliation	To what organizations do you belong?	What professional organizations do you belong to that would enhance your job performance?

When confronted with illegal questions, you can respond in a variety of ways. One way you can respond is to simply answer the question you have been asked. Be aware, however, that your response may lead to discrimination on the part of the employer. A second way you can respond is to refuse to answer the question. This choice may preserve your legal rights, but you may be perceived as uncooperative. A third way to respond is to consider why the employer might be asking the question and respond to your perception of the employer's intent. For example, when the interviewer asks if you have any children, you may respond by saying, "I have adequate child care that will not prevent me from working over-time." Another way to respond is by asking a question. For instance, you might say, "Could you explain how you think my having children would affect my job performance?"

In this section, we have examined the importance of the interview, the types of interviews you might encounter, and the types of questions you might be asked. In the next section, we will explore the skills involved in preparing for, participating in, and following-up after the interview.

INTERVIEWING TOOLS

Prepare for the Interview

Preparation for the interview process begins long before the initial contact with the employer. In fact, four major steps are involved in the preparation process: re-searching the company, updating your paperwork, rehearsing your responses, and ensuring a positive first impression.

According to Thomas Staffing, in his article "The 25 Worst Job Interview Mis-takes" (2002), "It isn't necessary to memorize the company's annual sale and profit figures, but you should know something about their products or services. One can-didate lost out an AT&T interview by mentioning their involvement in a news story that had been about ITT, and there was no way for the candidate to regain credibil-ity after such a glaring error. Check out information about large companies in busi-ness magazines or corporate directories at your public library, or call the company to ask for a copy of the annual report. For smaller organizations, you may have to rely on the grapevine: some of the best information can come from people who used to work there." Other ways to find out about a company include accessing online re-sources, such as company web pages; checking out company advertisements; and vis-iting the actual company facility to observe its layout. Company directories like *www.thomasregister.com* provide information about the size, location, products, and activities and assets of the company.

You may ask yourself why doing this research is so important before the inter-view. First, if you can show an employer you made the extra effort to learn about the company, you will increase your chances of making a positive first impression and avoid the embarrassment of the candidate mentioned above who confused AT&T with ITT. In addition, the information you gain from your research can help you de-termine if, in fact, this is a company that would be a good match for your skills, in-terests, and goals.

Your preparation would not be complete without determining what informa-tion you need from the prospective employer in order to decide whether or not to accept a job. Prepare yourself for that point in the interview when the employer asks, "Do you have any questions?" by listing several questions that will give you insight into the position, the company, and your future there. Questions you might consider asking include some of the following:

To find out about:	Consider asking:
Job Responsibilities	What are your expectations of a successful long-term employee in this position?
Work Environment	What uniforms or protective equipment are provided?
	How would you characterize the climate between workers and managers?
Education and Training	What opportunities might I have for professional growth?
Company Philosophy	What is the mission or vision of your company?
	To what extent does your company empower workers to share in decision-making?
Work Performance	How frequently do worker evaluations occur?
	On what competencies should I focus my attention during the first six months?

In general, avoid questions about salary or benefits until you have been offered a position.

Along with researching the company and preparing questions to ask the interviewer, you need to update your paperwork. Be certain that your resume includes your most recent employment, education, and related experience. Also, make sure you have a copy of the resume to take to the interview. In addition, you may be asked to complete an application form prior to the interview. Sometimes these forms require you to supply information that is not on your resume, such as your social security number, or specific addresses and phone numbers of schools or employers. It is a good idea to have this information on a separate sheet of paper that you can readily transfer to the application form. Finally, if you intend to send a letter of application prior to the interview, be sure to personalize this letter so that it speaks directly to the employer about the specific position rather than sending a generic letter suitable for a variety of jobs.

One of the most important steps in preparing for an interview is anticipating the questions you will likely be asked. A good place to start is by accessing the numerous websites that list the questions most frequently asked. One such site comes from the University of Maryland Career Center at *www.careercenter.umd.edu/STUDENT/ STEP5/QUESTION.htm*. Another excellent site is at *www.quintcareers.com/interview_ question_collections.html* where you will find traditional interview questions, sample behavioral questions, job interview questions for college seniors or recent graduates, and a job interview question database.

Once you have determined possible interview questions, you need to consider your own responses. Regardless of the question, you should attempt to highlight your qualifications and provide specific examples of those qualifications in your responses. For example, if you are asked by an employer, "What abilities do you bring to this position?" rather than saying, " I am well organized and a good problem solver," consider this response: "I have excellent organizational and problem solving skills. At my last job, I restructured the inventory system to reduce the inventory completion time by 50 percent." The best practice for responding to interview questions is to have someone ask you the questions and have you actually respond to them. Videotaping your mock interview gives you the added benefit of being able to review and revise your responses, along with observing your nonverbal behavior.

When scheduling the interview with the employer, you should note the time, place, and name of the person that you will meet. Write these down to be sure they are correct. Prior to the interview, consider traveling to the employer's address to know where it is and how long it takes to get there. Check for parking areas and entrances. Be sure that you arrive in plenty of time before the scheduled time. You do not want to be late or lost.

Your appearance is a very important consideration as you prepare for an interview. In fact, the first impression you make as you walk through the interviewer's door could determine whether or not you get the job. What should you wear to the interview? You choice of attire is determined in part by the job for which you are applying. Showing up in a three-piece suit for an auto body technician job is just as inappropriate as wearing jeans and a T-shirt to an interview for an executive position. The best rule of thumb is to be well groomed and dress conservatively. Consider contacting the company's human resources department and ask what you should wear. You could also pay a visit to the company as part of your research and observe how others are dressed. Follow their lead, and dress like you belong there too.

Create a Positive Impression

Creating a positive impression begins the moment you enter the company. For sure you will want to be on time, ideally 10 to 15 minutes early. If you did a travel-time dry run as a part of your preparation, you are likely to arrive in plenty of time. Even before you meet the interviewer, other employees may be observing you. Sometimes their feedback influences the employer's decision of who will be hired. So "put your best foot forward" by being pleasant and courteous to those you meet. In addition, if you brought along your updated resume and personal information sheet, you will be prepared to complete an application form. You may also want to bring along a portfolio as evidence of your past accomplishments: auto body technicians may keep a photo album of projects they have completed; interior design graduates may bring a sample board that shows design choices for a room they are redecorating; administrative assistants may bring samples of correspondence that they have prepared. Finally, knowing the interviewer's name and title ahead of time can be a plus when you are finally introduced.

When you are called into the interviewer's office, let the interviewer take the lead. If a hand is extended to you, extend yours. If you are asked to have a seat, do so. Wait to see which direction the interview goes. The interviewer may engage you in small talk or may provide you with valuable information about the company. Regardless of how the meeting proceeds, listen and respond accordingly.

During the interview, you will be asked a variety of questions. Respond with honesty and completeness. Also, a favorable first impression is achieved by being positive about yourself and your previous experiences at work and at school. Avoid any temptation to "bad mouth" former employers or teachers. Keep your previous complaints to yourself.

When answering the interviewer's questions, avoid one- or two-word responses. Rather, explain what qualifications you have and give concrete examples of those qualifications, as in the behavior-based formula discussed earlier. Use your responses to convince the interviewer that your previous accomplishments are accurate predictors of your future performance. If you're unsure of what the interviewer is asking, paraphrase the question to clarify any misunderstanding. Consider beginning such paraphrases with statements like these: "Let me make sure I understand what you're asking me . . ." or "In other words, you're wondering if I ever encountered a situation like this before." Regardless of the questions you are asked, however, limit your responses to about 30 seconds, and certainly no longer than two minutes to avoid rambling. In all of your answers, emphasize what you have to offer the company.

Even if an employer asks questions about your weaknesses, respond positively. Consider how you might respond to this question: "Tell me about a time when you had difficulty satisfying a disgruntled customer." Rather than saying, "I've never had any trouble satisfying customers," say, "I wasn't able to give a customer a refund because the customer didn't have a sales slip, which our store policy requires. I know that the customer was very unhappy. So after checking with my manager, I was able to offer the customer two discount coupons to apply to future purchases."

Your nonverbal communication also conveys much in the interview process. To show that you are confident, energetic, and enthusiastic about the prospects of employment, sit up in your chair and lean slightly forward. Make eye contact, smile, and keep an "open" body posture by avoiding crossed arms and legs. Use head nods and facial expressions that signal attentiveness and interest.

At the close of the interview, employers will give you a chance to ask questions. Use this opportunity to show interest in the company, and that you have listened to what the interviewer had said earlier. Prior research you did on the company will allow you to ask relevant and appropriate questions such as, "In what direction do you think the company is heading during the next five to ten years?" or "What recent innovations have affected the electronics department here?" Avoid questions about salary, vacation time, sick days, and so on. These are important questions that should be asked only after being offered the job.

End the interview on a positive note. Look the interviewer in the eye, express your sincere interest in the job, and reinforce your strongest qualifications for the position. Express thanks for the interviewer's time and attention, and find out when a decision will be made and how you will be contacted. Ask the interviewer for a business card, and use it for writing your follow-up letter.

Immediately after the interview, write a follow-up "Thank you" letter. If you don't hear from the interviewer when indicated, call and ask if a decision has been made.

As an applicant, you can prepare a list of five qualifications you want to call to the employer's attention. List these five qualities and provide CAR Stories—specific examples that will show the interviewer that you have the qualities you claim to have. For instance, if you tell the interviewer you are dependable, you might offer as an example your perfect attendance record during three years of employment at Ace Trucking. Providing a claim and an example like this gives the interviewer a "picture" of your past successes, unlike applicants who respond to the interviewer's questions with incomplete, brief, or vague replies. Specific replies are especially important during a "behavior-based" interview. This type of interview looks at job experiences of the past as predictors of future performance.

In addition to knowing the essential techniques for creating a positive impression, you should also be aware of the reasons that applicants are rejected in interviews. The Saint Louis University School of Law (2002) reported 11 reasons why candidates are rejected:

1. Not prepared for the interview
2. No real interest in the company
3. Lack of proper career planning
4. Lack of knowledge of field or specialization

5. Inability to express herself/himself clearly
6. Overbearing—over aggressive—conceited
7. Asks no or poor questions about the job
8. Unwilling to start at the bottom
9. Makes excuses—evasiveness
10. No confidence and poise
11. Poor personal appearance

Other reasons for rejection include criticizing former employers and co-workers, failure to make eye contact, sloppy application forms, lack of knowledge in field of specialization, low moral standards, strong prejudices, and being late to the interview without reason.

Follow-up After the Interview

"The follow-up is the way to turn interviews into jobs," says Kate Wendelton in her article, "Following-Up After a Job Interview: The *Only* Job Hunting Technique" (2002).

Unfortunately, many job applicants think their work is over after they leave the interview. This perception is especially true among those who feel confident about their performance during the interview. Most career counselors agree that the follow-up can be every bit as important as the interview itself. This follow-up should take place within 24 hours of the interview in the form of a phone call, an e-mail, or a thank you letter. Your contact should express your appreciation for the interview; share a positive comment about the people, place, product, or procedures of the company; express enthusiasm for the position; and remind the employer of your strongest qualifications (Simmons, 2002).

Whatever form your follow-up may take, (phone call, e-mail or letter), you will find the section in Chapter 8, titled *Select Elements for Follow-up Letters,* to be helpful.

In short, the best interview is one that is well planned, creates a positive impression, and follows up appropriately afterwards. Remember, employers are looking for reasons to hire you. Give them good reasons to do so!

"Being able to do the job well will not necessarily get you hired. The person who gets hired is often the one who knows the most about how to get hired" (Bolles, 2002).

CHAPTER 9 TOOL CHECK

Directions: Find the key words from the preceding chapter to complete the following sentences.

1. _____ interviews are the most common for recent graduates.
2. _____ interview questions are based on the theory that your past performance is the best indicator of your future behavior.
3. Asking an applicant, "Do you have any children?" is considered a(n) _____ question.
4. During an interview, applicants should avoid asking questions about _____ or _____ until they have been offered a position.
5. Preparing for an interview involves researching the company, updating your paperwork, _____, and _____.

6. List any two categories from which applicants can choose questions to ask an employer during an interview: _____ and _____.
7. Use CAR stories to provide _____ examples of your qualifications.
8. List any 2 of the 11 reasons cited in this chapter for rejecting applicants after an interview: _____ and _____.
9. Applicants should follow-up within _____ hours after an interview.
10. Follow-ups can be done by letters, phone calls, or _____.

CHAPTER 9 INTERACTIONS

The following interactions include the Interviewer's Plan Sheet, the Applicant's Plan Sheet, a videotaped mock interview, and a mock interview evaluation.

INTERACTION #1—Interviewer's Plan Sheet

Select 10 questions to be asked in an interview. Four questions should be behavior-based questions; one question should be an illegal question; and the remaining five may come from the list of frequently asked interview questions that follow or from any of the websites listed on page 217.

Note the interview questions that you will ask when you play the role of the interviewer with a partner. During the interview, jot down notes on the answers you receive. These notes will help you complete the Interview Report Form after the interview.

Interview questions and response notes

1. _____?
   _____

2. _____?
   _____

3. _____?
   _____

4. _____?
   _____

5. _____?
   _____

6. _____?
   _____

7. _____?
   _____

8. _____?
   _____

9. _____?
   _____

10. _____?
    _____

Include one illegal question, four behavior-based questions, and five of your choice. Note your impression of the applicant's responses in the space after each question.

Questions Frequently Asked During Employment Interviews

(Lindquist, V. R. (1994) *The Northwestern Lindquist-Endicott Report.* Retrieved from the World Wide Web September 16, 2002, at *www.drptech.com/career/ques.html*)

1. Why do you want to work for our company?
2. Tell me something about your last job.
3. How do you feel about your last employer?
4. Why did you leave your last job?
5. Do you feel that you are mature enough to handle the responsibilities of this job?
6. What salary do you expect to be getting here?
7. What are your future career plans?
8. How do you spend your spare time?
9. Are you taking any courses right now?
10. Tell me something about yourself.
11. At school, what courses did you like best? Least? Why?
12. What one person had the greatest influence on your life and why?
13. Why did you choose this particular field of work?
14. How did you finance your way through school?
15. How did you rate scholastically in your senior year in high school?
16. Where do you hope to be five years from now? Ten years from now?
17. What prompted you to apply for our company?
18. How does your family feel about your career choice and its requirements?
19. What, in your estimation, is the key to professional success, particularly in this job?
20. Are you looking for temporary or permanent work?
21. What is your concept of the ideal boss?
22. Do you have friends or relatives working for our company?
23. Have you ever been in trouble with the law? Explain.
24. Are you free to travel? Relocate? Any restrictions?
25. What, in your opinion, especially qualifies you for this job? Explain fully.
26. What books, magazines, or newspapers do you read regularly?
27. Have you ever been fired from a job? If so, why? Explain fully.
28. Are you in a position to work overtime when necessary?
29. What is your draft status? Are you registered? Do you have plans for the military?
30. Do you suffer from any allergies or recurring illnesses?

31. How far did you go with your formal education? Why did you stop at that point?

32. Is this a field of work you'll want to stay in? Explain why.

33. How is your memory for names and faces? Fine details?

34. How would you describe yourself as an employee?

35. Do you belong to any professional organizations related to this job? Are you willing to join such organizations?

36. What do you know about our product line and services? Explain fully.

37. Who are our competitors in this field? Explain how their product lines and services compete with ours.

38. Have you ever supervised people? Ever trained someone on the job? If so, how many?

39. What, in your opinion, is the value of your vocational education?

40. What foreign languages do you speak? Would you feel comfortable around people who speak a language other than your own?

41. How long would it take you to get to and from work? What kind of car do you have? Is it reliable? Are you punctual and reliable?

42. How will automation affect the future of our industry and your job? How are you preparing for this change?

43. How would you react to working under the supervision of a younger person?

44. What sports do you excel in? What do you get out of those sports?

45. What in your estimation is the outstanding achievement in your life?

46. What are your pet peeves?

47. Is it all right to call your previous employer for a reference? What do you think he'll tell me?

48. Do you picture yourself being promoted quickly in this company?

49. Have the people you've worked with ever made any difference to you on a job?

50. Have you ever applied here before? When? Did you follow-up on the application? Why or why not?

51. Would you want your salary increases to be based on merit, promotional examination, or length of commitment?

52. Would you object to a training or probationary period when we hire you?

53. Tell me what one outstanding quality should make me hire you rather than one of the other people applying for this job.

54. What is your best work quality?

55. What would you do if you found a co-worker taking home company tools against company policy?

For more questions, see the following websites:

little.nhlink.net/nhlink/employme/frequent.htm or

www.quintcareers.com/interview_question_collections.html

Illegal Questions

Not all questions that interviewers ask are as straightforward and honest. Unfortunately, illegal questions are still a part of the employment process. Although illegal questions may be asked mistakenly or unintentionally in the interview process, applicants must be aware of their right to maintain privacy and to be free from discriminatory employment practices. We include illegal questions in our mock interviews to provide you with the opportunity to practice responses to such questions. For more information see Types of Interview Questions discussed earlier in this chapter or check out the following websites:

www.collegegrad.com/ezine/23illega.shtml or

www.dreamjobcoaching.com/illegal.shtml

INTERACTION #2—Applicant's Plan Sheet

Note the five dominant skills or abilities that you intend to emphasize in your responses to the interviewer's questions. Then describe a situation from your past experience that required you to use each of the five skills or abilities, the actions you took, and the results you experienced. Below is an example.

SKILL/ ABILITY	SITUATION	ACTION	RESULTS
Example: Time Management	**Situation**: My last job required me to perform multiple tasks at the same time while meeting important deadlines.	**Action**: Each day at the start of my shift, I took about 10 minutes to review and prioritize the work I needed to get done that day, along with the amount of time I expected to spend on each assignment. Then I closed my office door and had my lab tech screen my calls for the next few hours and only answered urgent calls while I worked on the top priority items.	**Results**: I found that using this system gave me a sense of control over my work and kept me focused while screening out distractions that could wait for my attention later. I also consistently met the necessary deadlines.
1.			
2.			
3.			
4.			
5.			

INTERACTION #3—Mock Interview Assignment

Now that you have completed the Interviewer's Plan Sheet and the Applicant's Plan Sheet, you are ready to participate in a mock interview. Pair up with a partner in class and conduct two interviews, one in which you are the interviewer and your partner is the applicant and one where the roles are reversed. Establish rapport with your partner by introducing yourselves to one another, shaking hands, being seated, and briefly setting up the interview. Use the plan sheet that you had prepared earlier as a source of questions to ask and responses to make during the interviews. Videotape both interviews so that they may be reviewed and evaluated.

INTERVIEW REPORT FORM

After the interview, complete the Interview Report Form together with your partner. The form provides an opportunity for each of you to record observations about yourself and to receive feedback from your partner.

INTERVIEWER	APPLICANT
List two behaviors that you liked about the applicant's interviewing style. 1. 2.	List two behaviors that you liked about your interviewing style. 1. 2.
List two changes that would improve the applicant's interviewing style. 1. 2.	List two changes that would improve your interviewing style. 1. 2.
Note the five dominant qualifications that were emphasized in your applicant's responses to your questions. 1. 2. 3. 4. 5.	Note the five dominant qualifications that you emphasized in your responses to the interviewer's questions. 1. 2. 3. 4. 5.
Comment on how well you thought your applicant responded to the illegal question(s) in the interview.	Comment on how well you thought you responded to the illegal question(s) in the interview.

REFERENCES

Bolles, D. (2002).Two minute crash course on interviews. *Jobhuntersbible.com.* Retrieved September 6, 2002, from the World Wide Web: *www.jobhuntersbible.com/library/hunters/ crashcourse.shtml.*

Brown-Glaser, C. & Steinberg-Smalley, B. (August 1993). Four minutes that get you hired. *Reader's Digest,* 129–132.

Goyer, B. (November 1999). What are employers looking for? *The Job Market.* Retrieved August 13, 2002, from the World Wide Web: *www.mariononline.com/columnists/goyer/1999/ nov99.htm.*

Illegal interview questions. (January 29, 2001). *USA Today.* Retrieved August 26, 2001, from the World Wide Web: *www.usatoday.com/careers/resources/interviewillegal.htm.*

Job Service form, *Make the Most of a Job Interview.*

Lindquist, V. R. (1994). *The Northwestern Lindquist-Endicott Report* Retrieved from the World Wide Web September 16, 2002: *www.drptech.com/career/ques.html.*

Saint Louis University School of Law. (2002). Reasons for rejection. Retrieved September 11, 2002, from the World Wide Web: *http://lawlib.slu.edu/Community/CareerSvcs/Student/ Rejection.html.*

Simmons, B. (2002). Follow-up to the interview may clinch the job. *Workopolis.com.* Retrieved September 11, 2002 from the World Wide Web: *wysiwyg://6/http://www.workoplis.com/ servlet/News/ torontostar/20020209/ts5483.*

Staffing, T. (2002). The 25 worst job interview mistakes. Retrieved August 13, 2002, from the World Wide Web: *www.thomas-staffing.com/jobtip1.htm.*

University of Maryland Career Center at *www.careercenter.umd.edu/STUDENT/STEP5/ QUESTION.htm.*

Wendelton, K. (2002). Following-up after a job interview: The *only* job hunting technique. Retrieved August 13, 2002, from the World Wide Web: *www.fiveoclockclub.com/ careerCoach/10followingUp.htm.*

http://little.nhlink.net/nhlink/employme/frequent.htm

www.bernardhaldane.com/mycareer/38illegal.php

www.careercenter.umd.edu/STUDENT/STEP5/QUESTION.htm

www.collegegrad.com/ezine/23illega.shtml

www.dreamjobcoaching.com/illegal.shtml

www.mrichampions.com/behaviorbsd.html

www.nextlevel-consulting.com/interviewart.html

www.quintcareers.com/interview_question_collections.html

www.staffingworld.com/howtowin.htm

www.thomasregister.com

CHAPTER 10
CUSTOMER SERVICE BLUEPRINT

Establish Customer Service Background

Review the Customer Service Model

Establish the Need for Customer Service

CUSTOMER SERVICE TOOLS

Provide Quality Customer Service

Resolve Customer Complaints

TOOL CHECK

Company Research

Personal Experience Talk

INTERACTIONS

Company Inventory

Customer Service Survey

Article Review

CUSTOMER SERVICE BLUEPRINT

Establish Customer Service Background

In recent years, providing good customer service has become a top priority for many American businesses, small and large alike. While numerous companies have prided themselves on "putting the customer first," this philosophy experienced a resurgence in the early 1980s, when Detroit auto executives sought the input of W. Edwards Deming to help them understand why Japanese auto manufacturers were surpassing American auto manufacturers in both quality and design. Deming promoted a method of statistical analysis to reduce variation and to control the quality and consistency of production.

At the heart of Deming's approach are his Fourteen Points that "crystallize the key quality management practices that have come to be accepted at most high-quality companies in the United States and Japan" (Gabor, 1990, p. 17). These Fourteen Points represent what is commonly known today as Total Quality Management or TQM. What does TQM have to do with customer service? Quite simply, TQM defines quality as "anticipating the needs of the customer, translating those needs into a useful and dependable product, and creating a system that can produce the product at the lowest possible price, so that it represents 'good value' to the consumer and profits for the enterprise" (Gabor, 1990, p. 10).

A more current paradigm to assure quality is Six Sigma that provides a methodology for improving capability and reducing defects in any process. Six Sigma started with Motorola's manufacturing division "where millions of parts are made using the

same process repeatedly" (*http://sixsigmatutorial.com/Six-Sigma/Six-Sigma-Tutorial.aspx? ref=aw*). Subsequently, Six Sigma was applied to other non-manufacturing processes as well, including those in service, medical and insurance industries.

"Six Sigma methodology improves any existing business process by constantly reviewing and re-tuning the process. To achieve this, Six Sigma uses a methodology known as **DMAIC** (**D**efine opportunities, **M**easure performance, **A**nalyze opportunity, **I**mprove performance, **C**ontrol performance)" (*http://sixsigmatutorial.com/Six-Sigma/ Six-Sigma-Tutorial.aspx?ref=aw*).

In addition, Six Sigma strives for perfection and attempts to reduce defects and measure quality using statistical techniques. "It allows for only 3.4 defects per million opportunities for each product or service transaction" (*http://sixsigmatutorial.com/ Six-Sigma/Six-Sigma-Tutorial.aspx?ref=aw*).

Principles and techniques used in business, statistics, and engineering form the core elements of Six Sigma, in an attempt to improve process performance, decrease variation, and maintain consistent quality of the process output. The end result is defect reduction along with "improvement in profits, product quality, and customer satisfaction" (*http://sixsigmatutorial.com/Six-Sigma/Six-Sigma-Tutorial.aspx?ref=aw*).

Interestingly, however, the fundamentals of TQM are not relatively new. In fact, one can trace them as far back as 1913 and the seven tenets upon which the J. C. Penney stores were built:

1. "To serve the public, as nearly as we can, to its complete satisfaction."

2. "To expect for the service we render a fair remuneration and not all the profit the traffic will bear."

3. "To do all in our power to pack the customer's dollar full of value, quality, and satisfaction."

4. "To continue to train ourselves and our associates so that the services we give will be more and more intelligently performed."

5. "To improve constantly the human factor in our business."

6. "To reward men and women in our organization through participation in what the business produces."

7. "To test our every policy, method, and act in this way: 'Does it square with what is just and right?'" (Jablonski, 1992, pp. 9–10).

Review the Customer Service Model

Before examining the factors that contribute to good customer service, it might be helpful to develop a model that illustrates how good customer service evolves. It begins at the level of management, filters down into the organization, and then impacts those outside of the organization who use the products and services. This above-down-inside-out paradigm is actually one that was originally used to illustrate an optimally functioning nervous system within the human body; and in reality, this nervous system can serve as an apt comparison for an optimally functioning business or industry as well. For example, think of the brain and spinal cord as the central control unit of the body. It sends information to the smaller branches of nerves, which in turn communicate to all of the organs and cells within the body. When this communication flows smoothly, we are able to interface with our environment flexibly and with ease. In the same way, when a company's management team (brain and spinal cord) has a clearly established philosophy that supports quality, such information can be sent and promoted to all of the workers within that company (nerve branches) who, in turn, can reflect this philosophy to the external customers they serve. So while the process of TQM and subsequent good customer service begins with management, the active participation of every employee, division, and supplier is required in the improvement effort (Gabor, 1990, p. 5).

One final note, as we begin a more in-depth discussion of what constitutes good customer service. Customers fall into one of two categories: internal and external. An internal customer is "anyone within an organization who at any time is dependent on anyone else within the organization" (Hyken, 2002a). Conversely, external customers are those outside the organization who use the services or buy the products the company produces. For external customer service to be of top quality, it must be a reflection of the company's internal processes that promote quality on all levels. As we explore the ways to provide outstanding customer service, keep in mind that the suggestions discussed can be applied to both internal and external customers alike.

Establish the Need for Customer Service

Good customer service can be defined in many different ways, but for the sake of discussion, let us define it as service that goes above and beyond what the customer, whether internal or external, expects. In other words, it is not enough to simply satisfy the customer. Two professors from Vanderbilt University in Nashville, Tennessee, did an interesting study on customer service. Anthony J. Zahorak and Roland T. Rust studied service-oriented businesses such as retail stores, restaurants, and hotels and discovered that "approximately 25% to 40% of satisfied customers do not come back to the places of business where they have been satisfied" (Hyken, 2002c). One might logically question the reason for this phenomenon. Quite simply, a significant number of customers are looking not just for satisfaction but for products and services that are exceptional. Midwest Express Airlines is an example of one organization that went above and beyond what air travelers had come to expect in an airline. For example, the seats were larger and roomier than those found among most other airlines' coach seats. In addition, meals were served on "real" plates with silverware, glassware, linen napkins, and even tiny glass salt and pepper shakers. Complimentary choice of red or white wine accompanied meals that were more typically served in first-class accommodations only on other commercial flights. And of course, those who have traveled Midwest Express before are not likely to forget the hot chocolate chip cookies for which Midwest became famous. So you can see that Midwest Express examined what most travelers had come to expect when they flew coach and then went one step further to determine what they could do that would exceed those expectations.

Midwest Express is not alone in their customer service efforts. The Beta Consulting Group of Concord, New Hampshire, for example, conducted a survey in which they questioned "presidents, CEO's, owners, and other top executives at 139 companies in the manufacturing and service industries spread throughout the U.S. Of the 75 actual respondents, most were concentrated east of the Mississippi" (Beta Management Consulting, 2002). "Every company that responded to the survey that ranked in the A category of profits (presumably the highest profits) also cited high commitment to great customer service. In contrast, customer service was rated highly in strategic importance by only 65% of respondents ten years ago when the 'Business Outlook Survey' first began. Moreover, this time around, not one company responding to the survey ranked customer service as 'unimportant' to strategic development" (Beta Management Consulting, 2002). These examples show that providing quality customer service is becoming increasingly important to most businesses and industries.

CUSTOMER SERVICE TOOLS

Provide Quality Customer Service

So what exactly is required of a business or industry to provide top-notch customer service? Let's examine the following eight suggestions.

1. **Hire the right employees and provide proper training.** This first suggestion is largely dependent upon the efforts of management. No time and energy should be spared in filling positions with the most highly qualified individuals available. But simply hiring the best people for the job is not enough. All new employees should be given substantial training that includes becoming familiar with the company's philosophy. They also need to understand the protocol for day-to-day operations, especially in the area of internal and external customer service. And finally, all employees, both novices and veterans alike, should have opportunities for continual training that will provide them with the ability to enhance job performance and customer service on a consistent basis.

2. **Show appreciation for your customers.** Customers are what keep a company running smoothly and what keep a company in business, so never forget to let your customers know just how important they are. Remembering something as simple as saying, "Thank you" more frequently can be a good way to start. One local car dealership shows its customer appreciation by sending a plant or floral arrangement to all new buyers. Victoria's Secret, a nationally known retail business specializing in women's lingerie, recently showed their appreciation to loyal customers by inviting them to stop by for a free gift. In both these instances, customers are likely to bring return business.

3. **Ask how you're doing.** Soliciting feedback from your customers is a good way of finding out just how satisfied they are. This feedback is especially important when it comes to customer complaints. "A few years ago, there was a study commissioned by the White House Office of Consumer Affairs. The group that performed the study, TARP, the Technical Assistance Research Program, found that in an average business, 96% of people who have a complaint, don't complain—at least to the people who they do business with. This means that for every 26 complaints that are out there, we are only hearing from one. What do the other 25 do? They complain to their friends, associates, neighbors . . . " (Hyken, 2002b). In addition, "Some studies indicate a disgruntled customer will tell seven to 11 people about an unpleasant experience with your company. Dissatisfied e-commerce customers are even more vocal." (*www.localbusiness.com/Resource/Page/0,1383,PDX_3_6,00html*). Why not encourage customers to tell you about their concerns directly by surveys, e-mail, or telephone contacts?

4. **Guarantee your products or services.** Whatever products you produce or services you provide, stand behind them fully. Let your customers know that they can count on quality. If there should be a problem, make certain customers feel assured the problem will be addressed promptly, courteously, and to their complete satisfaction. While most reputable mail order companies, for example, gladly accept returns on merchandise that doesn't meet the customer's complete satisfaction, one company, Coldwater Creek, included in a customer's order a postage paid return mailing envelope in case the ordered article of clothing didn't fit.

5. **Give customers your full attention.** Whether dealing with internal or external customers, be fully attentive to them. For instance, put aside whatever paperwork you may be doing, put the phone on call-forwarding, and let your body language say you are ready and willing to focus exclusively on the customer's needs. Direct eye contact, an alert body posture, and a pleasant demeanor all communicate interest and thoughtful consideration of what the customer has to say.

6. **Listen carefully to the customer.** With distractions out of the way, you can now really listen to the customer. It is important to listen not only to the actual message but to the way the message is delivered. Most messages have two parts: the content (the information) and the intent (the feelings). Consequently, the good listener pays attention not only to the words being delivered but to the feelings behind the words. For instance, a customer may be calling to complain about a product that didn't meet his or her satisfaction. The caller may be upset, angry, frustrated, or just confused. You can respond more appropriately when you take into consideration not only the nature of the complaint but the emotional state of the caller as well. One useful technique in situations like these is paraphrasing. The listener restates to the customer's satisfaction both the content and intent of the message to verify complete understanding of the message. The paraphrase might sound something like this: "It seems as if you are disappointed with the fabric on the sofa and are feeling anxious about how we might remedy the problem."

7. **Speak in language the customer understands.** In order to establish rapport with your customer, it is important to avoid jargon or confusing technical terms your customer may not understand. Always try to put yourself in your customer's shoes by considering his or her level of expertise. For example, an employee selling a personal computer to a first-time buyer would need to keep explanations clear and simple to avoid overwhelming the buyer.

8. **Show that you care.** Last but not least, let your customers know that their concerns matter to you. Telling a customer, "Sorry, I can't help you; that's not my department," communicates that the customer doesn't matter. Keeping a customer on-hold for an extended period of time during a phone call also sends the message that the customer's time is less valuable than your own. And what about failing to reply promptly to an e-mail message where a customer has raised a question or voiced a concern? The message is still the same—you don't matter!

Resolve Customer Complaints

Even if a company follows all of the previous suggestions for providing good customer service, customer complaints are still bound to occur from time to time. In some instances, these complaints are perfectly legitimate—customers simply did not receive the quality of goods or services they expected. In other instances, customers may voice complaints that are unreasonable or have no basis in fact. For example, "The old saying, 'the customer is always right' has been revised at some companies, such as top carrier Southwest Airlines, whose Chairman Herb Kelleher has insisted that the customer isn't always right—some are outrageously demanding and rude" (*www.localbusiness.com/Resource/Page0,1383,PDX_3_6,00.html*). To complicate matters further, in both of these cases, customers may be upset, angry, and belligerent. Consequently, handling customer complaints involves addressing not only the complaint itself, but the emotions of the customer as well. Following are some strategies to keep in mind when handling customer complaints.

1. **Stay cool.** No matter how frustrating or upsetting a customer may be, maintain your own composure. Responding in a like manner only escalates the difficulty. Take a few slow, deep breaths, and remember that the customer's complaints are not about you personally.

2. **Listen for the feelings.** Let the customer voice his or her feelings first before attempting to deal with the nature of the complaint. Listen as empathically as possible and consider paraphrasing the emotions you are observing. For example, saying something like, "I sense you are really angry and upset about this situation" can diffuse an overly emotional reaction on the part of the customer. In addition, customers sometimes just need to know that someone cares about their concerns and is willing to acknowledge their feelings in order to calm down and discuss the problem more reasonably.

3. **Listen for the facts.** Once the customer has calmed down, ask him or her to explain the nature of the complaint in detail. Listen carefully to the information the customer provides, and if necessary, jot down a few notes. Then when you are sure the customer has finished, paraphrase the information you understood to the customer's satisfaction. You might say something like this: "If I hear you correctly, you're saying that the shipment you were promised on the 15th didn't arrive until the 30th and that you want to send back the parts that were custom-ordered, right?"

4. **Try to resolve the complaint.** If at all possible, try to fix the problem. Companies who give their employees the freedom to handle complaints judiciously without fear of reprisals can often provide the satisfaction the customer is seeking. Customer frustration is only increased when the customer is bumped from one department to the next in an effort to find the "right" party to resolve the issue. If you honestly are unable to remedy the problem directly, politely explain to the customer that you will personally find someone who can help. Then do so promptly. Avoid keeping customers waiting either in person or on the phone. And if a brief wait is unavoidable, try saying something like this: "Ms. Johnson, I know you are very concerned about this problem, so I am going to contact the supervisor in shipping to find out the cause for the delay. I'll need about five minutes to do this. Do you have time to wait? If not, I will call you back as soon as I talk to the supervisor."

5. **Offer explanations and alternatives.** Sometimes due to company policy or an unreasonable customer demand, you simply cannot do what the customer wants. In such cases, provide an explanation and offer an alternative to foster goodwill. Consider the problem of the shipping delay discussed above. You might provide an explanation and alternative as follows: "Ms. Johnson, I understand the inconvenience you experienced when the shipment arrived two weeks after the date you were promised. Apparently the manufacturer was behind schedule and sent us the parts ten days later than we had requested. We did send them out to you the day we received them. While we cannot provide a refund on custom orders, we will give you the phone number and address of the manufacturer so you can seek a refund directly."

6. **End on a cordial note.** Regardless of whether you were able to resolve the complaint or simply offer an alternative, try to close the conversation cordially. Let the customer know you truly value his or her business. Also make it clear you are always available should the customer need further assistance.

While the decision to provide quality customer service begins with management, everyone within the organization is responsible for ensuring that customer expectations are exceeded. Customer service is not something new, yet it continues to be the deciding factor that separates good businesses from outstanding businesses.

CHAPTER 10 TOOL CHECK

Directions: Use the key words from the preceding chapter to complete the sentences below.

1. Good customer service may be defined as _____.
2. An internal customer is _____.
3. An external customer is _____.
4. The Six Sigma methodology DMAIC stands for _____.
5. _____ was the man who developed the Fourteen Points upon which TQM is based.
6. According to TARP (Technical Assistance Research Program), the average business hears from only about _____ percent of unhappy customers while the other _____ percent do not complain directly to the places where they did business.
7. A listening technique that can be used to confirm understanding of a customer's message is called _____.
8. Before listening to the facts of a complaint voiced by an angry customer, one should listen first for the _____.
9. When one cannot resolve a problem the way a customer would like, one should offer _____ and _____.
10. Always end a conversation with a customer on a _____ note.

CHAPTER 10 INTERACTIONS

INTERACTION #1—Company Research

Select a company well known for its outstanding customer service. You can make your selection on the basis of companies you have done business with, companies that are highly reputable within your own community, or perhaps companies you investigate on the Internet or at your local public library. Most libraries will be able to supply you with various directories for manufacturing, business, and service-related companies that you can use as a starting point. (Harris Source or Info USA)

Once you have chosen a company, respond to the following questions.

1. What is the name of the company?

2. Is the company local, national, or international?

3. What products or services does the company provide?

4. How many workers does the company employ?

5. What kind of pre-employment training do new employees receive?

6. What kind of ongoing training opportunities are available for all employees?

7. Does the company have a statement of its philosophy? If so, what is it?

8. Does the company have a customer service policy? If so, what is it?

9. Provide an example or two of the kind of service a customer can expect to receive when doing business with this company.

10. What are your perceptions of the quality of this company's customer service?

After completing your research, share your information with others in the class.

INTERACTION #2—Company Inventory

Complete the following inventory to assess your own company's quality of customer service. The numbers below each item on the inventory represent 1 for Excellent, 2 for Average, and 3 for Needs Improvement. Circle the appropriate choice; then tally your scores at the end of the inventory.

1. My company has a philosophy statement that clearly emphasizes the importance of customer service.

   1   2   3

2. My company trains new employees to provide quality customer service.

   1   2   3

3. My company provides opportunities for continual customer service training.

   1   2   3

4. My company encourages employees to offer suggestions for new and better ways to provide customer service.

   1   2   3

5. My company rewards employees for providing quality customer service.

   1   2   3

6. My company provides a climate that encourages respect, appreciation, and value for all employees.

   1   2   3

7. My company encourages all employees to treat customers with respect, appreciation, and value.

   1   2   3

8. My company stands behind its products/services to ensure customer satisfaction.

   1   2   3

9. My company consistently seeks customer feedback.

   1   2   3

10. My company seriously considers the customer feedback it receives in order to improve upon the service it provides.

   1   2   3

Company Inventory Rating Scale:

10-12:   Providing excellent customer service
13-15:   Providing good customer service
16-18:   Providing acceptable customer service
19 or more: Needs work in improving customer service

INTERACTION #3—Customer Service Survey

As you have probably determined by now, soliciting customer feedback from both internal and external customers is important for companies seeking continuous improvement. If your company already has a survey or customer feedback form, join with two or three others in your class to analyze the form. In your analysis, consider the following questions:

1. Does the survey provide the kind of information the company is seeking in order to improve the quality of its goods and services?

2. Is the survey quick and easy for the customer to complete?

3. How does the company administer the survey and to which customers?

4. How is the information on the survey tabulated?

5. What follow-up procedure does the company have after tabulating the survey results?

If your company does not have a customer feedback survey, join with two or three others in your class to create a form. Consider these steps as you create the form:

1. Determine the kinds of information you want the form to solicit.

2. Brainstorm for a list of questions most likely to obtain the desired information.

3. Consider the format the survey should take (i.e., checklist, fill-in-the-blank, rating system, etc.).

4. Decide how the survey will be administered and to which customers.

5. Design the form.

INTERACTION #4—Article Review

To learn more about the quality movement and good customer service, find an article on TQM, W. Edwards Deming, the Fourteen Points, or Six Sigma. You can access this information on the Internet, in your public library's online magazine index, or in the *Reader's Guide to Periodical Literature.*

Make a photocopy of the article you have selected and then do the following.

1. Read the article carefully, noting the purpose of the article (i.e., key idea).

2. Highlight the main points and supporting facts.

3. Prepare a one-page, typed summary of the information contained in the article.

4. Include a personal reaction (about one paragraph) to the article in which you comment on what you learned, what you think about the information, what questions the article raised for you, and so on.

5. Submit the summary to your instructor for evaluation.

INTERACTION #5—Personal Experience Talk

Think of an experience you had in which you received good customer service. Briefly share with the entire class or in a group of three to four others the nature of your experience. Describe in detail what occurred that left you feeling highly satisfied and willing to do business with this person or company again. After the sharing, see if the class or your group can come up with a list of other customer service tips not already discussed in this chapter.

REFERENCES

Beta Management Consulting. (2002). Great customer service equals profits, survey says. Retrieved October 16, 2002, from the World Wide Web: *wysiwg://19/http://www.betacg.com/bet_a07.ph.*

Gabor, A. (1990). *The man who discovered quality: How W. Edwards Deming brought the quality revolution to America.* New York: Times Books/Random House.

Hyken, S. (2002b). The complaining customer. *Customer Service Articles.* Retrieved October 16, 2002, from the World Wide Web: *www.hyken.com/article14.htm.*

Hyken, S. (2002a) Internal customer service. *Customer Service Articles.* Retrieved October 16, 2002, from *www.hyken.com/article13htm.*

Hyken, S. (2002c). The dangerous customer. *Customer Service Articles.* Retrieved October 16, 2002, from *www.hyken.com/article05.htm.*

Jablonski, J. R. (1992). *Implementing TQM: Competing in the nineties through Total Quality Management.* San Diego: Pfeiffer.

Six Sigma Tutorial. (2001–2004). Retrieved February 25, 2005 from http://sixsigmatutorial.com/Six-Sigma/Six-Sigma-Tutorial.aspx?ref=aw.

www.localbusiness.com/Resource/Page/0,1383,PDX_3_6,00html.

INDEX